Varieties
of
Unbelief
FROM EPICURUS
TO SARTRE

PHILOSOPHICAL TOPICS
PAUL EDWARDS, GENERAL EDITOR

Varieties
of
Unbelief

FROM EPICURUS
TO SARTRE

Edited, with an Introduction,
Notes, and Bibliography by

J. C. A. Gaskin

FELLOW OF TRINITY COLLEGE DUBLIN

Macmillan Publishing Company
New York
Collier Macmillan Publishers
London

Macmillan Publishing Company
866 Third Avenue, New York, New York 10022

Collier Macmillan Canada, Inc.

Library of Congress Cataloging-in-Publication Data
Varieties of unbelief.
1. Religion—Controversial literature.   I. Gaskin,
J. C. A. (John Charles Addison)
BL2780.V29 1989   212′.7   88-8963
ISBN 0-02-340681-X

Printing: 1 2 3 4 5 6 7   Year: 9 0 1 2 3 4 5

ACKNOWLEDGMENTS

I am grateful for the following permissions to use copyright material: in Chapter 1 to Penguin Books, Ltd. with respect to various passages from R. E. Latham's translation of Lucretius' *On the Nature of the Universe* (Penguin Classics, 1981), copyright R. E. Latham, 1961, and to Macmillan Publishing Company with respect to parts of Epicurus' "Letter to Herodotus" from Epicurus' *Letters, Principal Doctrines and Vatican Sayings*, translated by Russel M. Geer, copyright 1964, Macmillan Publishing Company; in Chapter 14 to Lawrence and Wishart Ltd., London, with respect to the translations of various essays and short pieces by Karl Marx; in Chapter 16 to Copyrights Ltd., The Institute of Psycho-Analysis, and the Hogarth Press with respect to an extract from "The Future of an Illusion" from *The Complete Psychological Works of Sigmund Freud*, translated and edited by James Strachey, and for the same to W. W. Norton and Company, Inc.; in Chapter 17 to Unwin Hyman with respect to part of Chapter 5 of Bertrand Russell's *Human Society in Ethics and Politics* and also to Unwin Hyman and Simon and Schuster, Inc. for their permission to reprint part of "What I Believe" from Russell's *Why I am not a Christian*, copyright 1957 and 1985 by Allen and Unwin; in Chapter 19 to Verso Publishers and Random House, Inc., with respect to *The War Diaries of Jean-Paul Sartre* by Jean-Paul Sartre, translated by Quinton Hoare, English translation copyright 1984 by Verso Editions, reprinted by permission of Pantheon Books, a Division of Random House Inc.; in Chapter 20 A. E. Housman, "From far, from eve and morning." Copyright 1939, 1940, © 1965 by

Holt, Rinehart and Winston, Inc. Copyright © 1967, 1968 by Robert E. Symons. Reprinted from *The Collected Poems of A. E. Housman*, by permission of Henry Holt and Company, Inc.

I am also most grateful to the following for their generous permission to use copyright material — the passages in Chapter 2 from Cicero's *De Natura Deorum*, translated by H. Rackham (copyright 1933) and Sextus Empiricus' "Outlines of Pyrrhonism" (copyright 1933) are reprinted by permission of the publishers and the Loeb Classical Library, Cambridge, Massachusetts, Harvard University Press; in Chapter 18 the section from Chapter 6 of *Language Truth and Logic* is reprinted by the gracious permission of Sir Alfred Ayer. The sections from the *Complete Works of Nietzsche* in Chapter 15 were originally published in 1909 – 1911, but have been reprinted in the United States in 1974 by Gordon Press, New York, whose edition I am pleased to acknowledge.

I would also like to thank my colleague, Vincent Denard, for his translation of the passage by Critias that appears in the Introduction and David Berman for making available to me his copies of some of the rarer pieces that appear in this selection. I am also obliged to him for advice about one or two of the items that appear in the Bibliography.

At a time of life when most men have put down the pen and everything else, my father, Harry Gaskin, came to my aid in proofreading. I am very grateful to him and to my mother in this as in so much else.

PREFACE

This book is not intended merely as an *ad hoc* collection of choice pieces on atheism. It is an attempt to bring together and exhibit in historical sequence the main *ideas* that have challenged the claims of supernatural religions, or affirmed this-worldly concerns and human-centered values.

The selection of these pieces has been difficult. Some items thrust themselves forward. For example, it would be strange to construct a book on unbelief without *some* contribution from Hume, Marx, or Russell. But others, such as Collins and Palmer, could have been made to stand down in favor of . . . , and here each reader can submit his or her own particular preference. The choices I would, however, defend to the last are Epicurus himself and Lucretius. They stand at the fount of unbelief: the philosophical archetypes for looking at the world as a single natural system in which supernatural agents and bodiless spirits play no part.

Rarity as well as philosophical interest also attach to three items. Two are the suppressed essays, "Of the Immortality of the Soul" and "Of Suicide" by David Hume. These are printed here for the first time with the short paragraphs sanctioned by Hume and include the final corrections made in his own hand as preserved in the unique copy in the National Library of Scotland. The third is the splendid dialogue by the poet Shelley, *A Refutation of Deism*. This has always been difficult to find and is here reprinted for the first time in its original form in a collection of works of philosophical rather than literary importance.

An apology: One or two of the points made in the Introduction are repeated — very sparingly — in comments made about particular authors. This is done on the assumption that at least some readers will turn to selections by particular authors without first consulting the introductory remarks of *this* particular author.

J. C. A. Gaskin
Trinity College Dublin

CONTENTS

Varieties
of
Unbelief
FROM EPICURUS
TO SARTRE

INTRODUCTION

> Great and terrible systems of divinity and
> philosophy lie round about us, which, if true,
> might drive a wise man mad.
>
> *Walter Bagehot, 1879*

> Before accepting any belief one ought first to
> follow reason as a guide, for credulity without
> enquiry is a sure way to deceive oneself. We have
> plenty of deceivers in our own times. . . . Their
> favourite injunctions are. . . . "Salvation is
> through faith"; "The wisdom of this world is
> wickedness."
>
> *Celsus, c. 170* A.D.

There are five main varieties of unbelief: materialism, skepticism, academic or critical unbelief, social unbelief, and unbelief that is derived from the existence of natural explanations for the prevalent phenomenon of religion. I return to these in the third section of this Introduction, but two prior matters require attention before any real understanding of the progress of unbelief is possible. The first of these concerns the exact meaning of *unbelief* and its relation to atheism, deism, and certain other traditional stances about the existence and nature of god(s). The second concerns the difference between ancient and modern unbelief brought about by the intervening triumph of Christianity and Islam—what I have called the "historical dialectic." Ancient unbelief is social, skeptical, and critical; but at best it is also *positive*; an autonomous, free inquiry into the nature of the universe and the human relation to it. Modern unbelief is much of this, but it is also negative and reactive; a *denial* of the teaching of the religions which had for so long dominated the cultural, intellectual, and political life of the Western world. But first the mapwork of unbelief—the essential terminology of the subject.

1. The Mapwork of Unbelief and Atheism

A common dictionary definition of *unbelief* is "absence or lack of belief; disbelief, incredulity: most frequently with reference to matters of

1

religion." The same source defines *atheism* as "disbelief in the existence of God or gods; godlessness."

In this book the word "unbelief" (or its cognates) is regularly used rather than "atheism" (or its cognates). "Unbelief" however needs a more precise definition than the one given, and atheism has variations of meaning as well as a propensity to be used as a term of abuse that must be clearly indicated: partly to justify preference for "unbelief"; and partly to discern the several variations of opinion that constitute atheism and which are identical with the essential aspect of unbelief as the term is defined in the following section.

Unbelief is (A) lack of belief in supernatural agents — God, gods, demons, or any abstraction intended as a substitute for these, e.g. Tillich's "ground of our being"; (B) lack of belief in miracles, interventions in the natural order by supernatural agents; and (C) lack of belief in a future state, in the continuance of any individual person after that person's real bodily death. Let us refer to these as unbeliefs A, B, and C.

If someone is an unbeliever in sense A, it follows that he or she will also be an unbeliever in sense B since no one could consistently believe in interventions by nonexistent agents. Unbeliefs A and C, on the other hand, may be, and on occasions have been (see p. 215), entertained independently of each other. But however one looks at it, the essential unbelief is A. It is what we would normally think of as atheism but for the historical confusions associated with that much older term; confusions we must now examine.

Originally the Greek work *atheos* meant simply "without god" or, because of the close association between particular gods and the integrity of a state, "without piety toward the civic god(s)," i.e., to the god(s) of the state to which the "atheist" belonged. But even as early as Plato (c. 428–348 B.C.) distinctions were being drawn between different types of atheism. At the beginning of Book X of the *Laws*, Plato points out that anyone who deliberately performs an impious act must have supposed *either* that the gods do not exist, *or* that they take no care of man, *or* that they are easily appeased and turned aside from their purposes by sacrifices and prayers.

The first possibility, if it extended to *all* gods and not merely to the civic gods of the locality where the atheist happened to reside, would be atheism in the sense of unbelief A. (To some ears "atheism" would still carry the nuance of *denying* the existence of gods, whereas "unbelief" would convey the more neutral sense of *lacking* belief in gods. It is partly to avoid this nuance that I prefer the word *unbelief*.) The third possibility is a species of religious absurdity; an "impiety" that does not concern unbelief at all. But the second possibility is a potent source of confusion. Is someone really an unbeliever in sense A if he or she thinks — as the Epicureans did — that there are gods who live inactively in perfect happiness knowing and caring nothing of humanity; or if one thinks — as Voltaire and Paine and many other eighteenth-century deists did — that the deity brought into existence and designed the universe and all its processes, but takes no special care of men and women?

The Epicurean position is the easier one to assess. The Epicurean gods are natural. They are a product of the material universe and it would be *theoretically* possible for empirical investigation to show that they do not exist. If it turned out that in fact the gods do not exist, nothing would be lacking in the Epicurean system except blissful beings perhaps worthy of our contemplation as the embodiment of perfect happiness. More significantly, if they *do* exist, the Epicurean gods are mere inactive centers of permanent well-being neither demanding nor justifying any religious activity on earth. They do not respond to prayers. They are insensitive to sacrifice. They neither know nor care about humanity in any way. In short, the Epicurean belief in gods *is* unbelief A. It is a complete *lack* of belief in all supernatural agents since their "gods" were neither supernatural nor agents. When we remember that the Epicureans also had no recourse to divine interventions in natural events, and that they emphatically rejected belief in any sort of future state, the scale of their "impiety" (in Platonic or Christian terms) becomes evident: they were unbelievers in all three senses defined previously. For these reasons, the Epicureans play prominent roles in the first and last chapters of this book.

Deism presents a more difficult picture. Some four hundred years after Plato, the Stoic philosopher Epictetus (c. 55–135 A.D.) set out (*Discourses*, I, xii) what are in effect five belief possibilities including deism (he did not have the word at his disposal) and what may be called "attenuated deism":

> Concerning the gods, there are some who say that no divine being exists [i.e., full *atheism* or unbelief A without qualification]; and others that a divine being exists but is idle and uncaring and has no forethought for anything [*Epicureanism*]; and a third class that there is such a being, and he takes forethought also, but only in respect of great and heavenly things, but of nothing that is on earth [*attenuated deism*]; and a fourth class, that he takes thought of things both in heaven and earth, but only in general, and not of each particular individual [*deism*]. And there is a fifth class, whereof are Odysseus and Socrates, who say "Nor can I move without thy knowledge." [Homer, *Iliad* X, 279. See also Xenophon, *Memorabilia* I, i, 19: "Socrates thought that the gods know all things, our words and deeds and secret purposes; that they are present everywhere. . . ." With the substitution of the singular for "gods," this is also part of the Christian and Muslim view of things, i.e., it is part of *theism*: the other part being that this ever-present, all-seeing and caring supernatural agent is also creator and sustainer of all things].

Neither deism nor attentuated deism amounts to atheism in the sense of unbelief A. Despite the fact that virtually all to whom the title "deist" could be attached entertain unbelief B (lack of belief in miracles) and that very many would profess unbelief C (lack of belief in a future state), the vestigial belief in a potent supernatural agent, although far from Christian theism and in many cases stridently opposed to Christianity, is not straight lack of belief in supernatural agents. Indeed deistic arguments have been employed as a step on the way to theism: for example, the arguments from design and from cosmic origins, which convince the diest, are also built into the foundations of any reasoned commitment to Christian or Islamic theism.

Professed deists, Voltaire and Paine, for example, are included in this book, which is primarily concerned with unbelief A, because the ideological grip of Christian theism after the destruction of the ancient world was so complete and so tenacious that eighteenth-century deism represents, not the step *toward* a rationally based Christianity which it could have been, but a crucial historical step *away* from Christianity and toward modern unbelief.

The variety of meanings rolled up in the word *atheism* apart, its use as an accurate and acceptable description is deeply prejudiced by its long-standing employment as a term of abuse.

The ancient classical suspicions about the loyalty of anyone who denied the state gods have already been noted. in Judeo-Christian history the association of "the fool" with one who says "there is no God" is at least as old as Psalm XIV. But at the beginning of the eighteenth century, four influences still combined to make atheism both a serious criminal accusation and also a term of abuse for an imprecisely defined but loathed and dreaded minority persuasion (compare the present-day use of the terms "sexist and "racist"). The four influences were the deep conviction that a denial of Christianity was wicked, the prolonged enthusiasm of the Roman Church for rooting out heresy, the prevalence of state laws in defense of Christianity (of whatever species), and the habit of designating as "atheism" any deviation from some other article of Christian faith taken to be crucial (belief in a future state for example). *Atheism* was even used to refer to something as contingently connected with belief A as antisocial behavior. Thus the phrase "practical atheist" (used by Tillotson, Wollaston, and others) indicated those whose behavior was so bad that they denied God in their *actions*.

Confronted with the pejorative associations of the term, its vagueness, and later the tendency of religious apologists to define atheism so that no one could be an atheist, it is not surprising to find in English freethinking literature of the second half of the nineteenth century an attempt to restore to the word *atheism* a clear and *unemotive* sense identical in content and nuance to what we have called unbelief A. Sir

John Lubbock in his much-reprinted book *The Origins of Civilization* (London, 1870) speaks of the prereligious phase of the development of humanity as "*Atheism*; understanding by this term not a denial of the existence of a Deity, but an absence of any definite ideas on the subject" (p. 136). A little later, Charles Bradlaugh, the eminent Victorian secularist, insists — for contemporary, not anthropological uses — in *The Freethinkers' Text Book* (London, 1876) that:

> The Atheist does not say "There is no God," but he says "I know not what you mean by God; the word "God" is to me a sound conveying no clear or distinct affirmation. I do not deny God, because I cannot deny that of which I have no conception, and the conception of which, by its affirmer, is so imperfect that he is unable to define it to me." (p. 118)

Partly as a result of Bradlaugh's own activities and those of men and women who thought as he did, the word *atheist* still conveys mild disapproval, but of the sort now more adequately expressed by the phrase "militant atheist": one who cannot leave other people at peace with their own (harmless?) religious beliefs.

In the title and elsewhere in this book the word *unbelief* (where necessary differentiated as definition A, B, or C) is used rather than any qualified use of the word *atheism*. When no differentiation is offered, *at least* unbelief sense A will be intended. The terms *Epicurean, deist,* and *theist* (or their cognates whenever useful) are also used in the senses explained in the quotation from Epictetus.

2. The Historical Dialetic

Unbelief has gone through three distinct historical phases: (a) In classical antiquity a period of relatively unfettered development that ended between 300 and 450 A.D. During this period Skeptical and Epicurean unbelief is definitively set out; (b) A long period during which these classical schools, and any substitute for them, are resolutely and all but successfully suppressed by Christian and Islamic monotheistic dominion of the Western world; and (c) the modern period dating from the late sixteenth century in which initially Skeptical and Epicurean arguments are rediscovered, then the biblical claims of Christianity are challenged in order to establish deistic positions, and finally the deistic position themselves are rejected in a welter of discussion which results in (successful) investigations of the social and psychological causes of the prevalent phenomenon of religion.

(a) CLASSICAL ANTIQUITY   At least two interesting questions are presented for this period. The first is why unbelief shows up in Greek and Roman antiquity despite the prevalence of religion but is so little evident in later centuries because of the prevalence of religion. The second is where, when, and what were the earliest manifestations of unbelief.

The basic answer to the first question is that the multiple polytheisms of the classical world led to tolerance in matters of religion, and generally to tolerance concerning philosophical inquiry that resulted in lack of religion, provided that this lack did not extend to an unpatriotic defamation of the gods which protected the particular area where one happened to be. Thus (as Xenophon reports in *Memorabilia*, I, 3) when the Priestess of Delphi was asked such a question as "What is my duty about offering sacrifices?" she replied "Follow the custom of the State: that is the way to act piously." But there were many states and many customs, and there was no unified priesthood to impose any one custom, nor any popular claim about there being only one true God to justify universal worship. Even under the vast hegemony of Rome, the government required no more than the observance of a minimal official religion on official occasions: much more like an oath of allegiance and an expression of national unity than a serious commitment to some supernatural belief which it would be sinful to reject or blasphemous to treat with insincerity.

The difference between classical and Christian attitudes to atheism becomes clearer. The classical atheist—for example, the Christian in his dealings with the Roman state—is dangerous because his atheism puts in question his loyalty to the state. Thus Marcus Aurelius speaks about "those . . . who do not believe in gods and who fail their country in its need": almost certainly a reference (*Meditations*, III, 16) to Christians, and all the more noteworthy given the Emperor's known propensity to think rightly and act justly. On the other hand, the atheist who rejects Christian or Islamic beliefs is, from the point of view of those religions, dangerous because the atheist rejects an eternal truth and puts in jeopardy his own and perhaps other people's attainment of the Kingdom of Heaven. Hence under pagan Rome the Epicureans— real philosophical unbelievers—were left in peace, having no reason in conscience to reject customary observances. But the Christians had, or thought they had such reason, with the result, as Tacitus observes, that they were already universally despised (presumably as subversive) when the first of the occasional attempts at suppression of the sect began under Nero.

So unbelief was, to a certain extent, countenanced in antiquity. It had three main manifestations: the two philosophical schools of Epicureanism and Skepticism, and what one might call "social unbelief" or disillusion with the gods, first clearly evident in Athens of the sophists, i.e., c. 450–400 B.C.. We return to the philosophical schools in Chapters 1 and 2, but social unbelief deserves separate attention. It is apparent, for example, in Aristophanes' *Clouds* (423 B.C.), where a stage Socrates (very unfair to the real Socrates) tells a prospective pupil that "the gods are no longer current coin in my school," and again in several of Euripides tragedies where situations evolve that lead to skeptical comments about the nature or existence of the gods (see p. 87. For Schopenhauer on ancient religion see p. 142).

More importantly, the first sustained account of the possible *natural origins* of religious belief dates from this period. It occurs in a long speech recorded by Sextus Empiricus (q. v., p. 27) and attributed by him to the sophist politician Critias (c. 460 – 407 B.C.). The account is of such considerable interest in the history of unbelief that it is here quoted in its entirety. Some of the lines are attributed by Aetius (second century A.D.) to a lost play by Euripides, but apart from the fact that Critias and Euripides are almost exact contemporaries in Athens so that the piece may be a compilation from both sources, it is the existence and currency of such an idea, not its attribution, which concerns us.

> There was a time when the life of men was disorderly, beastly and ruled by force, when there was no prize for the good and no penalty for the wicked. Then men, I think, framed primitive laws, in order that justice should be sovereign over all alike and should shackle wanton violence, and those who sinned were punished.
>
> But then, since men committed furtively the acts of violence which the laws restrained them from doing openly, some shrewd and clever man, it seems to me, invented the dread of gods for mortals, so that the wicked should be afraid, even if their deeds, or words, or thoughts were in secret. And so he introduced the supernatural, saying that there is a god blessed with unceasing life, who with his mind hears and sees, takes careful notice of and heeds such things, possessing a divine nature; who will hear all that is said among mortals, and will be able to see all that is done. Even if you plan some wicked deed in silence, that will not escape the gods. For they take note of everything.
>
> By uttering these words he taught the happiest of lessons, concealing the truth with a falsehood. He said that the gods dwell in a place, the mention of which would strike most terror into men. From this place there came, he knew, the fears that mortals have and the things that benefit a wretched life: the vault of heaven above, where he saw the lightning to be and the dread rumblings of thunder, and the stormlit frame of the sky, the beautiful embroidery of that skilled craftsman, time; where the bright mass of the sun travels and from which the moist rain falls upon the earth.
>
> Such were the fears he surrounded men with, through which he both by his words gave the deity a fine dwelling and a suitable place, and quenched lawlessness with laws.
>
> In this way, I think, did someone first persuade mortal men to believe in the existence of the race of gods.

A hint of another naturalistic account of the origin of religion survives in a paraphrase of an idea attributed to the sophist Prodicus: "that things from which benefits to human life have been derived have come to be considered deities, such as Demeter [the corn-goddess, or corn itself] and Dionysus [the god of wine, or wine itself]." Diagoras, who is always dubbed "the Atheist" (very little is known about him) lived at this time. Cicero's telling use of an anecdote concerning him can be found on p. 31.

Drawing attention to the existence of social unbelief in the second half of the fifth century B.C. is not intended to give the impression of a world of unbelief or even of a world of Athenian unbelief. Religions were normal and everywhere encountered. Moreover, as already explained, atheism was associated with civic disloyalty. Atheism thus remained a largely unacceptable public position in the Greek city-states and prosecutions could and did take place (the most celebrated and certainly the least deserved being that of Socrates himself). But such prosecutions were rare, and were directed—sometimes with disguised political motives—at isolated individuals, not at ideas as such or at philosophical systems that took no account of the gods. The difference between the classical toleration of *ideas* and the closed minds of Christianity to the same ideas may be illustrated by the following paraphrase (by Bp. Hippolytus, third century) of Democratus' account of an infinite universe in which our world is one among many, and has no special status as a divine creation:

> In some of these worlds there is no sun or moon, in some they are larger than our sun and moon, and in some there are several suns and moons. The intervals between these worlds are irregular, and in some directions they are more numerous, in others less. In one place they are being born, in another dying. Some of them are growing, some are in their prime, and some declining. When they collide, they destroy one another. There are some worlds which are devoid of plants and animals and are completely waterless.

Contrast the ideological freedoms of a civilization that could entertain without fuss or commotion philosophical views of this sort with the situation that obtained two thousand years after Democritus—at the end of the sixteenth century—when Giordano Bruno was imprisoned by the Holy Inquisition for seven years, repeatedly tortured and eventually burned alive for suggesting somewhat similar ideas to those of Democritus but, by the time of Bruno, contrary to the long-received and almost universally enforced picture of the world as unique, anthropocentric, and expressing God's purposes for human life.

The point is thus not only that unbelief existed in various forms in the ancient world (which is obvious), but that it existed independently (which is less obvious) as one of several exciting philosophical accounts of the way things could be, not merely as a negative reaction to a religious consensus about the way things are. No such consensus existed; nor could it exist before the establishment of a monotheistic religion claiming both universal allegiance *and* a revelation that excluded the truth of every view incompatible with itself. Such a revelation was provided by Christianity; Islam followed with another.

(b) THE DOMINION OF MONOTHEISM   In the second century A.D. the arguments for and against the existence of god(s) could still be presented on a more or less equal footing, for example, in the anthology of skepticism by Sextus Empiricus (see, in particular, Book I of the work usually called *Against the Physicists*). But the intellectual climate is changing. Not only is Christianity itself emerging as a serious force but there is a tone of righteous indignation against unbelief that is evident even among Stoic monotheists. Plutarch strongly denounces the Epicureans, so does Epictetus:

> There are no gods [according to the Epicureans], or if there be, they have no care for men, nor we any communion with them; and thus religion and holiness, whereof the multitude babble, is the lying of imposters and sophists, or of legislators, for the frightening and restraining of evil-doers. By Zeus! What a monstrous impudence and imposture! [*Discourses*, II, xx]

The tone of intolerance can also be heard in St. Paul, but it is more emphatic, more precise, and of infinitely greater historical consequence:

> But even if we, or an angel from heaven, should preach to you a gospel contrary to that which we preached to you, let him be accursed. As we have said before, so now I say again, if any one is preaching to you a gospel contrary to that which you received, let him be accursed. [Galatians I; 8–9; see also, for example, Romans XVI; 17–20 and 2 John 10]

With injunctions of this sort at source, together with claims to be the exclusive and final revelation of the one and only true God, it is not surprising that almost as soon as Christianity achieved temporal power (at first, and somewhat precariously, under the Emperor Constantine in 313) it turned upon other religions and unsympathetic philosophies, and even upon variations of its own doctrines, with an ideological ferocity that was previously unknown in the world. For the Christian (and by the seventh century the Muslim as well), the total exclusive character of the religious truth now accepted made unbelief not merely false as a matter of fact, not merely socially disruptive, but also *wicked*: something that damned the unbeliever, and perhaps those influenced by him, in this world and the next.

Intolerance, the rational consequence of this position, was thus established as a religious virtue. Temples were torn down or coerced into Christian use, heresy was identified and suppressed, literature critical of the new religion was physically destroyed (e.g., copies of the powerful work *Against the Christians* by Porphyry were burned in 448), and the non-Christian schools of ancient philosophy at Athens were finally closed in 529. For a thousand years the voices of unbelief were effectively silenced by the, doubtlessly sincere, use of what can best be called the Principle of Intolerance: *We know what is right and true, and for your sake it is our duty to see to it that you know nothing else.* This does not mean that no persons cherished or circumspectly expressed thoughts that might provide obscure material for a scholarly history of unbelief in the period 500 to 1500. But the fact remains that no significant or influential literary unbelief can be identified in the Christian centuries that begin with Sextus Empiricus and end with Bruno and Vanini. When the religious monolith began to be chipped away, unbelief was no longer the comparatively free and autonomous search for philosophical truth that was evident in the best of the ancient world. It was a reaction *against* religion and against the tyranny of religion

(c) THE MODERN PERIOD Unless some of the main contributions to unbelief since about 1600 are read in chronological order (as they are presented in this book) the marked groupings of arguments and tactics among them are not immediately obvious.

At first, unbelief tends, for very understandable reasons of prudence, to be presented in a covert manner—as the "real" meaning of the gospels or as an illicit opinion quoted at length in order to show its "obvious" falsity by contrast with the "truth" of the Christian revelation. One or another of these tactics can be seen in the work of Hobbes, Collins, Hume, Voltaire, and in numerous English critical deists in the first half of the eighteenth century. The level of philosophical argument is often very high indeed, but the object is attacked indirectly. In the same century, positive deistic positions (positions that affirm the creative and designing activity of God but not that being's concern with man now) are urged (e.g., by Voltaire and Paine) *against* both the superstition of revealed religion and the scandal of atheism. However, among writers who influenced or were influenced by the violent eruption of anticlericalism that marked the French Revolution, new features of unbelief are discernible. The mask, where it was a mask, of deism can be removed in order to advocate full unbelief (e.g., D'Holbach), and the morality of Christianity can—still at some risk—be denounced (e.g., Paine and Palmer) not only as an aberration of institutionalized Christianity, but as flawed at its source. Shelley's learned and vigorous *A Refutation of Deism* stands both as a summary and culmination of all these movements toward unbelief.

In the nineteenth century the most important representations of unbelief—mostly German—took on a new character. It is almost as if it were tacitly agreed that religious beliefs in general and those of Christianity in particular were false, but it was no longer worth the social odium incurred by saying so. Instead the question became what account of religion could be given that would explain its existence and continuance as a conspicuous phenomenon of human society irrespective of its truth-claims. The various answers given by Schopenhauer,

Feuerback, Marx, Nietzsche, and Freud can be found in Chapters 12 and 16.

It is only in the final contributions from the present century that the sense of having to react against the demands of religion as a conscious preliminary to unbelief at last disappears. If not glad confident morning again, then at least the thing which made Hume so careful, which so appalled Nietzsche, which still angered Russell, and whose persistence so puzzled the thinkers of the nineteenth century, can be seen slipping away into relative unimportance while unbelief becomes an ordinary and more or less unemotive possibility among other possible points of view about the nature of things.

3. The Philosophical Debate

Whatever is said about the terminology and the history of unbelief, the same question remains at the end. It is: whether unbelief is the truth about the way things are, or nearer the truth, or at the very least more probably the truth than any of the more obvious religious accounts that it attempts to displace. A careful reading of the literature of unbelief shows that unbelief depends upon five main themes or argument-clusters.

(a) MATERIALISM   The only positive intellectual replacement for religion, as opposed to its mere rejection, is provided by accounts of the totality of things, with supporting arguments and evidence, whose truth would be incompatible with, in the old logic sense of "contrary to," belief in supernatural agents.

The earliest and most influential of such accounts is Epicurean Materialism. It is an anthropocentric value system (the Epicureans were the humanists of antiquity) combined with the thesis that the totality of things consists in void (empty space) and material entities (fundamental particles and their combinations) which exist and move in the void. This form of materialism holds that all processes and things in the universe, including all life and consciousness, must be explained if they are to be explained at all, in terms of material entities, their qualities, and their movements. It is evident that Epicurean Materialism is the precursor of the atomic theory in modern science, and that assumptions similar to those of Epicurean Materialism constitute the policy usually taken for granted in modern scientific research. Lucretius, Hobbes, D'Holbach, and Feuerbach, the many contemporary adherents of what is usually called the identity theory of mind, as well as some of the leading logical positivists, at least in their early days, are materialists in this sense.

Epicurean materialism is not the only form of the doctrine. In particular there are more recent, more philosophically complex forms which maintain that everything that exists is either itself material or depends

on matter for its existence. Let us call these forms "extended materialism." One of the most important results of such extension is that
materialists in this sense are *not* committed to the view that conscious
processes are identical with brain events or with publicly observable
behavior. But they *are* committed to the view that consciousness cannot
exist in the absence of a living brain. To put it another way: matter can
exist without mind, but not mind without matter. Hume in his essay
"Of the Immortality of the Soul" adopts extended materialism. So do
Marx and Freud and many leading contemporary philosophers including Russell and Ayer and various outspoken opponents of the identity
theory of mind. Both Epicurean and extended materialists agree on
what may be called the "ontological priority" or matter and in rejecting the dualist conception (typical of supernatural religions) that a
supernatural world exists alongside of or, in some metaphorical sense
that is difficult to explain, "beyond" the natural world. They also of
course agree in rejecting the possibility of life after death as a disembodied consciousness. It is perhaps worth noting that until the middle
of the twentieth century the majority of academic philosophers repudiated materialism in both forms. In recent decades, however, the
situation has been reversed. Philosophers who reject both kinds of
materialism can still be found, but they are now a small minority among
those who concern themselves with this topic.

(b) SKEPTICISM   A second but less obvious theme in unbelief is philosophical skepticism in its various forms, but originally Pyrrhonian
Skepticism (from Pyrrho of Elis, c. 365 – 275 B.C.). The main feature of
this position was argument to show that no justified true belief about
the god(s) *or anything else* can be attained by man. Hence only the
appearances of things can be the basis of action or forbearance from
action. Such skepticism has only to balance arguments for and against
the existence of god(s) (as Sextus Empiricus tries to do) to show that no
dogmatic religion is possible. Thus all religious beliefs are undermined.
But so is everything else, and it is no historical accident that the first
printing of Sextus — in a Latin translation in 1562 — shortly preceded
the appearance in European literature of a peculiar fideistic argument
for religious belief. *If* no justified true belief is possible, *then* we have
no better reason to believe in the existence of cats and dogs and other
material things than to believe in the existence of gods and supernatural spirits; and if we believe in the former, why not the latter? This
argument from equality of ignorance no more *supports* religion than it
supports any other position. But its existence did mean that the skepticism that is the strongest element in unbelief is not Pyrrhonian Skepticism but a mitigated version that argues that there is something special
about belief in god(s) and supernatural spirits which puts the content of
such belief "beyond our understanding" or deprives it of any distinct

meaning. Skepticism of this sort can be seen in a simple form in Hobbes, where it is a consequence of his materialist analysis of the universe; in a much more sophisticated form in Hume; and again, quite differently, in the writings of Sir Alfred Ayer.

(c) ACADEMIC OR CRITICAL UNBELIEF   Academic unbelief is the negative theme of unbelief that seeks to show (or reluctantly concludes from the ubiquitous problem presented to the believer by random evil and misfortune) that the view it rejects is incoherent, or lacks sound arguments and significant evidence to support itself. There is much of it in ancient Academic Skepticism — see, for example, Cicero's Cotta in Chapter 2. But Hume is the greatest single exponent of the position. He is followed by D'Holbach, Russell, and Ayer, and by virtually all modern philosophers of religion who reject the fundamental dualist assumptions of supernatural religion, namely that it *both* makes sense, *and* is unavoidable in a true account of reality, to talk about the activity of divine agents or supernatural beings which are in another category from ("in another order of being from") the material universe. Clearly no overall comment is possible here. The arguments must speak *ad hoc* for themselves.

(d) SOCIAL UNBELIEF OR DISILLUSION WITH GOD(s),   i.e., complete unbelief A and B, or the halfway house of nonreligious deism, devolved from perception of the adverse personal, political, social, or moral consequences of religious belief or from perception of the apparent uselessness of religious observances. In writing this book, I was surprised to notice how prominently and frequently this occasion for unbelief appears in the literature. The theme surfaces with Critias and recurs from Lucretius (with his concern to alleviate fear of death and fear of ever-watching gods, and his affirmation of anthropocentric values) to Russell (with his concern about the moral inadequacies of Christianity). Hume is profoundly critical of the frivolous merits and new crimes called into being by religion, and his *History of England* is in part a chronicle of the dark and contorted actions justified by religious beliefs. Voltaire is a master at exposing the moral cruelty that results from religious devotion and dogmatic creeds. Palmer and Paine find specific humanistic fault with biblical morality and the example of Jesus bar-Joseph as it is usually understood. Shelley denounces Judeo-Christian morality. Marx and Lenin argue that the whole edifice of religion is used to divert attention from what the people can and one day will do for themselves. Nietzsche has the most bitter and pungent insights into some of the darkest and nastiest influences of religion on the free spirit of man, *and so on.*

Now it may be asked firstly whether this condemnation of the effect of religion is justified; and secondly whether, if justified, the condemnation provides good grounds for rejecting religion in general.

Let us assume the first question, at least in part, to have been answered in the affirmative. If religion—Christianity and Islam in particular—has been responsible for some of the greatest artistic, literary, and idealistic achievements of humanity, it has also, by the common consent of historians and the witness of those still living, been responsible for horrific and protracted cruelty (e.g., upon countless poor creatures categorized as witches), for dreadful wars and other conflicts that would otherwise have had no occasion or less intensity (e.g., all the Crusades, the Thirty Years' War, and present conflicts in the Middle East and Ireland), and for individual guilt and misery about imagined sin. But does this provide in itself grounds for unbelief? May not a belief about the nature of things be true *and* sometimes result in dreadful actions by those who know about its truth, or suffering for those persuaded of its truth? If so, then the unbeliever may reply that in human terms it is better to deny or not to know about some truths. For example, if it could be shown decisively that some now existing race of men is vastly inferior in intelligence, emotional sensitivity, and ability to feel pain, weariness, or discomfort, to the rest of humanity, one could argue that it might well not be a good thing for this to become widely known. Thus, it could be argued that, *even if* some religion were true, it would be best denied or forgotten, given the consequences we can all perceive. But the unbeliever is not in fact forced into such a heroic or Promethean defiance of real gods. The arguments of academic unbelief coupled with materialist accounts of the nature of things are also parts of his or her total persuasion that supernatural religion is *not* true, or at least very unlikely to be true. Hence we do *not* have to suffer the consequences of religion so that truth might prevail.

The believer will contest the academic critic in order to maintain that his or her religion does indeed have arguments and evidence in its favor, or that it is part of an autonomous way of looking at things which needs no arguments or evidence. But the believer is also likely to say that all the old evils of religion are past. They were the results of two thousand years of misunderstandings, misuses, or mistranslations of the original sources and intentions: all is *now* social conscience and humanitarian light. Then we notice Iran; or we think what a pity God found so much difficulty in conveying his message clearly; or we wonder whether the new liberal-humanitarian religion is religion at all; or we ask how much free thought or happiness would remain in a society cherished by Marxist-Catholic priests given the past conduct of both ideologies.

(e) UNBELIEF FROM NATURAL EXPLANATION OF THE PHENOMENON OF RELIGION   There is strong evidence for unbelief of this sort in fifth-century Athens (p.7) and hints elsewhere, for example in Machiavelli (p. 153).

Hobbes traces religious belief to the need for ultimate explanations that no explanation from within the natural universe can give. Hume accounts for the original and sustaining cause of religious belief as the fear of the unknown causes of events upon which our life and expectations depend. But it is the nineteenth century that overflows with natural explanations of the phenomenon of religion. It is the metaphysic of the people that gives men and women external objectives and assures them that life means something (Schopenhauer). It is humanity's projection of itself onto an alien universe (Feuerbach). It is the superstition cherished by the ruling classes as the opium of the people (Marx). It is the projection onto the hostile universe of our need for a father figure (Freud).

But does an account — even if it is correct — of the causes of a set of beliefs absolve the believer (or anyone else) from taking seriously the truth claims of the beliefs? Evidently not. An account of what causes men to believe X (even if a true and sufficient account) says nothing about whether X itself is true or probably true or false. But the unbeliever's position is that in the case of religion the truth claims of X are at the very least highly questionable, and yet religion is unaffected. Religion is thus usually entertained independently of what are alleged to be the reasons and evidence in its favor. In *that* circumstance an account of causal origins — "a natual history" — is both needed, and all that is needed, in order to understand why the phenomenon persists.

But, it will be said, in all this, and in the writings of the unbelievers represented in this book, one area of evidence that is vital to theistic religions has been ignored except in Shelley's *Refutation*. This is the evidence consisting of special revelations of the existence and activity of God, the historical books of the Bible and the allegedly divinely inspired dreams of Mahomet recorded in the Koran, for examples. Biblical scholarship has itself, however, dealt with the Christian revelation without significant aid from unbelievers, at least since the eighteenth century (for an account of which see Sir Leslie Stephen's splendid *History of English Thought in the Eighteenth Century*, particularly Chapter IV). It is thus not necessary to include among *Varieties of Unbelief* arguments about the literal accuracy of biblical texts which no informed believer, on his or her own showing, now has a right to treat as literally accurate or as containing claims that no reasonable person could reject. On the other hand, allegedly inspired dreams recorded in the Koran present both an easier and a more difficult target for the unbeliever. They are an easier target inasmuch as dreams do not for the most part seek to pass the test of historicity in any ordinary sense. They are a more difficult target inasmuch as what is inspired will be in certain respects incorrigible. The pertinent questions that must remain are whether something is indeed inspired and how anyone is supposed to know that it is.

The overall stance of unbelief is thus very powerful. There is the possibility of a positive materialist/humanist account of the total nature of things. There are arguments for special skepticism about claims to justified true belief about supernatural agents or categories of being other than the natural. There is much academic doubt about the soundness of the arguments and the effectiveness of the evidence adduced for religious beliefs. There is vast historical and some contemporary evidence to show that the social and personal consequences of religion have at the very least involved much gratuitous misery in the world. Finally there are very good natural explanations for the phenomenon of religion that make no reference to its truth claims.

1

THE FOUNT OF UNBELIEF: EPICURUS AND LUCRETIUS ON CLASSICAL MATERIALISM

The Fourfold Epicurean Prescription
There is nothing to fear from gods, nothing
awaiting us in death; good can be attained, evil
fortune can be endured.

Philodemus (c. 110–35 B.C.*)*

Biographical Note

Epicurus (341–270 B.C.) grew up on the island of Samos. He came to Athens at the age of eighteen, probably in order to attend the Academy (the school of philosophy founded by Plato). After teaching for several years at Mytilene and Lampsacus, he returned to Athens in about 306, purchased a garden, and there established the school of philosophy whose location has ever since given an alternative name to Epicureanism: the Philosophy of the Garden. He remained in this community, quietly teaching his pupils, until his death in 270. He was the first philosopher to admit women to an organized school. A vast collection of writings was attributed to him in antiquity, but the great majority of them were lost: their loss being facilitated by the zealous hostility of Christianity to his philosophy.

Lucretius (c. 94–55 B.C.) was a Roman, a contemporary of Cicero's, and a faithful exponent for Latin readers of the Epicurean philosophy. His one work, which in translation takes up about two hundred modern printed pages, is the great didactic poem *De Rerum Natura (On the Nature of Things)*. This work survives more or less intact, although its survival can be traced to the existence of a single manuscript of the fifth century. Of the details of Lucretius' life nothing is known. Jerome's story about Lucretius' insanity and suicide has no evidence to support it and may well tell us more abut the taboos and fears of Christians than about the life of the pagan unbeliever.

17

Philosophical Note

Epicureanism is the archetype for almost all materialist unbelief. It differs from many of its modern counterparts by offering not only what it claims is a true account of the nature of the universe but also a prescription for human's happiness in such a universe. No supernatural agents of any kind are active in nature or interfere in human life; hence there is no Providence to be feared or divine powers to be propitiated. There is no more survival of the person after death than there was life before birth; hence there is nothing to be feared or hoped for in a future state. The universe consists in material things and void (i.e., the emptiness in which the material things exist and move). The ultimate constituents of things of all kinds are tiny, indestructible particles of which an infinite number are distributed in the void. The universe is infinite in extent, has no beginning, and will have no end. The earth and all living things are merely ephemera in the ever-changing configurations of particles in the void. The universe was not created by divine power, nor was the earth designed for our convenience. We evolved with it out of the primordial supply of matter, and will disappear with the earth's decay. Hence life can be lived without fear of death, or gods, or any supernatural powers. Life is best lived in quiet friendship with those about you. Nothing a person can do is evil or forbidden *per se*, but many things are not to be done because they hurt others, and many things are not to be done except in moderation because they hurt oneself.

The Epicurean acceptance of the evidence of the senses, its dismissal of metaphysical abstractions, and its rejection of Providence and immortality in favor of what we might now call "scientific materialism" are not positions merely asserted as beneficial credos. They are supported by observation and argued for in detail. But in this detail we should try to guard against at least two misconceptions.

The first concerns the Greek word *atomos* used by Epicurus and regularly translated as "atom." To the Greek, *atomos* conveyed the literal sense "uncuttable" and hence "indestructible," and that is what Epicurus meant: the ultimate building blocks of things were *indestructible*. But to us atoms are not indestructible; only too evidently they can be broken up into lesser entities. Lucretius too had problems with *atomos*. No readily available Latin word existed, and Lucretius had to resort to such phrases as "primary bodies," "first things," "primordial particle." In the following extracts we therefore followed Lucretius rather than Epicurus in order to avoid the *now* misleading connotations of "atom."

The second possible misconception concerns Epicurus' and Lucretius' references to, and naming of, gods. It may be that the Epicureans did not feel strong enough to deny the existence of gods, especially when these were so closely identified with the integrity of the state, or they may have genuinely concurred in this matter with the *vox populi*. But it is the account they give of gods, not any denial of their existence, which makes their system fundamentally atheistical not only from the viewpoint of most ancient cults but emphatically from the Christian or Muslim point of view. The Epicurean gods are not creators of the universe or of anything in it; they are a creation *of* the material universe having some sort of permanent body. Moreover these gods do not concern themselves with us. They exist in "complete tranquility, aloof and detached from our affairs . . . exempt from any need of us, indifferent to our merits and immune from anger" (Lucretius, II, 646–51). In short, the verbal appearance of gods remains in the Epicurean philosophy, but the appearance is only used for the purposes of poetic conceit or to instantiate an ideal of happiness which it may be useful for us to contemplate.

The account of physical nature that was adopted and made famous by Epicurus was not in fact originated by him, but by the little-known Leucippus and his younger contemporary Democritus (c. 460–370 B.C.). Only fragments by and short paraphrases of Democritus survive. But for our present purposes it is not necessary to distinguish his thought from that of Epicurus, nor that of Epicurus from his apparently faithful exponent Lucretius. We are concerned with the system as a whole and as a whole Epicureanism (or "Greek Atomism" or "Classical Materialism") is the principal representation of unbelief in the ancient world.

The Epicurean account of the universe and of humanity's place in it was all but extinguished by the religious "sickness" (the word is used by Diogenes of Oenoanda, one of the last of the ancient Epicureans) which overwhelmed free thought in the third to fifth centuries of our era. As republished in the sixteenth century, this account infused the revolutionary ideas of Giordano Bruno, Hobbes, Gassendi, and others, not only to give a tremendous ideological boost to the development of modern science, but also to suggest again the possibility of a totality in which the fear of death and concern with supernatural agencies need play no part.

One final point: The reader may feel that what follows — a sequence of passages from Epicurus followed in some cases with Lucretius' amplification of the same ideas — is not a real contribution to unbelief because it does not *explicitly* refute the religious beliefs that have been dominant since antiquity. That is precisely its significance. The Epicureans did not have to react against a monolithic religion which almost everyone had accepted as true. Theirs was a comparatively unfettered attempt to understand the nature of things without reference to supernatural agents: an attempt which no one would ever be able to make again in the same terms after the triumph of monotheism. But it is the attempt that provides the fundamental *alternative* to monotheism rather than merely a critical refutation of it.

Classical Materialism

From Epicurus' "Letter to Herodotus" and Lucretius' *De Rerum Natura*. The complete "Letter" is only about twenty pages long.

1. *Matter cannot be created or destroyed.*

Epicurus: Now that this [to use our senses as the foundation of all our investigations] has been established we must consider the phenomena that cannot be perceived by the senses. The first principle is that nothing can be created from the non-existent: for otherwise any thing would be formed from any thing without the need of seed. If all that disappears were destroyed into the non-existent, all matter would be destroyed, since that into which it would be dissolved has no existence. Truly this universe has always been such as it now is, and so it shall always be; for there is nothing into which it can change, and there is nothing outside the universe that can enter into it and bring about a change.

Lucretius I, 146–58, 215–6: This dread and darkness of the mind cannot be dispelled by the sunbeams, the shining shafts of day, but only by an understanding of the outward form and inner workings of nature. In tackling this theme, our starting point will be this principle: *Nothing can ever be created by divine power out of nothing.* The reason why all mortals are so gripped by fear is that they see all sorts of things happening on the earth and in the sky with no discernible cause, and these they attribute to the will of a god. Accordingly, when we have seen that nothing can be created out of nothing, we shall then have a clearer picture of the path ahead, the problem of how things are created and occasioned without the aid of the gods. . . . The second great principle is this: *nature resolves everything into its component particles and never reduces anything to nothing.*

2. *The universe consists of matter and void. Matter is composed of indestructible particles.*

Epicurus: Moveover, the universe consists of material bodies and void. That the bodies exist is made clear to all by sensation itself, on which reason must base its judgment in regard to what is imperceptible, as I have said above. If that which we call "void" and "space" and "the untouchable" did not exist, the particles of matter would have no place in which to exist or through which to move, as it is clear they do move.

In addition to these two, there is nothing that we can grasp in the mind, either through concepts or through analogy with concepts, that has real existence and is not referred to merely as a property or an accident of material things or of the void.

Of material things, some are compounds, others are the simple particles from which the compounds are formed. The particles are indivisible and unchangeable, as is necessary if all is not to be dissolved to nothing, but something strong is to remain after the dissolution of the compounds, something solid, which cannot be destroyed in any way. Therefore, it is necessary that the first beginnings be indivisible particles of matter.

3. *The universe is infinite.*

Epicurus: Moreover, the universe as a whole is infinite, for whatever is limited has an outermost edge to limit it, and such an edge is defined by something beyond. Since the universe does not have an edge, it has no limit; and since it lacks a limit, it is infinite and unbounded. Moreover, the universe is infinite both in the number of its indestructible particles and in the extent of its void. If, on the one hand, the void were infinite and matter finite, the particles would not remain anywhere but would be carried away and scattered through the infinite void, since there would be no atoms from without to support them and hold them together by striking them. If, on the other hand, the void were finite, there would not be room in it for an infinite number of atoms.

Lucretius I, 958–83: Learn, therefore, that *the universe is not bounded in any direction.* If it were, it would necessarily have a limit somewhere. But clearly a thing cannot have a limit unless there is something outside to limit it, so that the eye can follow it up to a certain point but not beyond. Since you must admit that there is nothing outside the universe, it can have no limit and is accordingly without end or measure. It makes no odds in which part of it you may take your stand: whatever spot anyone may occupy, the universe stretches away from him just the same in all directions without limit. Suppose for a moment that the whole of space were bounded and that someone made his way to its uttermost boundary and threw a flying dart. Do you choose to suppose that the missile, hurled with might and main, would speed along the course on which it was aimed? Or do you think something would block the way and stop it? You must assume one alternative or the other. But neither of them leaves you a loophole. Both force you to admit that the universe continues without end. Whether there is some obstacle lying on the boundary line that prevents the dart from going farther on its course or whether it flies on beyond, it cannot in fact have started from the boundary. With this argument I will pursue you. Wherever you may place the ultimate limit of things, I will ask you: "Well then, what does happen to the dart?" The upshot is that the boundary cannot stand firm anywhere, and final escape from this conclusion is precluded by the limitless possibility of running away from it.

4. *Particle types are limited; the number of particles of each type is infinite.*

Epicurus: In addition, the indivisible, solid particles of matter, from which composite bodies are formed and into which such bodies are dissolved, exist in so many different shapes that the mind cannot grasp their number; for it would not be possible for visible objects to exhibit such great variation in form and quality if they were made by repeated use of particles of conceivable variety. The number of particles of each shape is infinite; but the number of varieties cannot be infinite, only inconceivably great.

Lucretius II, 478–499: To the foregoing demonstration I will link on another fact which will gain credence from this context: *the number of different forms of primordial particles is finite.* If it were not so, some of them would have to be of infinite magnitude. Within the narrow limits of any single particle, there can be only a limited range of forms. Suppose that particles consist of three minimum parts, or enlarge them by a few more. When by fitting on parts at top or bottom and transposing left and right you have exhausted every shape that can be given to the whole body by all possible arrangements of the parts, you are obviously left with no means of varying its form further except by adding other parts. Thence it will follow, if you wish to vary its form still further, that the arrangement will demand still other parts in exactly the same way. Variation in shape goes with increase in size. You cannot believe, therefore, that the particles are distinguished by an infinity of forms; or you will compel some of them to be of enormous magnitude, which I have already proved to be demonstrably impossible.

5. *The particles which compose matter move continuously and without a beginning of motion.*

Epicurus: Indestructible particles move without interruption through all time. Some of them fall in a straight line; some swerve from their courses; and others move back and forth as the result of collisions. These last make up the objects that our senses recognize. Some of those that move in this way after collisions separate far from each other; the others maintain a vibrating motion, either closely entangled with each other or confined by other atoms that have become entangled. There are two reasons for this continued vibration. The nature of the void that separates each of the particles from the next permits it, for the void is not able to offer any resistance; and the elasticity that is characteristic of the particles causes them to rebound after each collision. The degree of entanglement of the particles determines the extent of the recoil from the collision. These motions had no beginning, for the primordial particles and the void have always existed.

If all these things are remembered, a statement as brief as this provides a sufficient outline for our understanding of the nature of that which exists.

6. *The number of worlds like or unlike our own is infinite.*

Epicurus: Finally, the number of worlds, some like ours and some unlike, is also infinite. For the particles are infinite in number, as has been shown above, and they move through the greatest distances. The particles suited for the creation and maintenance of a world have not been used up in the formation of a single world or of a limited number of them, whether like our world or different from it. There is nothing therefore that will stand in the way of there being an infinite number of worlds.

Lucretius II, 1052–1076: Granted, then, that empty space extends without limit in every direction and that seeds innumerable in number are rushing on countless courses through an unfathomable universe under the impulse of perpetual motion, *it is in the highest degree unlikely that this earth and sky is the only one to have been created* and that all those particles of matter outside are accomplishing nothing. This follows from the fact that our world has been made by nature through the spontaneous and casual collision and the multifarious, accidental, random and purposeless congregation and coalescence of particles whose suddenly formed combinations could serve on each occasion as the starting-point of substantial fabrics — earth and sea and sky and the races of living creatures. On every ground, therefore, you must admit that there exists elsewhere other congeries of matter similar to this one which the ether clasps in ardent embrace.

When there is plenty of matter in readiness, when space is available and no cause or circumstance impedes, then surely things must be wrought and effected. You have a store of particles that could not be reckoned in full by the whole succession of living creatures. You have the same natural force to congregate them in any place precisely as they have been congregated here. You are bound therefore to acknowledge that in other regions there are other earths and various tribes of men and breeds of beasts.

7. *Our sense perceptions are physical emissions from material things striking our sense organs. Thought itself is a species of particle movement.*
   [Epicurus' account of sense perception is here omitted as being too technical and not directly relevant to the theme of the present work.]

8. *The primary particles that compose matter themselves possess only the characteristics of size, mass, shape and motion. Matter is not infinitely divisible.*
   [omitted]

9. *The soul, or that which distinguishes a living thing from a dead thing, is a material entity of a refined sort. The possibility of sensation depends upon its union with the body. Death is the dissolution of that union and is therefore nothing to us.*
   Epicurus: Next, referring to the sensations and the feelings as the most certain foundation for belief, we must see that, in general terms,

the soul is a finely divided, material thing, scattered through the whole aggregation of particles that make up the body, most similar to breath with a certain admixture of heat, in some ways resembling the one, in some ways the other. But there is also a part of the soul that goes beyond even these two in fineness, and for this reason it is more ready to share in the feelings of the body. All this is made evident to us by the powers of the soul, that is, by its feelings, its rapidity of action, its rational faculties, and its possession of those things whose loss brings death to us.

Next, we must conclude that the primary cause of sensation is in the soul; yet it would not have acquired sensation if it had not been in some way enclosed by the rest of the body. But the rest of the body, having given the soul the proper setting for experiencing sensation, has itself also gained from the soul a certain share in this capacity. Yet it does not fully share with the soul, and for this reason when the soul departs, the body no longer experiences sensation; for the body did not have this capacity in itself but made sensation possible for that other that had come into existence along with it, namely the soul. The soul, thanks to the power perfected in it by the motions of the body, at once bringing to completion its own power to experience sensation, returned a share of this power to the body because of their close contact and common feelings, as I have said. For this reason, sensation is never lost while the soul remains, even though the other parts of the body have been destroyed. Indeed, even if a portion of the soul is lost with the loss in whole or in part of that portion of the body that enclosed it, if any part at all of the soul survives, it will still experience sensation; but when the rest of the body survives both as a whole and part by part, it has no sensation if that collection of particles, small though it be, that makes up the soul has been lost. However, if the whole body is destroyed, the soul is scattered and no longer enjoys the same powers and motions; and as a result, it no longer possesses sensation. Whenever that in which the soul has existed is no longer able to confine and hold it in, we cannot think of the soul as still enjoying sensation, since it would no longer be within its proper system and would no longer have the use of the appropriate motions.

Moreover, we must clearly observe this also, that the word "incorporeal" in its common use is applied only to that which we can think of as existing by itself. Now there is no incorporeal thing that we can think of as existing by itself except the void. The void can neither act nor be acted upon; it only gives to corporeal things a space though which to move. Therefore, those who say that the soul is incorporeal are talking nonsense; for in that case the soul would be unable to act or be acted upon, and we clearly see that the soul is capable of both.

Lucretius III, 94–7, 161–176, 445–58: First, I maintain that *the mind*, which we often call the intellect, the seat of the guidance and control of life, *is part of a man*, no less than hand or foot or eyes are parts of a whole living creature. . . .

The same reasoning proves that *mind and spirit are both composed of matter*. We see them propelling the limbs, rousing the body from sleep, changing the expression of the face and guiding and steering the whole man — activities that all clearly involve touch, as touch in turn involves matter. How then can we deny their material nature? You see the mind sharing in the body's experiences and sympathizing with it. When the nerve-racking impact of a spear gashes bones and sinews, even if it does not penetrate to the seat of life, there ensues faintness and a tempting inclination earthwards and on the ground a turmoil in the mind and an intermittent faltering impulse to stand up again. The substance of the mind must therefore be material, since it is affected by the impact of material weapons. . . .

Again, we are conscious that mind and body are born together, grow up together and together decay. With the weak and delicate frame of wavering childhood goes a like infirmity of judgment. The robust vigor of ripening years is accompanied by a steadier resolve and a maturer strength of mind. Later, when the body is palsied by the potent forces of age and the limbs begin to droop with blunted vigor, the understanding limps, the tongue falters and the mind totters: everything weakens and gives way at the same time. It is thus natural that the vital spirits should all evaporate like smoke, soaring into the gusty air, and we have seen that it shares the body's birth and growth and wearies with the weariness of age. [There follow about four hundred lines of concentrated argument to show that a person does not survive bodily death. Book III concludes with Lucretius' eloquent and justly famous plea to accept our mortality and free ourselves from fear of death. See a translation in the concluding section of this book.]

10. *No supernatural agent directs or is identical with any heavenly body or earthly event.*

Epicurus: Now as to celestial phenomena, we must believe that these motions, periods, eclipses, risings, settings, and the like do not take place because there is some divinity in charge of them, who so arranges them in order and will maintain them in that order, and who at the same time enjoys both perfect happiness and immortality; for activity and anxiety, anger and kindness are not in harmony with blessedness, but are found along with weakness, fear, and dependence on one's neighbors. We must also avoid the belief that masses of concentrated fire have attained a state of divine blessedness and undertaken these motions of their own free will. . . .

In addition to these general matters, we must observe this also, that there are three things that account for the major disturbances in men's minds. First, they assume that the celestial bodies are blessed and eternal yet have impulses, actions, and purposes quite inconsistent with divinity. Next, they anticipate and foresee eternal suffering as depicted in the myths, or even fear the very lack of consciousness that come with death as if this could be of concern to them. Finally, they suffer all this, not as a result of reasonable conjecture, but through some sort of unreasoning imagination; and since in imagination they set no limit to suffering, they are beset by turmoil as great as if there were a reasonable basis for their dread, or even greater. But it is peace of mind to have been freed from all this and to have constantly in memory the essential principles of the whole system of belief. We must therefore turn our minds to immediate feelings and sensations—in matters of general concern to the common feelings and sensations of mankind, in personal matters, to our own—and to every immediate evidence from each of the means of judgment. If we heed these, we shall rightly track down the sources of disturbance and fear, and when we have learned the causes of celestial phenomena and of the other occasional happenings, we shall be free from what other men most dread.

Lucretius V, 64–90, 195–99: The next stage in the argument is this. I must first demonstrate that the world also was born and is composed of a mortal body. Then I must deal with the concourse of matter that laid the foundation of land, sea and sky, stars and sun and globe of the moon. I must show what living things have existed on earth, and which have never been born; how the human race began to employ various utterances among themselves for denoting various things; and how there crept into their minds that fear of the gods which, all the world over, sanctifies temples and lakes, groves and altars and images of the gods. After that, I will explain by what forces nature steers the courses of the sun and the journeyings of the moon, so that we shall not suppose that they run their yearly races between heaven and earth of their own free will with the amiable intention of promoting the growth of crops and animals, or that they are rolled round in furtherance of some divine plan. For it may happen that men who have learnt the truth about the carefree existence of the gods fall to wondering by what power the universe is kept going, especially those movements that are seen overhead in the borderland of ether. Then the poor creatures are plunged back into their old superstitions and saddle themselves with cruel masters whom they believe to be all-powerful. All this because they do not know what can be and what cannot: how a limit is fixed to the power of everything and an immovable frontier post. . . .

Even if I knew nothing of primordial particles, I would venture to assert on the evidence of the celestial phenomena themselves, supported by many other arguments, that the universe was certainly not created for us by divine power: so great are the faults with which it stands endowed.

2

CLASSICAL SKEPTICISM: CICERO AND SEXTUS EMPIRICUS AGAINST KNOWLEDGE OF THE GODS

> It is overwhelmingly necessary to investigate our own capacity for knowledge. For if we are so constituted that we can know nothing, there is no call to enquire further into particular things.
>
> *Eusebius (c.* A.D. *260–340) quoting a skeptic*

Biographical Note

Cicero (106–43 B.C.), Roman aristocrat, politician, orator, and author of some of the best Latin prose ever written, was educated by talented teachers who represent all the main schools of philosophy, law and oratory, in Rome and Athens. His somewhat precarious public career spanned the last turbulent years of the Roman Republic. Because of the chance survival of over 800 of his private letters (rediscovered by Petrarch in 1345), perhaps more is known about Cicero as a person than about any other human being who lived before the seventeenth century. His contribution to philosophy was made in the last three years of his life, when in rural retirement he composed a number of treatises (several in dialogue form) to make Greek philosophy accessible to Latin audiences. One of these was *Concerning the Nature of the Gods* from which the following passages are taken.

Of the life of Sextus Empiricus, next to nothing is known except that he must have lived about A.D. 200 and that he was a physician, possibly of the empirical school as his name suggests. Three of his works survive: *Outlines of Pyrrhonism* (i.e. skepticism) from whose third Book the excerpt is taken, and two much longer and more detailed works generally grouped together under the title *Adversus Mathematicos* which, as R.G. Bury suggests, might be rendered *Against the Professors of all Arts and Sciences*. The value of Sextus' writings is that he records a great bulk of skeptical argument which would otherwise have been lost in antiquity.

Philosophical Note

Ancient skepticism has a long and complicated history going back to Pyrrho of Elis (c. 360 – 275 B.C.) or earlier. The philosophical thrust of skepticism was a rejection of all claims to knowledge that exceed a simple statement of each fact as it appears to us. The psychological thesis of skepticism was that "quietude" could only be achieved by not embracing positive opinions which inevitably conflict with other positive opinions. The opinions that were mainly criticized were the "dogmatisms" (i.e., positive beliefs) of the Epicureans and Stoics. But when the *Outlines* resurfaced in Western Europe — in print in a Latin translation in 1562 — its arguments were to provide ammunition against another dogmatism. The old skepticism also reappeared in the writings of Montaigne in the claim that Christian belief depends upon faith, not upon reason and evidence.

In the extracts from Cicero, skepticism appears as philosophically acute criticisms of the monotheistic dispositions of the Stoic philosophers. The criticisms almost certainly come from Carneades (c. 214 – 129 B.C.) *via* Clitomachus. They are, as it were, academic criticisms of theology in the ancient world. They reappear, for example, in Hume's *Dialogues concerning Natural Religion.*

The chapter quoted from Sextus does not attempt to argue against the common opinion *that there are gods* since that would itself involve the illegitimate positive affirmation *that there are not.* It simply seeks to oppose *arguments* that there are gods in order to lead to the typical skeptical suspense of judgment on the subject. Within three centuries of Sextus, and then for more than a thousand years, such a suspense of judgment would at best be regarded as a catastrophic misfortune for the unbeliever, and at worst as an evil to be eradicated by all the cruelty that human ingenuity could devise.

Sections 1 and 2 that follow are taken from Cicero's *De Natura Deorum* (*Concerning the Nature of the Gods*) Book III, Chapters 10 – 11 and 35 – 39, respectively. Both are from speeches by Cotta, who represents the skeptical critic. The Epicurean and Stoic views are put by other speakers. Section 3 is from Sextus Empiricus, *Outlines of Pyrrhonism,* Book I, Chapter 6 and Book III, Chapter 3.

1. The Natural Origin of Order

Cicero, *De Natura Deorum, III, Chapters 10 – 11*

10   If the world as a whole is not god, neither are the stars, which in all their countless numbers you wanted to reckon as gods, enlarging with delight upon their uniform and everlasting movements. And I protest you do this with good reason, for they display a marvelous and

extraordinary regularity. But not all things, Balbus, that have fixed and regular courses are to be accredited to a god rather than to nature.

What occurrence do you think could possibly be more regular than the repeated alternation of flow in the Euripus at Chalcis? or in the Straits of Messina? or than the eddying ocean-currents in the region where

> Europe and Libya by the hurrying wave
> Are sundered?

Cannot the tides on the coasts of Spain or Britain ebb and flow at fixed intervals of time without a god's intervention? Why, if all motions and all occurrences that preserve a constant periodic regularity are declared to be divine, pray shall we not be obliged to say that tertian and quartan agues are divine too, for nothing can be more regular than the process of their recurrence? But all such phenomena call for a rational explanation; and in your inability to give such an explanation you fly for refuge to a god.

Also you admired the cleverness of an argument of Chrysippus, who was undoubtedly an adroit and hardy thinker (I apply the adjective "adroit" to persons of nimble wit, and "hardy" to those whose minds have grown hard with use as the hand is hardened by work); well, Chrysippus argues thus: "If anything exists that man is not capable of creating, he that creates that thing is superior to man; but man is not capable of creating the objects that we see in the world; therefore he that was capable of so doing surpasses man; but who could surpass man save god? therefore god exists."

The whole of this is involved in the same mistake as the argument of Zeno; no definition is given of the meaning of "superior" and "more excellent," or of the distinction between nature and reason. Chrysippus furthermore declares that, if there be no gods, the natural universe contains nothing superior to man; but for any man to think that there is nothing superior to man he deems to be the height of arrogance. Let us grant that it is a mark of arrogance to value oneself more highly than the world; but not merely is it not a mark of arrogance, rather is it a mark of wisdom, to realize that one is a conscious and rational being, and that Orion and Canicula are not. Again, he says "If we saw a handsome mansion, we should infer that it was built for its masters and not for mice; so therefore we must deem the world to be the mansion of the gods." Assuredly I should so deem it if I thought it had been built like a house, and not constructed by nature, as I shall show that it was.

11   But then you tell me that Socrates, in Xenophon's account, asks the question, if the world contains no rational soul, where did we pick up ours? And I too ask the question, where did we get the faculty of speech, the knowledge of numbers, the art of music? unless indeed we suppose that the sun holds conversation with the moon when their

courses approximate, or that the world makes a harmonious music, as Pythagoras believes. These faculties, Balbus, are the gifts of nature — not nature "walking craftsmanlike manner" as Zeno says (and what this means we will consider in a moment), but nature by its own motions and mutations imparting motion and activity to all things. And so I fully agreed with the part of your discourse that dealt with nature's punctual regularity, and what you termed its concordant interconnexion and correlation; but I could not accept your assertion that this could not have come about were it not held together by a single divine breath. On the contrary, the system's coherence and persistencê is due to nature's forces and not to divine power; she does possess that "concord" (the Greek term is *sympatheia*) of which you spoke, but the greater this is as a spontaneous growth, the less possible is it to suppose that it was created by divine reason.

2. The Indifference of the Gods

Cicero, *De Natura Deorum*, III, Chapters 35–39

Now let us consider the next topics — first whether the world is ruled by divine providence, and then whether the gods have regard for the affairs of mankind. For these are the two that I have left of the heads into which you divided the subject; and if you gentlemen approve, I feel that they require a somewhat detailed discussion. . . .

35   Well, Dionysius was not struck dead with a thunderbolt by Olympian Jupiter, nor did Aesculapius cause him to waste away and perish of some painful and lingering disease. He died in his bed and was laid upon a royal pyre, and the power which he had himself secured by crime he handed on as an inheritance to his son as a just and lawful sovereignty. It is with reluctance that I enlarge upon this topic, since you may think that my discourse lends authority to sin; and you would be justified in so thinking, were not an innocent or guilty conscience so powerful a force in itself, without the assumption of any divine design. Destroy this, and everything collapses; for just as a household or a state appears to lack all rational system and order if in it there are no rewards for right conduct and no punishments for transgression, so there is no such thing at all as the divine governance of the world if that governance makes no distinction between the good and the wicked.

"But," it may be objected, "the gods disregard smaller matters, and do not pay attention to the petty farms and paltry vines of individuals, and any trifling damage done by blight or hail cannot have been a matter for the notice of Jupiter; even kings do not attend to all the petty affairs in their kingdom": this is how you argue. As if forsooth it was Publius Rutilius's estate at Formiae about which I complained a little time ago, and not his loss of all security!

36   But this is the way with all mortals: their external goods, their vineyards, cornfields and olive-yards, with their abundant harvests and fruits, and in short all the comfort and prosperity of their lives, they think of as coming to them from the gods; but virtue no one ever imputed to a god's bounty. And doubtless with good reason; for our virtue is a just ground for others' praise and a right reason for our own pride, and this would not be so if the gift of virtue came to us from a god and not from ourselves. On the other hand when we achieve some honor or some accession to our estate, or obtain any other of the goods or avoid any of the evils of fortune, it is then that we render thanks to the gods, and do not think that our own credit has been enhanced. Did anyone ever render thanks to the gods because he was a good man? No, but because he was rich, honored, secure. The reason why men give to Jupiter the titles of Best and Greatest is not that they think that he makes us just, temperate or wise, but safe, secure, wealthy, and opulent. Nor did anyone ever vow to pay a tithe to Hercules if he became a wise man! It is true there is a story that Pythagoras used to sacrifice an ox to the Muses when he had made a new discovery in geometry! but I don't believe it, since Pythagoras refused even to sacrifice a victim to Apollo of Delos, for fear of sprinkling the altar with blood. However, to return to my point, it is the considered belief of all mankind that they must pray to god for fortune but obtain wisdom for themselves. Let us dedicate temples as we will to Intellect, Virtue and Faith, yet we perceive that these things are within ourselves; hope, safety, wealth, victory are blessings which we must seek from the gods. Accordingly *the prosperity and good fortune of the wicked*, as Diogenes used to say, *disprove the might and power of the gods entirely.*

37   "But sometimes good men come to good ends." Yes, and we seize upon these cases and impute them with no reason to the immortal gods. Diagoras, named the Atheist, once came to Samothrace, and a certain friend said to him, "You who think that the gods disregard men's affairs, do you not remark all the votive pictures that prove how many persons have escaped the violence of the storm, and come safe to port, by dint of vows to the gods? "That is so," replied Diagoras; "it is because there are nowhere any pictures of those who have been shipwrecked and drowned at sea." On another voyage he encountered a storm which threw the crew of the vessel into a panic, and in their terror they told him that they had brought it on themselves by having taken him on board their ship. He pointed out to them a number of other vessels making heavy weather on the same course, and inquired whether they supposed that those ships also had a Diagoras on board. The fact really is that your character and past life make no difference whatever as regards your fortune good or bad.

"The gods do not take notice of everything, any more than do human rulers," says our friend. Where is the parallel? If human rulers knowingly overlook a fault they are greatly to blame, but as for god, he cannot even offer the excuse of ignorance. And how remarkably you champion his cause, when you declare that the divine power is such that even if a person has escaped punishment by dying, the punishment is visited on his children and grandchildren and their descendants! What a remarkable instance of the divine justice! Would any state tolerate a lawgiver who should enact that a son or grandson was to be sentenced for the transgression of a father or grandfather?

> Where shall the Tantalids' vendetta end?
> What penalty for Myrtilus's murder
> Shall ever glut the appetite of vengeance?

Whether the Stoic philosophers were led astray by the poets, or the poets relied on the authority of the Stoics, I should find it hard to say; for both tell some monstrous and outrageous tales. For the victim lashed by the lampoons of Hipponax or the verses of Archilochus nursed a wound not inflicted by a god but received from himself; and we do not look for any heaven-sent cause when we view the licentiousness of Aegisthus or of Paris, since their guilt almost cries aloud in our ears; and the bestowal of health upon many sick persons I ascribe to Hippocrates rather than to Aesculapius; and I will never allow that Sparta received the Lacedaemonian rule of life from Apollo rather than from Lycurgus. It was Critolaus, I aver, who overthrew Corinth, and Hasdrubal Carthage: those two glories of the sea-coast were extinguished by these mortals, not be some angry god — who according to your school is entirely incapable of anger. But at all events a god could have come to the aid of those great and splendid cities and have preserved them.

39   For you yourselves are fond of saying that there is nothing that a god cannot accomplish, and that without any toil; as a man's limbs are effortlessly moved merely by his mind and will, so, as you say, the gods' power can mould and move and alter all things. Nor do you say this as some superstitious fable or old wives' tale, but you give a scientific and systematic account of it: you allege that matter, which constitutes and contains all things, is in its entirety flexible and subject to change, so that there is nothing that cannot be molded and transmuted out of it however suddenly, but the moulder and manipulator of this universal substance is divine providence, and therefore providence, whithersoever it moves, is able to perform whatever it will. Accordingly either providence does not know its own powers, or it does not regard human affairs, or it lacks power of judgment to discern what is the best. "It does not care for individuals." This is no wonder; no more does it care for cities. Not for these? Not for tribes or nations either. And it is shall appear that it despises even nations, what wonder is it that it has scorned the entire human race?

3. The Incoherence of the Conception of God

Sextus Empiricus, *Outline of Pyrrhanism*, I, Chapter 6; III, Chapter 3

I, Ch. 6: *The Principle of Skepticism.* The originating cause of Skepticism is, we say, the hope of attaining quietude. Men of talent, who were perturbed by the contradictions in things, and in doubt as to which of the alternatives they ought to accept, were led on to inquire what is true in things and what false, hoping by the settlement of this question to attain quietude. The main basic principle of the Skeptic system is that of opposing to every proposition an equal proposition; for we believe that as a consequence of this we end by ceasing to dogmatize.

III, Ch. 3: *Concerning God.* Since, then, the majority have declared that God is a most efficient cause, let us begin by inquiring about God, first premising that although, following ordinary life, we affirm undogmatically that gods exist and reverence gods and ascribe to them foreknowledge, yet as against the rashness of the Dogmatists [mainly Stoics and Epicureans; Christians had not yet become an intellectual force worth attention] we argue as follows:

When we conceive objects we ought to form conceptions of their substances as well, as, for instance, whether they are corporeal or incorporeal. And also of their forms; for no one could conceive "Horse" unless he had first learnt the horse's form. And of course the object conceived must be conceived as existing somewhere. Since, then, some of the Dogmatists assert that God is corporeal, others that he is incorporeal, and some that he has human form, others not, and some that he exists in space, others not; and of those who assert that he is in space some put him inside the world, others outside; how shall we be able to reach a conception of God when we have no agreement about his substance or his form or his place of abode? Let them first agree and consent together that God is of such and such a nature, and then, when they have sketched out for us that nature, let them require that we should form a conception of God. But so long as they disagree interminably, we cannot say what agreed notion we are to derive from them.

But, say they, when you have conceived of a Being imperishable and blessed, regard this as God. But this is foolish; for just as one who does not know Dion is unable also to conceive the properties which belong to him as Dion, so also when we do not know the substance of God we shall also be unable to learn and conceive his properties. And apart from this, let them tell us what a "blessed" thing is — whether it is that which energizes according to virtue and foreknows what is subject to itself, or that which is void of energy and neither performs any work itself nor provides work for another. For indeed about this also they disagree interminably and thus render "the blessed" something we cannot conceive, and therefore God also.

Further, in order to form a conception of God one must necessarily
—so far as depends on the Dogmatists—suspend judgment as to his
existence or non-existence. For the existence of God is not pre-evident.
For if God impressed us automatically, the Dogmatists would have
agreed together regarding his essence, his character, and his place;
whereas the interminable disagreement has made him seem to us non-
evident and needing demonstration. Now he that demonstrates the
existence of God does so by means of what is either pre-evident or
non-evident. Certainly not, then, by means of the pre-evident; for if
what demonstrates God's existence were pre-evident, then—since the
thing proved is conceived together with that which proves it, and
therefore is apprehended along with it as well, as we have established
—God's existence also will be pre-evident, it being apprehended along
with the pre-evident fact which proves it. But, as we have shown, it is
not pre-evident; therefore it is not proved, either, by a pre-evident
fact. Nor yet by what is non-evident. For if the non-evident fact which
is capable of proving God's existence, needing proof as it does, shall be
said to be proved by means of a pre-evident fact, it will no longer be
non-evident but pre-evident. Therefore the non-evident fact which
proves his existence is not proved by what is pre-evident. Nor yet by
what is non-evident; for he who asserts this will be driven into circular
reasoning when we keep demanding proof every time for the non-evident fact which he produces as proof of the one last propounded.
Consequently, the existence of God cannot be proved from any other
fact. But if God's existence is neither automatically pre-evident nor
proved from another fact, it will be inapprehensible.

There is this also to be said. He who affirms that God exists either
declares that he has, or that he has not, forethought for the things in the
universe, and in the former case that such forethought is for all things
or for some things. But if he had forethought for all, there would have
been nothing bad and no badness in the world; yet all things, they say,
are full of badness; hence it shall not be said that God forethinks all
things. If, again, he forethinks some, why does he forethink these things
and not those? For either he has both the will and the power to
forethink all things, or else he has the will but not the power, or the
power but not the will, or neither the will nor the power. But if he had
had both the will and the power he would have had forethought for all
things; but for the reasons stated above he does not forethink all;
therefore he has not both will and the power to forethink all. And if he
has the will but not the power, he is less strong than the cause which
renders him unable to forethink what he does not forethink: but it is
contrary to our notion of God that he should be weaker than anything.
And if, again, he has the power but not the will to have forethought for
all, he will be held to be malignant; while if he has neither the will nor
the power, he is both malignant and weak—an impious thing to say

about God. Therefore God has no forethought for the things in the universe.

But if he exercises no forethought for anything, and there exists no work nor product of his, no one will be able to name the source of the apprehension of God's existence, inasmuch as he neither appears of himself nor is apprehended by means of any of his products. So for these reasons we cannot apprehend whether God exists. And from this we further conclude that those who positively affirm God's existence are probably compelled to be guilty of impiety; for if they say that he forethinks all things they will be declaring that God is the cause of what is evil, while if they say that he forethinks some things or nothing they will be forced to say that God is either malignant or weak, and obviously this is to use impious language.

3

"THE TRIUMPH OF BARBARISM AND RELIGION": EDWARD GIBBON ON THE SPREAD OF CHRISTIANITY AND THE NOBLE ARMY OF MARTYRS

But now, as I have said, the most of mankind lie
sick, as it were of a pestilence, in their false
beliefs about the world, and the tale of them
increases. For by imitation they take the disease
from one another like sheep.

Diogenes of Oenoanda, c. 200 A.D.

I beseech you therefore, brethren, by the mercies
of God, that you present your bodies a living
sacrifice, holy, acceptable to God, which is your
reasonable service.

St. Paul

Biographical Note

Edward Gibbon (1737–1794, author of the near-definitive *History of the Decline and Fall of the Roman Empire* published in six volumes between 1776 and 1788, attained a deep but irregular education from a succession of tutors at Oxford, and for five years at Lausanne in Switzerland. At the age of sixteen he experienced a temporary and brief conversion to Roman Catholicism. But his ever-increasing and eventually vast classical and historical learning seems to have made him in the long run a disinterested and skeptical observer of religion rather than a devotee of any part of it. In 1776 he sent a copy of the first volume of his *History,* containing the controversial Chapter 15 "The Progress of the Christian Religion, and the Sentiments, Manners, Numbers and Condition of the Primitive Christians," and 16 "The Conduct of the Roman Government towards the Christians, from the Reign of Nero to that of Constantine" to David Hume. Hume's comment on "the dignity of your style, the depth of your matter [and] the extensiveness of your learning" still stands. Concerning Chapters 15 and 16 Hume was also prophetic: "It was impossible to treat the subject so as not to give ground of suspicion against you, and you may expect that a clamour will arise." It did. Gibbon replied with a *Vindication* in January 1779, and the substitution of scholarship for the myths of Christian history had begun.

Philosophical Note

Gibbon's importance as a marker on the road to unbelief lies in the immense and impeccable learning he could bring to bear upon the natural and historical origins of Christianity. The conventional myth about the spread of Christianity in the Roman world referred to the providence of God and the convincing historical and personal testimony of its early followers. Gibbon replied that the providence of God is inscrutable and the testimony flawed. He then identified five causes for the spread of Christianity. These causes are independent of the supposed truth of the revelation delivered or of its excellence for mankind. The conventional myth about the prolonged and extensive persecution of Christians by the pagan emperors (a myth now unchallengeably replanted in popular imagination by Hollywood spectaculars) was also challenged by Gibbon. The persecution, he shows, was erratic, occasional, inconclusively pursued, and, most of all to the point, largely invited by Christians themselves in their iconoclastic attitude to the power symbols of the State, and by their own enthusiastic seeking after martyrdom in a world they expected soon to end.

The two crucial chapters of the *History* comprise about 150 pages. Their learned power and urbane skepticism can only be enjoyed when they are taken in full measure. The following extracts are therefore appetizers, not meals. Gibbon justifies almost everything he says by reference to authority. These footnotes are omitted.

1. The Spread of Christianity

From *History of the Decline and Fall of the Roman Empire*, Chapter 15 in which Gibbon argues that, "It was by the aid of these causes, (i) exclusive zeal, (ii) the immediate expectation of another world, (iii) the claim of miracles, (iv) the practice of rigid virtue, and (v) the constitution of the primitive Church, that Christianity spread itself with so much success in the Roman Empire." Part of the argument for cause (ii) is as follows:

When the promise of eternal happiness was proposed to mankind, on condition of adopting the faith and of observing the precepts of the gospel, it is no wonder that so advantageous an offer should have been accepted by great numbers of every religion, of every rank, and of every province in the Roman empire. The ancient Christians were animated by a contempt for their present existence, and by a just confidence of immortality, of which the doubtful and imperfect faith of modern ages cannot give us any adequate notion. In the primitive church, the influence of truth was very powerfully strengthened by an opinion which, however it may deserve respect for its usefulness and antiquity, has not been found agreeable to experience. It was universally believed that the end of the world and the kingdom of Heaven were at hand. The near approach of this wonderful event had been predicted by the apostles; the tradition of it was preserved by their earliest disciples, and those who understood in their literal sense the discourses of Christ himself were obliged to expect the second and glorious coming of the Son of Man in the clouds, before that generation was totally extinguished, which had beheld his humble condition upon earth, and which might still be witness of the calamities of the Jews under Vespasian or Hadrian. The revolution of seventeen centuries has instructed us not to press too closely the mysterious language of prophecy and revelation; but, as long as, for wise purposes, this error was permitted to subsist in the church, it was productive of the most salutary effects on the faith and practice of Christians, who lived in the awful expectation of that moment when the globe itself, and all the various race of mankind, should tremble at the appearance of their divine judge.

The ancient and popular doctrine of the Millennium was intimately connected with the second coming of Christ. As the works of the creation had been finished in six days, their duration in their present state, according to a tradition which was attributed to the prophet Elijah, was fixed to six thousand years. By the same analogy it was inferred that this long period of labour and contention, which was now almost elapsed, would be succeeded by a joyful Sabbath of a thousand years; and that Christ, with the triumphant band of the saints and the elect who had escaped death, or who had been miraculously revived, would reign upon earth till the time appointed for the last and general resurrection. So pleasing was this hope to the mind of believers that the *New Jerusalem*, the seat of this blissful kingdom, was quickly adorned with all the gayest colours of the imagination. A felicity consisting only of pure and spiritual pleasure would have appeared too refined for its inhabitants, who were still supposed to possess their human nature and senses. A garden of Eden, with the amusements of the pastoral life, was no longer suited to the advanced state of society which prevailed under the Roman empire. A city was therefore erected of gold and precious stones, and a supernatural plenty of corn and wine was bestowed on the adjacent territory; in the free enjoyment of whose spontaneous productions the happy and benevolent people was never to be restrained by any jealous laws of exclusive property. The assurance of such a Millennium was carefully inculcated by a succession of fathers from Justin

Martyr and Irenaeus, who conversed with the immediate disciples of the apostles, down to Lactantius, who was preceptor to the son of Constantine. Though it might not be universally received, it appears to have been the reigning sentiment of the orthodox believers; and it seems so well adapted to the desires and apprehensions of mankind that it must have contributed, in a very considerable degree, to the progress of the Christian faith. But, when the edifice of the church was almost completed, the temporary support was laid aside. The doctrine of Christ's reign upon earth was at first treated as a profound allegory, was considered by degrees as a doubtful and useless opinion, and was at length rejected as the absurd invention of heresy and fanaticism. A mysterious prophecy, which still forms a part of the sacred canon, but which was thought to favour the exploded sentiment, has very narrowly escaped the proscription of the church.

Whilst the happiness and glory of a temporal reign were promised to the disciples of Christ, the most dreadful calamities were denounced against an unbelieving world. The edification of the new Jerusalem was to advance by equal steps with the destruction of the mystic Babylon; and, as long as the emperors who reigned before Constantine persisted in the profession of idolatry, the epithet of Babylon was applied to the city and to the empire of Rome. A regular series was prepared of all the moral and physical evils which can afflict a flourishing nation; intestine discord, and the invasion of the fiercest barbarians from the unknown regions of the North; pestilence and famine, comets and eclipses, earthquakes and inundations. All these were only so many preparatory and alarming signs of the great catastrophe of Rome, when the country of the Scipios and Caesars should be consumed by a flame from Heaven, and the city of the seven hills, with her palaces, her temples, and her triumphal arches, should be buried in a vast lake of fire and brimstone. It might, however, afford some consolation to Roman vanity, that the period of their empire would be that of the world itself; which, as it had once perished by the element of water, was destined to experience a second and a speedy destruction from the element of fire. In the opinion of a general conflagration, the faith of the Christian very happily coincided with the tradition of the East, the philosophy of the Stoics, and the analogy of Nature; and even the country which, from religious motives, had been chosen for the origin and principal scene of the conflagration, was the best adapted for that purpose by natural and physical causes; by its deep caverns, beds of sulphur, and numerous volcanoes, of which those of Ætna, of Vesuvius, and of Lipari, exhibit a very imperfect representation. The calmest and most intrepid sceptic could not refuse to acknowledge that the destruction of the present system of the world by fire was in itself extremely probable. The Christian, who founded his belief much less on the fallacious arguments of reason than on the authority of tradition and the interpretation of scripture, expected it with terror and confidence, as a certain and approaching event; and, as his mind was perpetually filled with the solemn idea, he considered every disaster that happened to the empire as an infallible symptom of an expiring world.

The condemnation of the wisest and most virtuous of the Pagans, on account of their ignorance or disbelief of the divine truth, seems to offend the reason and the humanity of the present age. But the primitive church, whose faith was of a much firmer consistence, delivered over, without hesitation, to eternal torture the far greater part of the human species. A charitable hope might perhaps be indulged in favour of Socrates, or some other sages of antiquity, who had consulted the light of reason before that of the gospel had arisen. But it was unanimously affirmed that those who, since the birth or the death of Christ, had obstinately persisted in the worship of the dæmons, neither deserved, nor could expect, a pardon from the irritated justice of the Deity. These rigid sentiments, which had been unknown to the ancient world, appear to have infused a spirit of bitterness into a system of love and harmony. The ties of blood and friendship were frequently torn asunder by the difference of religious faith; and the Christians, who, in this world, found themselves oppressed by the power of the Pagans, were sometimes seduced by resentment and spiritual pride to delight in the prospect of their future triumph. "You are fond of spectacles," exclaims the stern Tertullian; "except the greatest of all spectacles, the last and eternal judgment of the universe. How shall I admire, how laugh, how rejoice, how exult, when I behold so many proud monarchs, and fancied gods, groaning in the lowest abyss of darkness; so many magistrates, who persecuted the name of the Lord, liquefying in fiercer fires than they ever kindled against the Christians; so many sage philosophers blushing in red hot flames, with their deluded scholars; so many celebrated poets trembling before the tribunal, not of Minos, but of Christ; so many tragedians, more tuneful in the expression of their own sufferings; so many dancers ———!" But the humanity of the reader will permit me to draw a veil over the rest of this infernal description, which the zealous African pursues in a long variety of affected and unfeeling witticisms.

Doubtless there were many among the primitive Christians of a temper more suitable to the meekness and charity of their profession. There were many who felt a sincere compassion for the danger of their friends and countrymen, and who exerted the most benevolent zeal to save them from the impending destruction. The careless Polytheist, assailed by new and unexpected terrors, against which neither his priests nor his philosophers could afford him any certain protection, was very frequently terrified and subdued by the menace of eternal tortures. His fears might assist the progress of his faith and reason; and, if he could once persuade himself to suspect that the Christian religion might possibly be true, it became an easy task to convince him that it was the safest and most prudent party that he could possibly embrace.

2. The Noble Army of Martyrs

From *History of the Decline and Fall of the Roman Empire*, Chapter 16 in which Gibbon argues "(i) that a considerable time elapsed before [the Roman authorities] considered the new sectaries as an object deserving of the attention of government, (ii) that in the conviction of any of their subjects who were accused of so very singular a crime, they proceeded with caution and reluctance, (iii) that they were moderate in the use of punishments, and (iv) that the afflicted church enjoyed many intervals of peace and tranquility." He concludes:

In this general view of the persecution, which was first authorized by the edicts of Diocletian, I have purposely refrained from describing the particular sufferings and deaths of the Christian martyrs. It would have been an easy task, from the history of Eusebius, from the declamations of Lactantius, and from the most ancient acts, to collect a long series of horrid and disgustful pictures, and to fill many pages with racks and scourges, with iron hooks, and red-hot beds, and with all the variety of tortures which fire and steel, savage beasts and more savage executioners, could inflict on the human body. These melancholy scenes might be enlivened by a crowd of visions and miracles destined either to delay the death, to celebrate the triumph, or to discover the relics, of those canonized saints who suffered for the name of Christ. But I cannot determine what I ought to transcribe, till I am satisfied how much I ought to believe. The gravest of the ecclesiastical historians, Eusebius himself, indirectly confesses that he has related whatever might redound to the glory, and that he has suppressed all that could tend to the disgrace, of religion. Such an acknowledgment will naturally excite a suspicion that a writer who has so openly violated one of the fundamental laws of history has not paid a very strict regard to the observance of the other; and the suspicion will derive additional credit from the character of Eusebius, which was less tinctured with credulity, and more practised in the arts of courts, than that of almost any of his contemporaries. On some particular occasions, when the magistrates were exasperated by some personal motives of interest or resentment, when the zeal of the martyrs urged them to forget the rules of prudence, and perhaps of decency, to overturn the altars, to pour out imprecations against the emperors, or to strike the judge as he sat on his tribunal, it may be presumed that every mode of torture, which cruelty could invent or constancy could endure, was exhausted on those devoted victims. Two circumstances, however, have been unwarily mentioned, which insinuate that the general treatment of the Christians who had been apprehended by the officers of justice was less intolerable than it is usually imagined to have been. 1. The confessors who were condemned to work in the mines were permitted, by the humanity or the negligence of their keepers, to build chapels and freely to profess their religion in the midst of those dreary habitations. 2. The bishops were obliged to check and to censure the forward zeal of the Christians, who voluntarily threw themselves into the hands of the magistrates. Some of these were persons oppressed by poverty and debts, who blindly sought to terminate a miserable existence by a glorious death. Others were allured by the hope that a short confinement would expiate the sins of a whole life; and others, again, were actuated by the less honourable motive of deriving a plentiful subsistence, and perhaps a considerable profit, from the alms which the charity of the faithful bestowed on the prisoners. After the church had triumphed over all her enemies, the interest as well as vanity of the captives prompted them to magnify the merit of their respective suffering. A convenient distance of time or place gave an ample scope to the progress of fiction; and the frequent instances which might be alleged of holy martyrs, whose wounds had been instantly healed, whose strength had been renewed, and whose lost members had miraculously been restored, were extremely convenient for the purpose of removing every difficulty and of silencing every objection. The most extravagant legends, as they conduced to the honor of the church, were applauded by the credulous multitude, countenanced by the power of the clergy, and attested by the suspicious evidence of ecclesiastical history.

The vague descriptions of exile and imprisonment, of pain and torture, are so easily exaggerated or softened by the pencil of an artful orator that we are naturally induced to inquire into a fact of a more distinct and stubborn kind: the number of persons who suffered death, in consequence of the edicts published by Diocletian, his associates, and his successors. The recent legendaries record whole armies and cities, which were at once swept away by the undistinguishing rage of persecution. The more ancient writers content themselves with pouring out a liberal effusion of loose and tragical invectives, without condescending to ascertain the precise number of those persons who were permitted to seal with their blood their belief of the gospel. From the history of Eusebius, it may however be collected that only nine bishops were punished with death; and we are assured, by his particular enumeration of the martyrs of Palestine, that no more than ninety-two Christians were entitled to that honorable appellation. As we are unacquainted with the degree of episcopal zeal and courage which prevailed at that time, it is not in our power to draw any useful inferences from the former of these facts; but the latter may serve to justify a very important and probable conclusion. According to the distribution of

Roman provinces, Palestine may be considered as the sixteenth part of the Eastern empire; and since there were some governors who, from a real or affected clemency, had preserved their hands unstained with the blood of the faithful, it is reasonable to believe that the country which had given birth to Christianity produced at least the sixteenth part of the martyrs who suffered death within the dominions of Galerius and Maximin; the whole might consequently amount to about fifteen hundred: a number which, if it is equally divided between the ten years of the persecution, will allow an annual consumption of one hundred and fifty martyrs. Allotting the same proportion to the provinces of Italy, Africa, and perhaps Spain, where, at the end of two or three years, the rigour of the penal laws was either suspended or abolished, the multitude of Christians in the Roman empire on whom a capital punishment was inflicted by a judicial sentence will be reduced to somewhat less than two thousand persons. Since it cannot be doubted that the Christians were more numerous, and their enemies more exasperated, in the time of Diocletian, than they had ever been in any former persecution, this probable and moderate computation may teach us to estimate the number of primitive saints and martyrs who sacrificed their lives for the important purpose of introducing Christianity into the world.

We shall conclude this chapter by a melancholy truth which obtrudes itself on the reluctant mind; that even admitting, without hesitation, or inquiry, all that history has recorded, or devotion has feigned, on the subject of martyrdoms, it must still be acknowledged that the Christians, in the course of their intestine dissensions, have inflicted far greater severities on each other than they had experienced from the zeal of infidels. During the ages of ignorance which followed the subversion of the Roman empire in the West, the bishops of the Imperial city extended their dominion over the laity as well as clergy of the Latin church. The fabric of superstition which they had erected, and which might long have defied the feeble efforts of reason, was at length assaulted by a crowd of daring fanatics, who, from the twelfth to the sixteenth century, assumed the popular character of reformers. The church of Rome defended by violence the empire which she had acquired by fraud; a system of peace and benevolence was soon disgraced by proscriptions, wars, massacres, and the institution of the holy office. And, as the reformers were animated by the love of civil, as well as of religious, freedom, the Catholic princes connected their own interest with that of the clergy, and enforced by fire and the sword the terrors of spiritual censures. In the Netherlands alone, more than one hundred thousand of the subjects of Charles the Fifth are said to have suffered by the hand of the executioner; and this extraordinary number is attested by Grotius, a man of genius and learning, who preserved his moderation amidst the fury of contending sects, and who composed the annals of his own age and country, at a time when the invention of printing had facilitated the means of intelligence and increased the danger of detection. If we are obliged to submit our belief to the authority of Grotius, it must be allowed that the number of Protestants who were executed in a single province and a single reign far exceeded that of the primitive martyrs in the space of three centuries and of the Roman empire. But, if the improbability of the fact itself should prevail over the weight of evidence; if Grotius should be convicted of exaggerating the merit and sufferings of the Reformers; we shall be naturally led to inquire what confidence can be placed in the doubtful and imperfect monuments of ancient credulity; what degree of credit can be assigned to a courtly bishop, and a passionate declaimer, who, under the protection of Constantine, enjoyed the exclusive privilege of recording the persecutions inflicted on the Christians by the vanquished rivals or disregarded predecessors of their gracious sovereign.

4

THOMAS HOBBES ON THE NATURAL CAUSES OF RELIGION AND THE ABSURDITY OF SPEECH ABOUT GOD

Fear of power invisible, feigned by the mind, or imagined from tales publicly allowed, RELIGION; not allowed, SUPERSTITION.

Leviathan, Chapter 6

Biographical Note

The irascible and, by his own estimation, timid Hobbes was born in 1588 — suddenly according to report, his mother being startled by the approach of the Spanish Armada. He died in 1679, pensioned by Charles II and sustained by the Cavendish family. Tutorships, foreign travel, translations from the classics, controversy with Descartes, the (largely erroneous) pursuit of mathematics, politics, tennis, and an apparently inexhaustible energy for anything life put in his way, marked Hobbes' career from first to last.

His massive publications (in English and in Latin) on political philosophy, general philosophy, mechanics, and human nature are prickly, witty, controversial, at times belligerent, and in many respects highly original and unorthodox. Of these, the best known in *Leviathan*, but among his other works *Human Nature*, written much earlier but only published in 1650, one year before *Leviathan*, deserves to be more widely read.

It is remarkable, given the religious and political passions of his time, and given his own uncomfortable opinions and litigious character, that Hobbes managed to guide his way through so long a life without disaster. But he did manage to survive, despite a committee of Parliament being instructed in 1666 to investigate his "atheism" as a possible provocation of divine wrath leading to the outbreak of the plague in London. "There was a report," says his friend Aubrey, "that some of the bishops made a motion to have the good old gentleman burned for a heretic." But Hobbes lived on, befriended by the rich and powerful, to die of natural causes in his ninety-second year.

Philosophical Note

The enormous period of time that separates the last utterances of ancient unbelief from its first recognizable manifestations in seventeenth-century Europe (Montaigne 1533–1592, Bruno 1548–1600, and Vanini (1585–1619) in the sixteenth century being debatable cases) is partly explained by Gibbon at the end of the previous section. The Roman Church triumphantly adopted what we have called the Principle of Intolerance: *We know what is right and true, and for your sake it is our duty to see to it that you know nothing else.* The Principle is utterly unknown in ancient religion, where the variety and local importance of particular gods preclude its application. But the principle is appropriate to the exclusive claims of monotheism, and was effectively used by the Roman Church, in due course adopted by Protestant reformers, and passed on to some of the nastiest and most brutal of modern secular ideologies. Unbelief was thus silenced, and became almost unthinkable for many centuries, and heresy was contained by the fires that served Christianity more effectively than the secret police of our century have served political masters.

I express this matter strongly and without academic qualification because without an awareness of the temporal and coercive power of Christianity, it is not possible to understand the often coded and always indirect criticisms of religion that were all that even a courageous man who was not a fool could at first risk. Thus Hobbes always sets passages that, if read in isolation, would sound sharply hostile to religion, in a context or with an escape clause which could identify him with the "true" Christian. For example, having dismantled (*Leviathan*, Chapter 4) one of the favored philosophical accounts of man's immortality (that man is material, perishable body, *plus* immaterial, immortal soul) he later argues (Chapter 38) that this is orthodox because scripture has nothing to say about immortal souls and only mentions "[bodily] resurrection on the last day" as an expectation. After Hobbes the devices for avoiding unequivocal confrontation with religious belief become almost standard. Thus Anthony Collins contrives to avow beliefs that he had evidently been arguing against. Voltaire produces a scandalously critical article (see p. 59) on the Divinity of Jesus by condemning *and quoting* the opinions of others. Hume directs us to revelation and faith as a means of believing what he shows is plainly contrary to reason, and so on. It is not really until after the French Revolution that avowed atheism became permissible and even then — and perhaps still — it was not the best way to commend oneself as a school teacher, a politician, a television personality, or a president of the United States.

So Hobbes is equivocal. His accounts of the natural causes of religion and of the language we can use about God sound (and I would contend really were) directly calculated to make religious belief uncomfortable. But he could have denied and for his own safety would have had to deny this objective. The evidence of other passages gives Hobbes his escape. Some modern scholars accept his protestations as genuine: he was more like a religious reformer seeking to isolate the essential belief than a barbed unbeliever. But it seems incredible that a man of Hobbes' vast learning and sharpness of mind could have been unconscious of, or not genuinely intended, the damning criticisms of religion that his contemporaries unanimously read into his works. The more Hobbes' "true" religion requires quotation marks, the less his "atheism" needs such absolution.

Section 1 is taken from *Leviathan*, the conclusion of Chapter 11 and the first half of Chapter 12. Section 2 is from *Human Nature*, the beginning of Chapter 11.

1. The Natural Causes of Religion

From *Leviathan*, Chapters 11, 12

Ignorance of natural causes, disposeth a man to credulity, so as to believe many times impossibilities: for such know nothing to the contrary, but that they may be true; being unable to detect the impossibility. And credulity, because men like to be hearkened unto in company, disposeth them to lying: so that ignorance itself without malice, is able to make a man both to believe lies, and tell them; and sometimes also to invent them.

Anxiety for the future time, disposeth men to inquire into the causes of things: because the knowledge of them, maketh men the better able to order the present to their best advantage.

Curiosity, or love of the knowledge of causes, draws a man from the consideration of the effect, to seek the cause; and again, the cause of that cause; till of necessity he must come to this thought at last, that there is some cause, whereon there is no former cause, but is eternal; which is it men call God. So that it is impossible to make any profound inquiry into natural causes, without being inclined thereby to believe there is one God eternal; though they cannot have any idea of him in their mind, answerable to his nature. For as a man that is born blind, hearing men talk of warming themselves by the fire, and being brought to warm himself by the same, may easily conceive, and assure himself, there is somewhat there, which men call *fire*, and is the cause of the heat he feels; but cannot imagine what it is like; not have an idea of it in his mind, such as they have that see it: so also by the visible things in this world, and their admirable order, a man may conceive there is a cause of them, which men call God; and yet not have an idea, or image of him in his mind.

And they that make little, or no inquiry into the natural causes of things, yet from the fear that proceeds from the ignorance itself, of what it is that hath the power to do them much good or harm, are inclined to suppose, and feign unto themselves, several kinds of powers invisible; and to stand in awe of their own imaginations; and in time of distress to invoke them; as also in the time of an expected good success, to give them thanks; making the creatures of their own fancy, their gods. By which means it hath come to pass, that from the innumerable variety of fancy, men have created in the world innumerable sorts of gods. And this fear of things invisible, is the natural seed of that, which every one in himself calleth religion; and in them that worship, or fear that power otherwise than they do, superstition.

And this seed of religion, having been observed by many; some of those that have observed it, have been inclined thereby to nourish, dress, and form it into laws; and to add to it of their own invention, any opinion of the causes of future events, by which they thought they should be best able to govern others, and make unto themselves the greatest use of their powers.

CHAPTER XII. OF RELIGION SEEING there are no signs, nor fruit of *religion*, but in man only; there is no cause to doubt, but that the seed of *religion*, is also only in man; and consisteth in some peculiar quality, or at least in some eminent degree thereof, not to be found in any other living creatures.

And first, it is peculiar to the nature of man, to be inquisitive into the causes of the events they see, some more, some less; but all men so much, as to be curious in the search of the causes of their own good and evil fortune.

Secondly, upon the sight of anything that hath a beginning, to think also it had a cause, which determined the same to begin, then when it did, rather than sooner or later.

Thirdly, whereas there is no other felicity of beasts, but the enjoying of their quotidian food, ease, and lusts; as having little or no foresight of the time to come, for want of observation, and memory of the order, consequence, and dependence of the things they see; man observeth how one event hath been produced by another; and remembereth in them antecedence and consequence; and when he cannot assure himself of the true causes of things, (for the causes of good and evil fortune for the most part are invisible,) he supposes causes of them, either such as his own fancy suggesteth; or trusteth the authority of other men, such as he thinks to be his friends, and wiser than himself.

The two first, make anxiety. For being assured that there be causes of all things that have arrived hitherto, or shall arrive hereafter; it is impossible for a man, who continually endeavoreth to secure himself against the evil he fears, and procure the good he desireth, not to be in a perpetual solicitude of the time to come; so that every man, especially those that are over provident, are in a state like to that of Prometheus.

For as Prometheus, which interpreted, is, *the prudent man*, was bound to the hill Caucasus, a place of large prospect, where, an eagle feeding on his liver, devoured in the day, as much as was repaired in the night: so that man, which looks too far before him, in the care of future time, hath his heart all the day long, gnawed on by fear of death, poverty, or other calamity; and has no repose, nor pause of his anxiety, but in sleep.

This perpetual fear, always accompanying mankind in the ignorance of causes, as it were in the dark, must needs have for object something. And therefore when there is nothing to be seen, there is nothing to accuse, either of their good, or evil fortune, but some *power*, or agent *invisible*: in which sense perhaps it was, that some of the old poets said, that the gods were at first created by human fear: which spoken of the gods, that is to say, of the many gods of the Gentiles, is very true. But the acknowledging of one God, eternal, infinite, and omnipotent, may more easily be derived, from the desire men have to know the causes of natural bodies, and their several virtues, and operations; than from the fear of what was to befall them in time to come. For he that from any effect he seeth come to pass, should reason to the next and immediate cause thereof, and from thence to the cause of that cause, and plunge himself profoundly in the pursuit of causes; shall at last come to this, that there must be, as even the heathen philosophers confessed, one first mover; that is, a first, and an eternal cause of all things; which is that which men mean by the name of God: and all this without thought of their fortune; the solicitude whereof, both inclines to fear, and hinders them from the search of the causes of other things; and thereby gives occasion of feigning of as many gods, as there be men that feign them.

And for the matter, or substance of the invisible agents, so fancied; they could not by natural cogitation, fall upon any other conceit, but that it was the same with that of the soul of man; and that the soul of man, was of the same substance, with that which appeareth in a dream, to one that sleepeth; or in a looking-glass, to one that is awake; which, men not knowing that such apparitions are nothing else but creatures of the fancy, think to be real, and external substances; and therefore call them ghosts; as the Latins called them *imagines*, and *umbræ*; and thought them spirits, that is, thin aerial bodies; and those invisible agents, which they feared, to be like them; save that they appear, and vanish when they please. But the opinion that such spirits were incorporeal, or immaterial, could never enter into the mind of any man by nature; because, though men may put together words of contradictory signification, as *spirit*, and *incorporeal*; yet they can never have the imagination of any thing answering to them: and therefore, men that by their own meditation, arrive to the acknowledgment of one infinite, omnipotent, and eternal God, chose rather to confess he is incomprehensible, and above their understanding, than to define his nature by *spirit incorporeal*, and then confess their definition to be unintelligible: or if they give him such a title, it is not *dogmatically*, with intention to make the divine nature understood; but *piously*, to honor him with attributes, of significations, as remote as they can from the grossness of bodies visible.

Then, for the way by which they think these invisible agents wrought their effects; that is to say, what immediate causes they used, in bringing things to pass, men that know not what it is that we call *causing*, that is, almost all men, have no other rule to guess by, but by observing, and remembering what they have seen to precede the like effect at some other time, or times before, without seeing between the antecedent and subsequent event, any dependence or connexion at all: and therefore from the like things past, they expect the like things to come; and hope for good or evil luck, superstitiously, from things that have no part at all in the causing of it: as the Athenians did for their war at Lepanto, demand another Phormio; the Pompeian faction for their war in Africa, another Scipio; and others have done in divers other occasions since. In like manner they attribute their fortune to a stander by, to a lucky or unlucky place, to words spoken, especially if the name of God be amongst them; as charming and conjuring, the liturgy of witches; insomuch as to believe, they have power to turn a stone into bread, bread into a man, or any thing into any thing.

Thirdly, for the worship which naturally men exhibit to powers invisible, it can be no other, but such expressions of their reverence, as they would use towards men; gifts, petitions, thanks, submission of body, considerate addresses, sober behavior, premeditated words, swearing, that is, assuring one another of their promises, by invoking them. Beyond that reason suggesteth nothing; but leaves them either to rest there; or for further ceremonies, to rely on those they believe to be wiser than themselves.

Lastly, concerning how these invisible powers declare to men the things which shall hereafter come to pass, especially concerning their good or evil fortune in general, or good or ill success in any particular undertaking, men are naturally at a stand; save that using to conjecture of the time to come, by the time past, they are very apt, not only to take casual things, after one or two encounters, for prognostics of the like encounter ever after, but also to believe the like prognostics from other men, of whom they have once conceived a good opinion.

And in these four things, opinion of ghosts, ignorance of second causes, devotion towards what men fear, and taking of things casual for prognostics, consisteth the natural seed of *religion*: which by reason of the different fancies, judgments, and passions of several men, hath grown up into ceremonies so different, that those which are used by one man, are for the most part ridiculous to another.

2. The Absurdity of Speech About God

From *Human Nature*, Chapter 11

1. Hitherto of the knowledge of things *natural*, and of the passions that arise naturally from them. Now forasmuch as we give names not only to things natural, but also to *supernatural*; and by all names we ought to have some meaning and conception: it followeth in the next place, to consider what thoughts and imaginations of the mind we have, when we take into our mouths the most blessed name of GOD, and the names of those *virtues* we attribute unto him; as also, what *image* cometh into the mind at hearing the name of *spirit*, or the name of *angel*, good or bad.

2. And forasmuch as God Almighty is *incomprehensible*, it followeth, that we can have *no* conception or *image* of the *Deity*, and consequently, all *his attributes* signify our *inability* and defect of power to *conceive* anything concerning his nature, and not any conception of the same, excepting only this, that *there is a God*: for the effects we acknowledge naturally, do include a power of their producing, before they were produced; and that power presupposeth something existent that hath such power: and the thing so existing with power to produce, if it were not eternal, must needs have been produced by somewhat before it, and that again by something else before that, till we come to an eternal, that is to say, the first power of all powers, and first cause of all causes: and this is it which all men conceive by the name of GOD, implying eternity, incomprehensibility, and omnipotency. And thus all that will consider, may know *that* God is, though not *what* he is: even a man that is born blind, though it be not possible for him to have any imagination what kind of thing fire is; yet he cannot but know that somewhat there is that men call fire, because it warmeth him.

3. And whereas we attribute to God Almighty, *seeing, hearing, speaking, knowing, loving,* and the like, by which names we understand something in *men* to whom we attribute them, we understand *nothing* by them in the nature of God: for, as it is well reasoned, *Shall not the God that made the eye, see; and the ear, hear?* So it is also, if we say, shall God, which made the eye, not see without the eye; or that made the ear, not hear without the ear; or that made the brain, not know without the brain; or that made the heart, not love without the heart? The *attributes* therefore given unto the *Deity*, are such as *signify* either *our incapacity* or our *reverence*: our incapacity, when we say incomprehensible and infinite; our reverence, when we give him those names, which amongst us are the names of those things we most magnify and commend, as omnipotent, omniscient, just, merciful, &c. And when God Almighty giveth those names to himself in the Scriptures, it is but ἀνθρωποπαθῶς, that is to say, by descending to our manner of speaking; without which we are not capable of understanding him.

4. By the name of *spirit*, we understand a *body natural*, but of such *subtilty*, that it worketh not upon the senses; but that filleth up the place which the image of a visible body might fill up. Our conception therefore of spirit consisteth of *figure without color*; and in figure is understood dimension, and consequently, to conceive a spirit, is to conceive something that hath dimension. But *spirits supernatural* commonly signify some *substance without* dimension; which two words do flatly contradict one another: and therefore when we attribute the name of spirit unto God, we attribute it not as the name of anything we conceive, no more than we ascribe unto him sense and understanding; but as a signification of our reverence, we desire to abstract from him all corporal grossness.

5. Concerning other things, which some men call *spirits incorporeal*, and some *corporeal*, it is not *possible* by *natural* means only, to come to *knowledge* of so much, as that *there are such* things. We that are Christians *acknowledge* that there be angels good and evil, and that there are spirits, and that the soul of a man is a spirit, and that those spirits are immortal: *but*, to *know* it, that is to say, to have natural evidence of the same, it is *impossible*: for, all *evidence* is *conception*, as it is said, chap. vi. sect. 3, and all conception is imagination, and proceedeth from *sense*, chap. iii. sect. 1. And *spirits* we suppose to be those substances which work *not* upon the *sense*, and therefore not conceptible. But though the Scripture acknowledges spirits, yet doth it nowhere say, that they are incorporeal, meaning thereby, without dimension and quality; nor, I think, is that word incorporeal at all in the Bible; but it is said of the spirit, that it abideth in men; sometimes that it dwelleth in them, sometimes that it cometh on them, that it descendeth, and goeth, and cometh; and that spirits are angels, that is to say messengers: all which words do imply *locality*; and locality is *dimension*; and whatsoever hath dimension, is *body*, be it never so subtile. To me therefore it seemeth, that the Scripture favoreth them more, that hold angels and spirits corporeal, than them that told the contrary. And it is a plain *contradiction* in natural discourse, to say of the soul of man; that it is *tota in toto, et tota in qualibet parte corporis*, grounded neither upon reason nor revelation, but proceeding from the ignorance of what those things are which are called *spectra*, images, that appear in the dark to children, and such as have strong fears, and other strange imaginations, as hath been said, chapter iii. sect. 5, where I call them phantasms: for, taking them to be things real, without us, like bodies, and seeing them to come and vanish so strangely as they do, unlike to bodies; what could they call them else, but *incorporeal bodies*? which is not a name, but an absurdity of speech.

5

ANTHONY COLLINS ON MORTALITY AND FREE THOUGHT

That which befalleth the sons of men befalleth
beasts; even one thing befalleth them: as the one
dieth, so dieth the other; yea, they have all one
breath; so that a man has no pre-eminence above
a beast: for all is vanity. All go unto one place; all
are of the dust, and all turn to dust again. . . .
For the living know that they shall die: but the
dead know not anything. . . . For there is no
work, nor device, nor knowledge, nor wisdom, in
the grave, whether thou goest.

Ecclesiastes 3, 19–21; 9. 5, 10

Surely such a wide diversity of opinion among
men of the greatest learning on a matter of the
first importance [piety and ritual, and the nature
of the gods] must influence with a sense of doubt
even those who think they possess certain
knowledge.

Cicero, De Natura Deorum, I, 6

Biographical Note

A pleasant and well-liked English gentleman, educated at Eton and
King's College, Cambridge, Anthony Collins (1676–1729) was acquainted with some of the leading radical thinkers of the period including John Toland, Matthew Tindal, Thomas Chubb, and John Locke.
Although he trained for a legal career, Collins never practiced, and his
energies were divided between the duties of a country landowner
(which he took very seriously) and the writing of controversial publications (which others took very critically) in which he disputed with
Samuel Clarke, Archbishop King, et al. In these publications Collins
argued for positions that were as close to unbelief senses B and C, and
possibly even A, as prudence would allow — and at times a bit closer.
His books include *A Letter to Dodwell* (1707) concerning immortality,
the *Discourse of Freethinking* (1713) advocating freedom of intellectual
inquiry, *Philosophical Inquiry Concerning Human Liberty* (1717) con-

cerning freedom and determinism, and the *Grounds and Reasons of the Christian Religion* (1724), concerning Christianity's supposed completion of Old Testament prophecies.

Philosophical Note

Collins is a perfect example of the propensity already noted in the case of Hobbes for the literature of unbelief to disguise itself in the early modern period behind protestations of faith. Collins' contemporaries thought he wrote like an infidel and argued with him accordingly. But what he writes always permits him to deny the "charge" of atheism. In recent years scholars remain divided (see Bibliography). But there can be little real doubt about the intention of the irony in the following passage, or about the sincerity of Collins' pleas for free-thinking in matters of religion, or the direction such free-thinking would take in his case.

The term *charge* of atheism is used advisedly. Atheism, apart from the earlier and more savage penalties against it that were repealed or disused after the Restoration, was made an offense under the laws of England by an Act of 1696, which prescribed penalties for persons who shall "assert or maintain that there are more gods than one, or shall deny the Christian religion to be true." The English Act was liberal in comparison with the law as enforced in France and most other Christian countries. But what constituted "atheism" in the seventeenth and eighteenth centuries is never clearly defined. It sometimes meant as little as "one who rejects Christianity as *I* understand it." Sometimes the word denoted those associated with the ideas of Epicurus; sometimes those who denied the providence of God; sometimes those who questioned the *arguments* for belief in God or immortality. But it is always a term of contumely. (It is not until the late nineteenth century that "atheism" even begins to suggest the nonemotive absence of any idea of God or gods.) As such, even unbelievers sought to avoid the designation. It was not until the *salons* of mid-eighteenth-century France began to give the protection of privacy to like-minded men and women that atheism began to be avowed. But Collins had no such protection.

1. Mortality

From *A Discourse of Freethinking* (1713), a note to page 152

It is possible the reader who is fully persuaded, as he has reason to be, of the immortality of the Soul, upon the authority of Jesus Christ, who has brought immortality to light, may be surprised that so wise a man as Solomon should deny so important a truth. Wherefore, for the vindication of Solomon's want of knowledge in this point, I observe:

First, that the immortality of the Soul was nowhere plain in the Old

Testament, was denied by the Sadducees, the most philosophical part of the Jewish Nation, and of whom their magistrates principally consisted; was thought doubtful by most sects of the Greek philosophers, and denied by the Stoics, the most religious sect of them all; had never, according to Cicero, been asserted in writing by any Greek author extant *in his time* before Pherecydes of the island of Syros; and was first taught by the Egyptians or, according to our learned Sir John Marsham, was their most noble invention. No wonder therefore if Solomon reasoned like the learned men of his own country and the more learned philosophers of the neighboring nations!

Secondly, I observe, that the true principles upon which the immortality of the Soul depends are only to be fetched from the New Testament. We learn in the Old Testament that Adam, by eating the forbidden fruit, subjected himself and all his posterity to death. But the New Testament teaches us to understand by death, eternal life in misery; and from thence we know that God had but one way to put mankind in a capacity of enjoying immortal happiness, *viz.* by sending Jesus Christ into the world, who (as God and man, and God's Son, and the same numerical Being with that God whose Son he was, and yet personally distinct from him) only could by his sufferings and death give an infinite satisfaction to an infinitely offended God, appease his wrath and thereby save the elect. Now I would ask how any man without revelation could know that death signified eternal life in misery; or that Adam's posterity should be liable to eternal damnation for his transgression; or how without revelation so wonderful a scheme as the gospel scheme (which alone lays the foundation of a happy immortality) could enter into the wisest man's imagination?

2. Free Thought

From *The Independent Whig,* number XIX, 25th May 1720, "Queries concerning Authority in Matters of Faith."

1. Is there any authority among men in matters of faith?
2. Wherein does that authority consist?
3. Who are the men that have that authority? and particularly, who are the men that have that authority in China, Turkey, France, Scotland, England, Hanover, Holland, and Sweden?
4. Have men in one country authority over others in another country in matters of faith? And who are those men that have that authority?
5. Are there any persons in the Roman Communion, who have authority, in matters of faith, over the other members of that communion? And who are they?
6. Are there any persons in the communion of the Church of England, who have authority, in matters of faith, over the other members of that communion? And who are they?

7. Have any persons in the Roman Church authority, in matters of faith, over the members of the Church of England?

8. If some persons of the Church of England have an authority, in matters of faith, over the other members of the Church of England; and if no person of the Roman Church have such an authority over the other members of the Roman Church; what reason can be assigned, for giving such authority to some persons of the Church of England, that will not equally hold for giving such authority to some persons in the Church of Rome, over the other members of the Church of Rome?

9. If any person in the Roman Church have now authority, in matters of faith, over the other members of the Roman Church; were there not persons in the Roman Church, who had such authority, before the Reformation?

10. Have private people in the Roman Church (that is, all but those who have an authority in matters of faith) any right to oppose those persons in the exercise of their authority, who have an authority in matters of faith in that Church? Are not private people obliged to submit to such, exercising their authority?

11. Have private people in the Church of England any right to oppose those persons in the exercise of their authority who have an authority in matters of faith in that Church? Are not private people obliged to submit to such, exercising their authority?

12. Have private men in all churches a right to judge, whether the matters of faith of their church be erroneous or no?

13. Have private men a right to separate from the communion of a church, whose matters of faith they judge to be erroneous?

14. Have private men a right to separate from the communion of all churches, if they deem them all erroneous in matters of faith?

15. Have private people, separating from the communion of all churches, as deeming them erroneous in matters of faith, a right to form a new church among themselves? Or ought they to live without public worship, and without being members of any particular church?

16. If private men have a right to judge, whether the matters of faith received in their church be erroneous or no; if they have a right to separate from the communion of a church, whose matters of faith they judge to be erroneous; and from all churches, if they deem them erroneous in matters of faith: And if private people have a right to form a new church upon such separation from all churches: What authority in matters of faith can there be in any persons of any church?

17. Will it not follow, from the answer that shall be given to the foregoing queries, that there can be no authority at all among men in matters of faith; or, that all authority in matters of faith rests in some person or persons in the Roman Church?

18. If there be an authority in matters of faith in some person or persons of the Roman Church; must not that person or those persons,

be infallible in the exercise of it; that is, Is not infallibility a consequence of authority? Or, at least, must not the said authority have the
same effect as infallibility, namely, produce an intire submission of
mind and actions in the people subject to the said authority?

19. If there be no authority among men in matters of faith; and if
every man has a right to judge for himself in matters of faith; can the
civil magistrate have a right to enact by law any articles (meaning such
articles as have no relation to the peace of civil society) as matters of
faith, by rewarding men to maintain them, and by punishing those who
oppose them, or any way putting them upon a worse foot for their
opposition, than other subjects? Does he not hereby set up for an
authority in matters of faith, and invade the right of private judgment?

20. If men have a right of private judgment in matters of faith, ought
the civil magistrate to hinder them from being free and impartial in the
use of their private judgment?

21. Is being rewarded for maintaining certain articles as matters of
faith, and being punished, or suffering for opposing them, proper to
produce a free and impartial use of our judgments, in relation to the
truth or falsehood of those matters of faith?

6

FRANÇOIS-MARIE VOLTAIRE AND THE BITTER RIDICULE OF BELIEF

> There is a great difference between seeking how
> to raise a laugh from every thing; and seeking, in
> every thing, what justly may be laughed at. For
> nothing is ridiculous except what is deformed: nor
> is any thing proof against raillery, except what is
> handsome and just. And therefore 'tis the hardest
> thing in the world, to deny fair honesty the use of
> this weapon, which can never bear an edge
> against himself, and bears against every thing
> contrary.
>
> *Shaftesbury, Characteristics,* 1711

> One must destroy one's opponents' seriousness
> with laughter, and their laughter with seriousness.
>
> *Gorgias, fifth century* B.C.

Biographical Note

François-Marie Arouet (1694–1778), universally known by his pen name Voltaire, was the most brilliant, prolific, and long-lived figure among the group of French intellectuals which at various times included Diderot, D'Alembert, Helvetius, and D'Holbach: the "Encyclopedists" or "Philosophes." Voltaire himself attained early literary success with his plays before embarking—with the epic poem *La Henriade* (1723)—on a lifelong crusade against the cruelty, repression, and absurdity of Christianity as it then existed. Although himself a believer in a designer-god, Voltaire's enormous outpouring of writings was unrelentingly and increasingly hostile to institutionalized religion. But so rich and famous was he by the last two decades of his life that he was suffered to live unmolested by authority on the borders of Switzerland and France. After his death his body was, however, buried outside Paris in unconsecrated ground—to be moved to the Pantheon in 1791, and then once more cast out after the Restoration in 1814. Voltaire's enormous output includes the well-known story *Candide* (1759), the manifesto against Christianity known as *The Sermon of the Fifty* (1762), and the *Philosophical Dictionary* (1764 onwards) from which the three following sections are taken.

Philosophical Note

The figure of Voltaire so dominates the European Enlightenment that any brief note about him must be invidious or superfluous or both. Suffice to say that he is not the philosopher whose profound, cautious, and extensive criticisms all but destroyed the rational foundations of theistic religion as a whole. To that achievement the name and writings of David Hume are ineradicably attached. Nor is Voltaire the philosopher who finally advocated and published a completely atheistic system; that was the work of Baron D'Holbach. Voltaire's work was seldom profound. It is deistic rather than atheistic. It is certainly not cautious, and contains few completely argued positions. But it is the effective lever—the superb propaganda for active humanity against pious cruelty—which exposed facile lies and bigotry. His weapons are usually simple arguments supported by learning, irony, mocking wit, and astringent ridicule. Voltaire does not explicitly adopt Shaftesbury's test of ridicule, but it is the fulcrum upon which much of his effect is achieved: religious lies, cruelty, and bigotry are evil; but they are also absurd. They are laughable because they are deformed. They are sanctified by seriousness but destroyed by laughter. Almost anything Voltaire wrote could be used to illustrate this characteristic. He was witty even when he was angry with the grossest folly. But his wit, fame and the sheer volume of his literary work probably spread more unbelief in France than the careful philosophizing of a hundred lesser men.

The following three articles are from the *Philosophical Dictionary* in its final expanded form. The article on "The Divinity of Jesus" has a flavor reminiscent of Collins on immortality (see p. 54); that on "Martyrs" vividly illustrates the Enlightenment's distaste for improbable prodigies and pious myths. The same feeling is succinctly expressed in Ambrose Bierce's *Devil's Dictionary:* "Martyr, noun. One who moves along the path of least resistance to a desired death." The article on "Optimism" is a theme that frequently recurs in Voltaire's works, namely that suffering cannot be given an easy or perhaps *any* explanation by Christianity.

1. Divinity of Jesus

From *The Philosophical Dictionary*

The Socinians, who are regarded as blasphemers, do not recognize the divinity of Jesus Christ. They dare to pretend, with the philosophers of antiquity, with the Jews, the Mahometans, and most other nations, that the idea of a god-man is monstrous; that the distance from

God to man is infinite; and that it is impossible for a perishable body to be infinite, immense, or eternal.

They have the confidence to quote Eusebius, bishop of Caesarea, in their favor, who, in his *Ecclesiastical History*, Book I, Chapter 9, declares that it is absurd to imagine the uncreated and unchangeable nature of Almighty God taking the form of a man. They cite the fathers of the church, Justin and Tertullian, who have said the same thing: Justin, in his Dialogue with Triphonius, and Tertullian, in his Discourse against Praxeas.

They quote St. Paul, who never calls Jesus Christ God, and who calls him man very often. They carry their audacity so far as to affirm that the Christians passed three entire ages in forming by degrees the apotheosis of Jesus; and that they only raised this astonishing edifice by the example of the pagans,who had deified mortals. At first, according to them, Jesus was only regarded as a man inspired by God, and then as a creature more perfect than others. They gave him some time after a place above the angels, as St. Paul tells us. Every day added to his greatness. He in time became an emanation, proceeding from God. This was not enough; he was even born before time. At last he was made God consubstantial with God. Crellius, Voquelsius, Natalis Alexander, and Hornbeck, have supported all these blasphemies by arguments, which astonish the wise and mislead the weak. Above all, Faustus Socinus spread the seeds of this doctrine in Europe; and at the end of the sixteenth century, a new species of Christianity was established. There were already more than three hundred species.

2. Martyrs

From *The Philosophical Dictionary*

I. Martyr, "witness"; martyrdom, "testimony." The early Christian community at first gave the name of "martyrs" to those who announced new truths to mankind, who gave testimony to Jesus, who confessed Jesus; in the same manner as they gave the name of "saints" to the presbyters, to the supervisors of the community, and to their female benefactors; this is the reason why St. Jerome, in his letters, often calls his initiated Paul, Saint Paul. All the first bishops were called saints.

Subsequently, the name of martyr was given only to deceased Christians, or to those who had been tortured for punishment; and the little chapels that were erected to them, received afterwards the name of "martyrion."

It is a great question, why the Roman empire always tolerated in its bosom the Jewish sect, even after the two horrible wars of Titus and Adrian; why it tolerated the worship of Isis at several times; and yet frequently persecuted Christianity. It is evident, that the Jews, who paid dearly for their synagogues, denounced the Christians as mortal foes, and excited the people against them. It is moreover evident that the Jews, occupied with the trade of brokers and usury, did not preach against the ancient religion of the empire, and the Christians, who were all busy in controversy, preached against the public worship, sought to destroy it, often burned the temples, and broke the consecrated statutes, as St. Theodosius did at Amasia, and St. Polyeuctus in Mitylene.

The orthodox Christians, sure that their religion was the only true one, did not tolerate any other. In consequence, they themselves were hardly tolerated. Some of them were punished and died for the faith — and these were the martyrs.

This name is so respectable, that it ought not to be prodigally bestowed: it is not right to assume the name and arms of a family to which one does not belong. Very heavy penalties have been established against those who have the audacity to decorate themselves with the cross of Malta or of St. Louis, without being chevaliers of those orders.

The learned Dodwell, the dextrous Middleton, the judicious Blondel, the exact Tillemount, the scrutinizing Launoy, and many others, all zealous for the glory of the true martyrs, have excluded from their catalogue an obscure multitude on whom this great title had been lavished. We have remarked, that these learned men were sanctioned by the direct acknowledgment of Origen, who, in this *Against Celsus*, confesses that there are very few martyrs, and those at a great distance of time, and that it is easy to reckon them. [Examples of the absurd stories attached to martyrs are here omitted.]

II. How does it happen that, in the enlightened age in which we live, learned and useful writers are still found who nevertheless follow the stream of old errors, and who corrupt many truths by admitted fables? They reckon the era of the martyrs from the first year of the empire of Dioclesian, who was then far enough from inflicting martyrdom on anybody. They forget that his wife Prisca was a Christian, that the principal officers of his household were Christians; that he protected them constantly during eighteen years; that they built at Nicomedia a church more sumptuous than his palace; and that they would never have been persecuted if they had not outraged the Caesar Valerius.

Is is possible that anyone should still dare to assert, "that Dioclesian died of age, despair, and misery"; he who was seen to quit life like a philosopher, as he had quitted the empire; he who, solicited to resume the supreme power, loved better to cultivate his fine gardens as Salona, than to reign over the whole of the then known world?

Oh ye compilers! will you never cease to compile? You have usefully employed your three fingers; employ still more usefully your reason!

What! You repeat to me that St. Peter reigned over the faithful at Rome for twenty-five years, and that Nero had him put to death together with St. Paul, in order to revenge the death of Simon the magician, whose legs they had broken by their prayers?

To report such fables, though with the best motive, is to insult Christianity.

The poor creatures who still repeat these absurdities, are copyists who review in octavo and duodecimo old stories that honest men no longer read, and who have never opened a book of wholesome criticism. They rake up the antiquated tales of the church; they know nothing of either Middleton, or Dodwell, or Bruker, or Dumoulin, or Fabricius, or Grabius, or even Dupin, or of any one of those who have lately carried light into the darkness.

III. We can only burst into laughter at all the humbug we are told about martyrs. The Tituses, the Trajans, the Marcus Aureliuses are painted as monsters of cruelty. Fleuri, abbe of Loc Bieu, has disgraced his ecclesiastical history by tales which a sensible old woman would not tell to little children.

Can it be seriously repeated, that the Romans condemned seven virgins, each seventy years old, to pass through the hands of all the young men of the city of Ancyra—those Romans who punished the Vestals with death for the least gallantry?

A hundred tales of this sort are found in the martyrologies. The narrators have hoped to render the ancient Romans odious, and they have rendered themselves ridiculous. Do you want good well-authenticated barbarities—good and well-attested massacres, rivers of blood which have actually flowed—fathers, mothers, husbands, wives, infants at the breast, who have in reality had their throats cut, and been heaped on one another? Persecuting monsters! Seek these only in your own annals: you will find them in the crusades against the Albigenses, in the massacres of Merindol and Cabrière, in the frightful day of St. Bartholomew, in the massacres of Ireland, in the vallies of the Pays de Vaud. It becomes you well, barbarians as you are, to impute extravagant cruelties to the best of emperors; you who have deluged Europe with blood, and covered it with corpses, in order to prove that the same body can be in a thousand places at once, and that the pope can sell indulgences!

3. Optimism

From *The Philosophical Dictionary*

I beg of you, gentlemen, to explain to me how everything is for the best; for I do not understand it.

Does it signify, that everything is arranged and ordered according to the laws of the impelling power? That I comprehend and acknowledge.

Do you mean, that every one is well and possesses the means of living—that nobody suffers? You know that such is not the case.

Are you of opinion, that the lamentable calamities which afflict the earth are good in reference to God; and that he takes pleasure in them? I credit not this horrible doctrine, nor you either.

God, according to Plato, necessarily chose the best of all possible worlds; and this system has been embraced by many Christian philosophers, although it appears repugnant to the doctrine of original sin. After this transgression, our globe was no more the best of all possible worlds, If it was ever so, it might be so still; but many people believe it to be the worst of worlds instead of the best.

Leibnitz takes the part of Plato: more readers than one complain their inability to understand either of them; and for ourselves, having read both more than once, we avow our ignorance according to custom; and since the gospel has reveled nothing on the subject, we remain in darkness without remorse.

Leibnitz, who speaks of everything, has treated of original sin; and as every man of systems introduces into his plan something contradictory, he imagined that the disobedience towards God, with the frightful misfortunes which followed it, were integral parts of the best of worlds, and necessary ingredients of all possible felicity: — "Calla, calla, senor don Carlos: todo che se haze es por su ben."

What! to be chased from a delicious place, where we might have lived for ever only for the eating of an apple? What! to produce in misery wretched children, who will suffer everything, and in return produce others to suffer after them? What! to experience all maladies, feel all vexations, die in the midst of grief, and by way of recompense be burned to all eternity — is this lot the best possible? It certainly is not good for us, and in what manner can it be so for God?

Leibnitz felt that nothing could be said to these objections, but nevertheless made great books, in which he did not even understand himself.

Lucullus, in good health, partaking of a good dinner with his friends and his mistress in the hall of Apollo, may jocosely deny the existence of evil; but let him put his head out of the window and he will behold wretches in abundance; let him be seized with a fever, and he will be one himself.

I do not like to quote; it is ordinarily a thorny proceeding. What precedes and what follows the passage quoted is too frequently neglected; and thus a thousand objections may arise. I must notwithstanding quote Lactantius, one of the fathers, who, in the thirteenth chapter of *The Anger of God*, makes Epicurus speak as follows: "God can either take away evil from the world and will not; or being willing to do so cannot. If he is willing and cannot, then he is not omnipotent. If he can but will not, then he is not benevolent. If he is neither willing nor able, then he is neither benevolent nor omnipotent. If he is both willing and able, whence then evil?"

The argument is weighty, and Lactantius replies to it very poorly, by saying that God wills evil, but has given us wisdom to secure the good. it must be confessed, that this answer is very weak in comparison with the objection; for it implies that God could bestow wisdom only by allowing evil — a pleasant wisdom truly! The origin of evil has always been an abyss, the depth of which no one has been able to sound. [Some examples of failure to sound the abyss are here omitted.]

The Syrians pretended, that man and woman having been created in the fourth heaven, they resolved to eat a cake in lieu of ambrosia, their natural food, which went to waste via the pores of the skin. But after eating cake, they were obliged to relieve themselves in the usual manner. The man and the woman requested an angel to direct them to a water-closet. Behold, said the angel, that petty globe which is almost of no size at all; it is situated about sixty millions of leagues from this place, and is the privy of the universe — go there as quickly as you can. The man and women obeyed the angel and came here, where thy have ever since remained: since which time the world has been what we now find it.

The Syrians will eternally be asked, why God allowed man to eat the cake, and experience such a crowd of formidable ills?

I pass with speed from the fourth heaven to Lord Bolingbroke. This writer, who doubtless was a great genius, gave to the celebrated Alexander Pope his plan of "all for the best," as it is found word for word in the posthumous works of Lord Bolingbroke, and recorded by Lord Shaftesbury in his *Characteristics*. Read in Shaftesbury's chapter of the Moralists, the following passage:

> Much may be replied to these complaints of the defects of nature — How came it so powerless and defective from the hands of a perfect Being? - But I deny that it is defective. Beauty is the result of contrast, and universal concord springs out a perpetual conflict. . . . It is necessary that everything be sacrificed to other things — vegetables to animals, and animals to the earth. . . . The laws of the central power of gravitation, which give to the celestial bodies their weight and motion, are not to be deranged in consideration of a pitiful animal, who, protected as he is by the same laws, will soon be reduced to dust.

Bolingbroke, Shaftesbury, and Pope, their working artisan, resolve the general question no better than the rest. Their "all for the best" says no more than that all is governed by immutable laws; and who did not know that? We learn nothing when we remark, after the manner of little children, that flies are created to be eaten by spiders, spiders by swallows, swallows by hawks, hawks by eagles, eagles by men, men by one another to afford food to worms; and at last, at the rate of about a thousand to one, to be the prey of devils everlastingly.

There is a constant and regular order established among animals of all kinds — an universal order. When a stone is formed in my bladder, the mechanical process is admirable: sandy particles pass by small degrees into my blood; they are filtered by the reins; and passing the urethra, deposit themselves in my bladder; where, uniting agreeably to the Newtonian attraction, a stone is formed which gradually increases, and

I suffer pains a thousand times worse then death by the finest arrangement in the world. A surgeon, perfect in the art of Tubal-cain, thrusts into me a sharp instrument; and cutting into the perineum, seizes the stone with his pincers, which breaks during the endeavors, by the necessary laws of mechanism; and owing to the same mechanism, I die in frightful torments. All this is "for the best," being the evident result of unalterable physical principles, agreeably to which I know as well as you that I perish.

If we were insensitive, there would be nothing to say against this system of physics; but this is not the point on which we treat. We ask, if there are not physical evils, and whence do they originate? There is no absolute evil, says Pope in his *Essay on Man*; or if there are particular evils, they compose a general good.

It is a singular general good which is composed of the stone, and the gout, — of all sorts of crimes and sufferings, and of death and damnation.

The fall of man is our placebo for all these particular maladies of body and soul, which you call "the general health"; but Shaftesbury and Bolingbroke have attacked original sin. Pope says nothing about it; but it is clear that their system saps the foundations of the Christian religion, and explains nothing at all.

In the meantime, this system has been since approved by many theologians, who willingly embrace contradictions. Be it so; we ought to leave to everybody the privilege of reasoning in their own way upon the deluge of ills which overwhelms us. It would be as reasonable to prevent incurable patients from eating what they please. "God," says Pope, "beholds, with an equal eye, a hero perish or a sparrow fall; the destruction of an atom, or the ruin of a thousand planets; the bursting of a bubble, or the dissolution of a world."

This, I must confess, is a pleasant consolation. Who does not find a comfort in the declaration of Lord Shaftesbury, who asserts, "that God will not derange his general system for so miserable an animal as man?" It must be confessed at least, that this pitiful creature has a right to cry out humbly, and to endeavour, while bemoaning himself, to understand why these eternal laws do nor comprehend the good of every individual.

This system of "all for the best" represents the Author of Nature as a powerful and malevolent monarch, who cares not for the destruction of four or five hundred thousand men, nor of the many more who in consequence spend the rest of their days in penury and tears, provided that he succeeds in his designs.

Far therefore from the doctrine — that this is the best of all possible worlds — being consolatory, it is a hopeless one to the philosophers who embrace it. The question of good and evil remains in remediless chaos for those who seek to fathom it in reality. It is a mere mental sport to the disputants, who are captives that play with their chains. As to unreasoning people, they resemble the fish which are transported from a river to a reservoir, with no more suspicion that they are to be eaten during the approaching Lent, than we have ourselves of the facts which originate our destiny.

Let us place at the end of every chapter of metaphysics, the two letters used by the Roman judges when they did not understand a pleading. L.N. *non liquet* — it is not clear. Let us above all silence the fools who, overloaded like ourselves with the weight of human calamities, add the mischief of their calumny: let us refute their execrable imposture, by having recourse to faith and providence.

Some reasoners are of opinion, that it agrees not with the nature of the Great Being of beings, for things to be otherwise than they are. It is a rough system, and I am too ignorant to venture to examine it.

7

DAVID HUME ON NATURAL ORDER AND SECULAR MORALITY

Therefore, given that matter has been in motion
for all eternity and that in that time there may
have occurred an infinite number of marvelous
arrangements proceeding from the infinite number
of possible combinations, if anything ought to be
repugnant to reason, it is the supposition that
none of these admirable arrangements was in fact
included among the infinite multitude of those
that matter did successfully achieve. It follows
therefore that the mind ought to be more
astonished at the hypothetical duration of chaos
than at the actual birth of the universe.

Diderot, Philosophical Thoughts, 1746, **XXI**

Let me write out word for word every one of the
commandments which Moses says were written by
God himself. . . . Now except for the commands
"Thou shalt not worship other gods" and
"Remember the sabbath day," what nation is
there, I ask in the name of the gods, *what nation
is there that does* NOT *think it ought to keep these
other commands?* To such an extent that
punishments have been ordained against those
that disobey: some more severe, some the same,
but some more humane than those prescribed by
Moses.

Julianus Caesar, Against the Galileans c. 360 A.D.

Biographical Note

David Hume, perhaps the greatest philosopher to have written in the
English language, was born in the Scottish borders in 1711. He may
well have attended Edinburgh University, although the evidence for
this is somewhat equivocal. Between 1726 and 1729 he made an attempt at a legal career, and in 1734 he spent a few miserable months in
a Bristol countinghouse before he finally embarked on the literary
career that began with the *Treatise of Human Nature* (1739/40). In

1779, three years after his death, his final work *The Dialogues concerning Natural Religion*—the most important critical work on the philosophy of religion in English or perhaps in any language—was published. Between these two works, Hume's literary output included several collections of essays, the skeptical *Enquiry concerning Human Understanding* (the "first *Enquiry*", 1748), a wholly secular account of morality in the *Enquiry concerning the Principles of Morals* (the "second *Enquiry*," 1751), the immense *History of England*, and an account of the phenomenon of religion in *The Natural History of Religion* (1757). Hume was also at various times a tutor, a civil servant attached to two military expeditions, the librarian of the Advocates' Library in Edinburgh, and the first secretary to the British Embassy in Paris. His publications put him continually at variance with official Christianity, and he died beloved by his friends and condemned by most of the devout: the final affront being his candid rejection of immortality to the very end. Adam Smith's encomium on him—"as approaching as nearly to the idea of a perfectly wise and virtuous man, as perhaps the nature of human frailty will permit" echoes with good reason the final judgment on Socrates at the end of Plato's *Phaedo*.

Philosophical Note

In Hume the influence of classical skepticism, revived and refined by seventeenth-century writers, reaches its careful apotheosis. But it is not the excessive skepticism that Diogenes Laertius ascribes to Pyrrho, determining nothing and suspending all judgment. Rather it is a cautious and balanced doubting of man's ability to produce reliable conclusions concerning subjects that are very remote from everyday sense and experience: the nature of god, the origin of the universe, or ultimate metaphysical or religious explanations, for examples. Hume's is the urbane skepticism of Cicero's Cotta (see pp. 28–32) not the psychological recipe for quietude in the ancient (Pyrrhonian) or modern (fideistic) forms.

In the first *Enquiry* and in the *Dialogues*, the principal reasons for believing in a god or gods *concerned with man* are subjected to devastating critical analysis. The *Natural History of Religion* is a detailed attempt to explain the existence and progress of religion from the operation of natural causes that take no account of the truth (or falsity) of what is believed. In the second *Enquiry*, at the end of the *Dialogues*, and in his essays Hume argues that religion and morality are independent and that religion has a pernicious effect upon morality. Some of these pernicious effects are documented in the *History of England*.

Hume's overall contribution to unbelief is thus immense, but the selection of material from his works is difficult. He seldom concentrates all he has to say on a given subject in one place, and some of the most radical things Hume has to say — about the relation of morality and religion, for example — have to be worked for by the reader.

The first section is *Dialogues*, part 8. Hume (equivocally in the person of Philo) having dissected the design argument, takes up the old and supposedly unsatisfactory Epicurean thesis that order could emerge from randomness without a guiding intelligence. Thought on the subject up to the time of Hume is expressed succinctly by Diderot (the French *philosophe*) in the first epigraph to this chapter. Hume takes the matter further with the suggestion that order may be self-selecting (Darwin's theory then becomes a special case of this applied to living organisms) or an inseparable feature of being any sort of material thing.

The overall strategy of Hume's argument is to break the fundamental theistic demand that existent things and order *need* an explanation in the activity of an intelligent agent. It is remotely probable that such an agent exists, but *if* it does then "the original source . . . has no more regard to good above ill than to heat above cold." It does not concern us nor we it.

The second section is Hume's essay "Of Suicide," which is included for three reasons. (1) It can stand by itself as a piece of radical thinking. (2) It challenges one of the most deeply held Christian taboos in a way that can still shock. (3) In the second *Enquiry*, in the last section of the *Dialogues* and in some private letters, Hume contends that what is moral simply is what brings about the happiness and welfare of society, and that this happiness (and our interest in promoting it) has little to do with the prohibitions or condemnations (or the rewards or punishments) of religion. Moreover, religion sets up frivolous species of merit (merits that contribute nothing to happiness or well-being) and false species of crime ("crimes" such as sabbath breaking, heresy, and *suicide*). But suicide, Hume argues, is *not* a crime on any humanistic view; it is not even a crime on the religious hypothesis, although it has always been treated as man's ultimate sin since Augustine's denunciation of it.

The essay "Of Suicide" was intended to be published by Hume in 1757 along with, "Of the Immortality of the Soul." Both works were withdrawn at the very last moment, possibly because of threats against their author or publisher. Neither was published in Hume's lifetime. The text followed here is from printed sheets corrected by Hume himself that he directed "to be considered as a manuscript." As far as can be determined, it has never before been published in exactly this form. (For the other suppressed essay, see pp. 225–230.)

Sections 3 and 4 are respectively the penultimate and final parts of the *Natural History of Religion*. They indicate Hume's thoughts about "frivolous merits" and his final skepticism about the "sophistry and illusion" of theology and "school metaphysics."

1. The Natural Origin of Order

Dialogues concerning Natural Religion, Part 8

What you ascribe to the fertility of my invention, replied Philo, is entirely owing to the nature of the subject. In subjects, adapted to the narrow compass of human reason, there is commonly but one determination, which carries probability or conviction with it; and to a man of sound judgment, all other suppositions, but that one, appear entirely absurd and chimerical. But in such questions as the present, a hundred contradictory views may preserve a kind of imperfect analogy; and invention has here full scope to exert itself. Without any great effort of thought, I believe that I could, in an instant, propose other systems of cosmogony, which would have some faint appearance of truth; though it is a thousand, a million to one, if either yours or any one of mine be the true system.

For instance; what if I should revive the old Epicurean hypothesis? This is commonly, and I believe, justly, esteemed the most absurd system, that has yet been proposed; yet, I know not, whether, with a few alternations, it might not be brought to bear a faint appearance of probability. Instead of supposing matter infinite, as Epicurus did; let us suppose it finite. A finite number of particles is only susceptible of finite transpositions: And it must happen, in an eternal duration, that every possible order or position must be tried an infinite number of times. This world, therefore, with all its events, even the most minute, has before been produced and destroyed, and will again be produced and destroyed, without any bounds and limitations. No one, who has a conception of the powers of infinite, in comparison of finite, will ever scruple this determination.

But this supposes, said Demea, that matter can acquire motion, without any voluntary agent or first mover.

And where is the difficulty, replied Philo, of that supposition? Every event, before experience, is equally difficult and incomprehensible; and every event, after experience, is equally easy and intelligible. Motion, in many instances, from gravity, from elasticity, from electricity, begins in matter, without any known voluntary agent; and to suppose always, in these cases, an unknown voluntary agent, is mere hypothesis; and hypothesis attended with no advantages. The beginning of motion in matter itself is as conceivable *a priori* as its communication from mind and intelligence.

Besides, why may not motion have been propagated by impulse through all eternity, and the same stock of it, or nearly the same, be still upheld in the universe? As much as is lost by the composition of motion, as much is gained by its resolution. And whatever the causes are, the fact is certain, that matter is, and always has been in continual agitation, as far as human experience or tradition reaches. There is not probably, at present, in the whole universe, one particle of matter at absolute rest.

And this very consideration too, continued Philo, which we have stumbled on in the course of the argument, suggests a new hypothesis of cosmogony, that is not absolutely absurd and improbable. Is there a system, an order, an economy of things, by which matter can preserve that perpetual agitation, which seems essential to it, and yet maintain a constancy in the forms, which it produces? There certainly is such an economy: For this is actually the case with the present world. The continual motion of matter, therefore, in less than infinite transpositions, must produce this economy or order; and by its very nature, that order, when once established, supports itself, for many ages, if not to eternity. But wherever matter is so poised, arranged, and adjusted as to continue in perpetual motion, and yet preserve a constancy in the forms, its situation must, of necessity, have all the same appearance of art and contrivance which we observe at present. All the parts of each form must have a relation to each other, and to the whole: And the whole itself must have a relation to the other parts of the universe; to the element, in which the form subsists; to the materials, with which it repairs its waste and decay; and to every other form, which is hostile or friendly. A defect in any of these particulars destroys the form; and the matter, of which it is composed, is again set loose, and is thrown into irregular motions and fermentations, till it unite itself to some other regular form. If no such form be prepared to receive it, and if there be a great quantity of this corrupted matter in the universe, the universe itself is entirely disordered; whether it be the feeble embryo of a world in its first beginnings, that is thus destroyed, or the rotten carcass of one, languishing in old age and infirmity. In either case, the chaos ensures; till finite, though innumerable revolutions produce at last some forms, whose parts and organs are so adjusted as to support the forms amidst a continued succession of matter.

Suppose (for we shall endeavor to vary the expression), that matter were thrown into any position, by a blind, unguided force; it is evident that this first position must in all probability be the most confused and most disorderly imaginable, without any resemblance to those works of human contrivance, which, along with a symmetry of parts, discover an adjustment of means to ends and a tendency to self-preservation. If the actuating force cease after this operation, matter must remain for ever in disorder, and continue an immense chaos, without any proportion or activity. But suppose, that the actuating force, whatever it be, still continues in matter, this first position will immediately give place to a second, which will likewise in all probability be as disorderly as the first, and so on, through many successions of changes and revolutions. No particular order or position ever continues a moment unaltered. The original force, still remaining in activity, gives a perpetual restlessness to matter. Every possible situation is produced, and instantly destroyed. If a glimpse or dawn of order appears for a moment, it is instantly hurried away, and confounded, by that never-ceasing force, which actuates every part of matter.

Thus the universe goes on for many ages in a continued succession of chaos and disorder. But is it not possible that it may settle at last, so as not to lose its motion and active force (for that we have supposed inherent in it), yet so as to preserve an uniformity of appearance, amidst the continual motion and fluctuation of its parts? This we find to be the case with the universe at present. Every individual is perpetually changing, and every part of every individual, and yet the whole remains, in appearance, the same. May we not hope for such a position, or rather be assured of it, from the eternal revolutions of unguided matter, and may not this account for all the appearing wisdom and contrivance which is in the universe? Let us contemplate the subject a little, and we shall find, that this adjustment, if attained by matter, of a seeming stability in the forms, with a real and perpetual revolution or motion of parts, affords a plausible, if not a true solution of the difficulty.

It is in vain, therefore, to insist upon the uses of the parts in animals or vegetables, and their curious adjustment to each other. I would fain know how an animal could subsist, unless its parts were so adjusted? Do we not find, that it immediately perishes whenever this adjustment ceases, and that its matter corrupting tries some new form? It happens, indeed, that the parts of the world are so well adjusted, that some regular form immediately lays claim to this corrupted matter: And if it were not so, could the world subsist? Must it not dissolve as well as the animal, and pass through new positions and situations; till in a great, but finite succession, it fall at last into the present or some such order?

It is well, replied Cleanthes, you told us, that this hypothesis was suggested on a sudden, in the course of the argument. Had you had leisure to examine it, you would soon have perceived the insuperable objections, to which it is exposed. No form, you say, can subsist, unless it posses those powers and organs, requisite for its subsistence: Some new order or economy must be tried, and so on, without intermission; till at last some order, which can support and maintain itself, is fallen upon. But according to this hypothesis, whence arise the many conveniences and advantages which men and all animals possess? Two eyes, two ears, are not absolutely necessary for the subsistence of the species. Human race might have been propagated and preserved, without horses, dogs, cows, sheep, and those innumerable fruits and products which serve to our satisfaction and enjoyment. If no camels had been created for the use of man in the sandy deserts of Africa and Arabia, would the world have been dissolved? If no loadstone had been framed to give that wonderful and useful direction to the needle, would human society and the human kind have been immediately extinguished? Though the maxims of nature be in general very frugal, yet instances of this kind are far from being rare; and any one of them is sufficient proof of design, and of a benevolent design, which gave rise to the order and arrangement of the universe.

At least, you may safely infer, said Philo, that the foregoing hypothesis is so far incomplete and imperfect; which I shall not scruple to allow. But can we ever reasonably expect greater success in any attempts of this nature? Or can we ever hope to erect a system of cosmogony, that will be liable to no exceptions, and will contain no circumstance repugnant to our limited and imperfect experience of the analogy of nature? Your theory itself cannot surely pretend to any such advantage; even though you have run into *anthropomorphism*, the better to preserve a conformity to common experience. Let us once more put it to trial. In all instances which we have ever seen, ideas are copied from real objects, and are ectypal, not archetypal, to express myself in learned terms: You reverse this order, and give thought the precedence. In all instances which we have ever seen, thought has no influence upon matter, except where that matter is so conjoined with it, as to have an equal reciprocal influence upon it. No animal can move immediately any thing but the members of its own body; and indeed, the equality of action and re-action seems to be an universal law of nature: But your theory implies a contradiction to this experience. These instances, with many more, which it were easy to collect (particularly the supposition of a mind or system of thought that is eternal, or in other words, an animal ingenerable and immortal), these instances, I say, may teach, all of us, sobriety in condemning each other, and let us see, that as no system of this kind ought ever to be received from a slight analogy, so neither ought any to be rejected on account of a small incongruity. For that is an inconvenience from which we can justly pronounce no one to be exempted.

All religious systems, it is confessed, are subject to great and insuperable difficulties. Each disputant triumphs in his turn; while he carries on an offensive war, and exposes the absurdities, barbarities, and pernicious tenets of his antagonist. But all of them, on the whole, prepare a complete triumph for the sceptic; who tells them, that no system ought ever to be embraced with regard to such subjects: For this plain reason, that no absurdity ought ever to be assented to with regard to any subject. A total suspense of judgment is here our only reasonable resource. And if every attack, as is commonly observed, and no defence, among theologians, is successful; how complete must be *his* victory, who remains always, with all mankind, on the offensive, and has himself no fixed station or abiding city, which he is ever, on any occasion, obliged to defend?

2. Religious Morality: False Crimes

"Of Suicide"

One considerable advantage, that arises from philosophy, consists in the sovereign antidote, which it affords to superstition and false religion. All other remedies against that pestilent distemper are vain, or, at least, uncertain. Plain good-sense, and the practice of the world, which alone serve most purposes of life, are here found ineffectual: History, as well as daily experience, affords instances of men, endowed with the strongest capacity for business and affairs, who have all their lives crouched under slavery to the grossest superstition. Even gaiety and sweetness of temper, which infuse a balm into every other wound, afford no remedy to so virulent a poison; as we may particularly observe of the fair sex, who, tho' commonly possessed of these rich presents of nature, feel many of their joys blasted by this importunate intruder. But when sound philosophy has once gained possession of the mind, superstition is effectually excluded; and one may safely affirm, that her triumph over this enemy is more complete than over most of the vices and imperfections, incident to human nature. Love or anger, ambition or avarice, have their root in the temper and affections, which the soundest reason is scarce ever able fully to correct. But superstition, being founded on false opinion, must immediately vanish, when true philosophy has inspired juster sentiments of superior powers. The contest is here more equal between the distemper and the medicine: And nothing can hinder the latter from proving effectual, but its being false and sophisticated.

It will here be superfluous to magnify the merits of philosophy, by displaying the pernicious tendency of that vice, of which it cures the human mind. The superstitious man, says Tully[a] [i.e., Cicero], is miserable in every scene, in every incident of life. Even sleep itself, which banishes all other cares of unhappy mortals, affords to him matter of new terror; while he examines his dreams, and finds in those visions of the night, prognostications of future calamities. I may add, that, tho' death alone can put a full period to his misery, he dares not fly to this refuge, but still prolongs a miserable existence, from a vain fear, lest he offend his maker, by using the power, with which that beneficent being has endowed him. The presents the God and Nature are ravished from us by this cruel enemy; and notwithstanding that one step would remove us from the regions of pain and sorrow, her menaces still chain us down to a hated being, which she herself chiefly contributes to render miserable.

It is observed of such as have been reduced by the calamities of life to the necessity of employing this fatal remedy, that, if the unseasonable

[a]*De Divinatione*, Book II.

care of their friends deprive them of that species of death, which they proposed to themselves, they seldom venture upon any other, or can summon up so much resolution, a second time, as to execute their purpose. So great is our horror of death, that when it presents itself under any form, besides that to which a man has endeavoured to reconcile his imagination, it acquires new terrors, and overcomes his feeble courage. But when the menaces of superstition are joined to this natural timidity, no wonder it quite deprives men of all power over their lives; since even many pleasures and enjoyments, to which we are carried by a strong propensity, are torn from us by this inhuman tyrant. Let us here endeavour to restore men to their native liberty, by examining all the common arguments against Suicide, and shewing, that that action may be free from every imputation of guilt or blame; according to the sentiments of all ancient philosophers.

If Suicide be criminal, it must be a transgression of our duty, either of God, our neighbor, or ourselves.

To prove, that Suicide is no transgression of our duty to God, the following considerations may perhaps suffice. In order to govern the material world, the almighty creator has established general and immutable laws, by which all bodies, from the greatest planet to the smallest particle of matter, are maintained in their proper sphere and function. To govern the animal world, he has endowed all living creatures with bodily and mental powers; with senses, passions, appetites, memory, and judgment; by which they are impelled or regulated in that course of life, to which they are destined. These two distinct principles of the material and animal world continually encroach upon each other, and mutually retard or forward each other's operation. The powers of men and of all other animals are restrained and directed by the nature and qualities of the surrounding bodies; and the modifications and actions of these bodies are incessantly altered by the operation of all animals. Man is stopped by rivers in his passage over the surface of the earth; and rivers, when properly directed, lend their force to the motion of machines, which serve to the use of man. But tho' the provinces of the material and animal powers are not kept entirely separate, there result from thence no discord or disorder in the creation. On the contrary, from the mixture, union, and contrast of all the various powers of inanimate bodies and living creatures, arises that surprising harmony and proportion, which affords the surest argument of supreme wisdom.

The providence of the deity appears not immediately in any operation, but governs every thing by those general and immutable laws, which have been established from the beginning of time. All events, in one sense, may be pronounced the action of the almighty. They all proceed from those powers, with which he has endowed his creatures. A house, which falls by its own weight, is not brought to ruin by his providence more than one destroyed by the hands of men; nor are the human faculties less his workmanship than the laws of motion and gravitation. When the passions play, when the judgment dictates, when the limbs obey; this is all the operation of God; and upon these animate principles, as well as upon the inanimate, has he established the government of the universe.

Every event is alike important in the eyes of that infinite being, who takes in, at one glance, the most distant regions of space and remotest periods of time. There is no one event, however important to us, which he has exempted from the general laws that govern the universe, or which he has peculiarly reserved for his own immediate action and operation. The revolutions of states and empires depend upon the smallest caprice or passion of single men; and the lives of men are shortened or extended by the smallest accident of air or diet, sunshine or tempest. Nature still continues her progress and operation; and if general laws be ever broke by particular volitions of the deity, it is after a manner which entirely escapes human observation. As on the one hand, the elements and other inanimate parts of the creation carry on their action without regard to the particular interest and situation of men; so men are entrusted to their own judgment and discretion in the various shocks of matter, and may employ every faculty, with which they are endowed, in order to provide for their ease, happiness, or preservation.

What is the meaning, then, of that principle, that a man, who, tired of life, and hunted by pain and misery, bravely overcomes all the natural terrors of death, and makes his escape from this cruel scene; that such a man, I say, has incurred the indignation of his creator, by encroaching on the office of divine providence, and disturbing the order of the universe? Shall we assert, that the Almighty has reserved to himself, in any peculiar manner, the disposal of the lives of men, and has not submitted that event, in common with others, to the general laws, by which the universe is governed? This is plainly false. The lives of men depend upon the same laws as the lives of all other animals; and these are subjected to the general laws of matter and motion. The fall of a tower or the infusion of a poison will destroy a man equally with the meanest creature: An inundation sweeps away every thing, without distinction, that comes within the reach of its fury. Since therefore the lives of men are for ever dependent on the general laws of matter and motion; is a man's disposing of his life criminal, because, in every case, it is criminal to encroach upon these laws, or disturb their operation? But this seems absurd. All animals are entrusted to their own prudence and skill for their conduct in the world, and have full authority, as far as their power extends, to alter all the operations of nature. Without the exercise of this authority, they could not subsist a moment. Every action, every motion of a man innovates in the order of some parts of matter, and diverts, from their ordinary course, the general laws of motion. Putting together, therefore, these conclusions, we find, *that* human life depends upon the general laws of matter and motion, and *that* 'tis no encroachment on the office of providence to disturb or alter these general laws. Has not every one, of consequence, the free disposal of his own life? And may he not lawfully employ that power with which nature has endowed him?

In order to destroy the evidence of this conclusion, we must show a reason, why this particular case is expected. Is it because human life is of so great importance, that it is a presumption for human prudence to dispose of it? But the life of man is of no greater importance to the universe than that of an oyster. And were it of ever so great importance, the order of nature has actually submitted it to human prudence, and reduced us to a necessity, in every incident, of determining concerning it.

Were the disposal of human life so much reserved as the peculiar province of the almighty that it were an encroachment on his right for man to dispose of their own lives; it would be equally criminal to act for the preservation of life as for its destruction. If I turn aside a stone, which is falling upon my head, I disturb the course of nature, and I invade the peculiar province of the almighty, by lengthening out my life, beyond the period, which, by the general laws of matter and motion, he had assigned to it.

A hair, a fly, an insect is able to destroy this mighty being, whose life is of such importance. Is it an absurdity to suppose, that human prudence may lawfully dispose of what depends on such insignificant causes?

It would be no crime in me to divert the Nile or Danube from its course, were I able to effect such purposes. Where then is the crime of turning a few ounces of blood from their natural channels!

Do you imagine that I repine at providence or curse my creation, because I go out of life, and put a period to a being, which, were it to continue, would render me miserable? Far be such sentiments from me. I am only convinced of a matter of fact, which you yourself acknowledged possible, that human life may be unhappy, and that my existence, if farther prolonged would become uneligible. But I thank providence, both for the good, which I have already enjoyed, and for the power, with which I am endowed, of escaping the ill that threatens me[a]. To you it belongs to repine at providence, who foolishly imagine that you have no such power, and who must still prolong a hated being, tho' loaded with pain and sickness, with shame and poverty.

Do you not teach, that when any ill befalls me, tho' by the malice of my enemies, I ought to be resigned to providence; and that the actions of men are the operations of the almighty as much as the actions of inanimate beings? When I fall upon my own sword, therefore, I re-

---

[a] *Agamus Deo gratias, quod nemo in vita teneri potest.* Senaca, *Epist.* xii. [Let us thank God no man can be kept in life.]

ceived my death equally from the hands of the diety, as if it had proceeded from a lion, a precipice, or a fever.

The submission, which you require to providence, in every calamity, that befalls me, excludes not human skill and industry; if possibly, by their means, I can avoid or escape the calamity. Any why may I not employ one remedy as well as another?

If my life be not my own, it were criminal for me to put it in danger, as well as to dispose of it: nor could one man deserve the appellation of *Hero*, whom glory or friendship transports into the greatest dangers, and another merit the reproach of *Wretch* or *Miscreant*, who puts a period to his life, from the same or like motives.

There is no being, which possesses any power or faculty, that it receives not from its creator; nor is there any one, which, by ever so irregular an action, can encroach upon the plan of his providence, or disorder the universe. Its operations are his work equally with that chain of events, which it invades; and which ever principle prevails, we may, for that very reason, conclude it to be most favoured by him. Be it animate or inanimate, rational or irrational, 'tis all a case: Its power is still derived from the supreme creator, and is alike comprehended in the order of his providence. When the horror of pain prevails over the love of life: When a voluntary action anticipates the effect of blind causes; it is only in consequence of those powers and principles, which he has implanted in his creatures. Divine providence is still inviolate, and placed far beyond the reach of human injuries.

It is impious, says the old Roman superstition[a], to divert rivers from their course, or invade the prerogative of nature. 'Tis impious, says the French superstition, to innoculate for the small-pox, or usurp the business of providence, by voluntarily producing distempers and maladies. 'Tis impious, says the modern European superstition, to put a period to our own life, and thereby rebel against our creator. And why not impious, say I, to build houses, cultivate the ground, and sail upon the ocean? In all these actions, we employ our powers of mind and body to produce some innovation in the course of nature; and in none of them do we any more. They are all of them, therefore, equally innocent or equally criminal.

But you are placed by providence, like a sentinel, in a particular station: and when you desert it, without being recalled, you are guilty of rebellion against your almighty sovereign, and have incurred his displeasure. I ask, why do you conclude, that Providence has placed me in this station? For my part, I find, that I owe my birth to a long chain of causes, of which many and even the principal, depended upon voluntary actions of men. *But Providence guided all these causes, and nothing happens in the universe without its consent and co-operation.* If so, then

[a]*Tacit. Ann.*, Book i.

neither does my death, however voluntary, happen without its consent; and whenever pain and sorrow so far overcome my patience as to make me tired of life, I may conclude, that I am recalled from my station, in the clearest and most express terms.

It is providence, surely, that has placed me at present in this chamber: But may I not leave it, when I think proper, without being liable to the imputation of having deserted my post or station? When I shall be dead, the principles, of which I am composed, will still perform their part in the universe, and will be equally useful in the grand fabric, as when they composed this individual creature. The difference to the whole will be no greater than between my being in a chamber and in the open air. The one change is of more importance to me than the other; but not more so to the universe.

It is a kind of blasphemy to imagine, that any created being can disturb the order of the world, or invade the business of providence. It supposes, that that being possesses powers and faculties, which it received not from its creator, and which are not subordinate to his government and authority. A man may disturb society, no doubt; and thereby incur the displeasure of the almighty: But the government of the world is placed far beyond his reach and violence. And how does it appear, that the almighty is displeased with those actions, that disturb society? By the principles which he has implanted in human nature, and which inspire us with a sentiment of remorse, if we ourselves have been guilty of such actions, and with that of blame and disapprobation, if we ever observe them in others. Let us now examine, according to the method proposed, whether Suicide be of this kind of actions, and be a breach of our duty to our *neighbour* and to society.

A man, who retires from life, does no harm to society. He only ceases to do good; which, if it be an injury, is of the lowest kind.

All our obligations to do good to society seem to imply something reciprocal. I receive the benefits of society, and therefore ought to promote its interest. But when I withdraw myself altogether from society, can I be bound any longer?

But allowing, that our obligations to do good were perpetual, they have certainly some bounds. I am not obliged to do a small good to society, at the expense of a great harm to myself. Why then should I prolong a miserable existence, because of some frivolous advantage, which the public may, perhaps, receive from me? If upon account of age and infirmities, I may lawfully resign any office, and employ my time altogether in fencing against these calamities, and alleviating, as much as possible, the miseries of my future life: Why may I not cut short these miseries at once by an action, which is no more prejudicial to society?

But suppose, that it is no longer in my power to promote the interest of the public. Suppose, that I am a burthen to it. Suppose, that my life hinders some person from being much more useful to the public. In such cases my resignation of life must not only be innocent but laudable. And most people, who lie under any temptation to abandon existence, are in some such situation. Those, who have health, or power, or authority, have commonly better reason to be in humour with the world.

A man is engaged in a conspiracy for the public interest; is seized upon suspicion; is threatened with the rack; and knows, from his own weakness, that the secret will be extorted from him: Could such a one consult the public interest better than by putting a quick period to a miserable life? This was the case of the famous and brave Strozzi of Florence.

Again, suppose a malefactor justly condemned to a shameful death; can any reason be imagined, why he may not anticipate his punishment, and save himself all the anguish of thinking on its dreadful approaches? He invades the business of providence no more than the magistrate did, who ordered his execution; and his voluntary death is equally advantageous to society, by ridding it of a pernicious member.

That Suicide may often be consistent with interest and with our duty to *ourselves,* no one can question, who allows, that age, sickness, or misfortune may render life a burthen, and make it worse even than annihilation. I believe that no man ever threw away life, while it was worth keeping. For such is our natural horror of death, that small motives will never be able to reconcile us to it. And tho' perhaps the situation of a man's health or fortune did not seem to require this remedy, we may at least be assured, that any one, who, without apparent reason, has had recourse to it, was curst with such an incurable depravity or gloominess of temper, as must poison all enjoyment, and render him equally miserable as if he had been loaded with the most grievous misfortunes.

If Suicide be supposed a crime, it is only cowardice can impel us to it. If it be no crime, both prudence and courage should engage us to rid ourselves at once of existence, when it becomes a burthen. It is the only way, that we can then be useful to society, by setting an example, which, if imitated, would preserve to every one his chance for happiness in life, and would effectually free him from all danger of misery.[a]

[a] It would be easy to prove, that Suicide is as lawful under the *christian* dispensation as it was to the heathens. There is not a single text of scripture, which prohibits it. That great and infallible rule of faith and practice, which must controul all philosophy and human reasoning, has left us, in this particular, to our natural liberty. Resignation to providence is, indeed, recommended in scripture; but that implies only submission to ills, which are unavoidable, not to such as may be remedied by prudence or courage. *Thou shalt not kill* is evidently meant to exclude only the killing of others, over whose life we have no authority. That this precept like most of the scripture precepts, must be modified by reason and common sense, is plain from the practice of magistrates, who punish criminals capitally, notwithstanding the letter of the law. But were this commandment ever so express against Suicide, it could now have no authority. For all the law of *Moses* is

3. Religious Morality: Frivolous Merits

Natural History of Religion, Part 14

XIV. Here I cannot forbear observing a fact, which may be worth the attention of such as make human nature the object of their inquiry. It is certain, that in every religion, however sublime the verbal definition which it gives of its divinity, many of the votaries, perhaps the greatest number, will still seek the divine favor, not by virtue and good morals, which alone can be acceptable to a perfect being, but either by frivolous observances, by intemperate zeal, by rapturous ecstacies, or by the belief of mysterious and absurd opinions. The least part of the *Sadder*, as well as of the *Pentateuch*, consists in precepts of morality; and we may also be assured, that that part was always the least observed and regarded. When the old Romans were attacked with a pestilence, they never ascribed their sufferings to their vices, or dreamed of repentance and amendment. They never thought, that they were the general robbers of the world, whose ambition and avarice made desolate the earth, and reduced opulent nations to want and beggary. They only created a dictator[1], in order to drive a nail into a door; and by that means, they thought that they had sufficiently appeased their incensed deity.

In Ægina, one faction forming a conspiracy, barbarously and treacherously assassinated seven hundred of their fellow-citizens; and carried their fury so far, that, one miserable fugitive having fled to the temple, they cut off his hands, by which he clung to the gates, and carrying him out of holy ground, immediately murdered him. *By this impiety*, says Herodotus[2], (not by the other many cruel assassinations) *they offended the gods, and contracted an inexpiable guilt.*

Nay, if we should suppose, what never happens, that a popular religion were found, in which it was expressly declared, that nothing but morality could gain the divine favour; if an order of priests were instituted to inculcate this opinion, in daily sermons, and with all the arts of persuasion; yet so inveterate are the people's prejudices, that, for want of some other superstition, they would make the very attendance on these sermons the essentials of religion, rather than place them in virtue and good morals. The sublime prologue of Zaleucus's[3] laws

---

abolished, except so far as it is established by the law of nature; and we have already endeavored to prove, that Suicide is not prohibited by that law. In all cases, *Christians* and *Heathens* are precisely upon the same footing; and if *Cato* and *Brutus*, *Arria* and *Portia* acted heroically, those who now imitate their example ought to receive the same praises from posterity. The power of committing Suicide is regarded by *Pliny* as an advantage which men possess even above the deity himself. *Deus non sibi potest mortem consciscere, si velit, quod homini dedit optimum in tantis vitae poenis.* Lib.ii. Chap. 7. [God himself is not able to kill himself if he wishes: that greatest good is given to compensate human life]

[1] Called Dictator clavis figendae causes. T. Livii. 1. vii. c, 3.

[2] Lib. vi.

[3] To be found in Diod. Sie, lib, xii.

inspired not the Locrians, so far as we can learn, with any sounder notions of the measures of acceptance with the deity, than were familiar to the other Greeks.

This observation, then, holds universally: But still one may be at some loss to account for it. It is not sufficient to observe, that the people every where degrade their deities into a similitude with themselves, and consider them merely as a species of human creatures, somewhat more potent and intelligent. This will not remove the difficulty. For there is no *man* so stupid, as that, judging by his natural reason, he would not esteem virtue and honesty the most valuable qualities which any person could possess. Why not ascribe the same sentiment to his deity? Why not make all religion, or the chief part of it, to consist in these attainments?

Nor is it satisfactory to say, that the practice of morality is more difficult than that of superstition, and is therefore rejected. For, not to mention the excessive penances of the *Brachmans* and *Talapoins*; it is certain, that the *Rhamadan* of the Turks, during which the poor wretches, for many days, often in the hottest months of the year, and in some of the hottest climates of the world, remain without eating or drinking from the rising to the setting sun; this *Rhamadan*, I say, must be more severe than the practice of any moral duty, even to the most vicious and depraved of mankind. The four lents of the Muscovites, and the austerities of some *Roman Catholics*, appear more disagreeable than meekness and benevolence. In short, all virtue, when men are reconciled to it by ever so little practice, is agreeable: All superstition is for ever odious and burdensome.

Perhaps the following account may be received as a true solution of the difficulty. The duties which a man performs as a friend or parent, seem merely owing to his benefactor or children; nor can he be wanting to these duties, without breaking through all the ties of nature and morality. A strong inclination may prompt him to the performance: A sentiment of order and moral obligation joins its force to these natural ties: And the whole man, if truly virtuous, is drawn to his duty without any effort or endeavour. Even with regard to the virtues which are more austere, and more founded on reflection, such as public spirit, filial duty, temperance, or integrity; the moral obligation, in our apprehension, removes all pretension to religious merit; and the virtuous conduct is deemed no more than what we owe to society and to ourselves. In all this, a superstitious man finds nothing which he has properly performed for the sake of his deity, or which can peculiarly recommend him to the divine favor and protection. He considers not, that the most genuine method of serving the Divinity is by promoting the happiness of his creatures. He still looks out for some more immediate service of the Supreme Being, in order to allay those terrors with which he is haunted. And any practice recommended to him, which either serves to no purpose in life, or offers the strongest violence to his natural inclinations; that practice he will the more readily embrace, on account of those very circumstances which should make him absolutely reject it. It seems the more purely religious, because it proceeds from no mixture of any other motive or consideration. And if, for its sake, he sacrifices much of his ease and quiet, his claim of merit appears still to rise upon him in proportion to the zeal and devotion which he discovers. In restoring a loan, or paying a debt, his divinity is nowise beholden to him; because these acts of justice are what he was bound to perform, and what many would have performed, were there no god in the universe. But if he fast a day, or give himself a sound whipping; this has a direct reference, in his opinion, to the service of God. No other motive could engage him to such austerities. By these distinguished marks of devotion he has now acquired the divine favour; and may expect, in recompence, protection and safety in this world, and eternal happiness in the next.

Hence the greatest crimes have been found, in many instances, compatible with a superstitious piety and devotion: Hence it is justly regarded as unsafe to draw any certain inference in favor of a man's morals from the fervour or strictness of his religious exercises, even though he himself believe them sincere. Nay, it has been observed, that enormities of the blackest dye have been rather apt to produce superstitious terrors, and increase the religious passion. Bomilcar having formed a conspiracy for assassinating at once the whole senate of Carthage, and invading the liberties of his country, lost the opportunity from a continual regard to omens and prophecies. *Those who undertake the most criminal and most dangerous enterprises are commonly the most superstitious*, as an ancient historian[a] remarks on this occasion. Their devotion and spiritual faith rise with their fears. Catiline was not contented with the established deities, and received rites of the national religion: His anxious terrors made him seek new inventions of this kind, which he never probably had dreamed of, had he remained a good citizen, and obedient to the laws of his country.

To which we may add, that after the commission of crimes, there arise remorses and secret horrors, which give no rest to the mind, but make it have recourse to religious rites and ceremonies, as expiations of its offenses. Whatever weakens or disorders the internal frame promotes the interests of superstition: And nothing is more destructive to them, than a manly, steady virtue, which either preserves us from disastrous melancholy accidents, or teaches us to bear them. During such calm sunshine of the mind, these specters of false divinity never make their appearance. On the other hand, while we abandon ourselves to the natural undisciplined suggestions of our timid and anxious hearts, every kind of barbarity is ascribed to the Supreme Being, from

[a]Diod. Sic. l ib. xv.

the terrors with which we are agitated; and every kind of caprice, from the methods which we embrace in order to appease him. *Barbarity, caprice;* these qualities, however nominally disguised, we may universally observe, form the ruling character of the Deity in popular religions. Even priests, instead of correcting these depraved ideas of mankind, have often been found ready to foster and encourage them. The more tremendous the divinity is represented, the more tame and submissive do men become to his ministers: And the more unaccountable the measures of acceptance required by him, the more necessary does it become to abandon our natural reason, and yield to their ghostly guidance and direction. Thus it may be allowed, that the artifices of men aggravate our natural infirmities and follies of this kind, but never originally beget them. Their root strikes deeper into the mind, and springs from the essential and universal properties of human nature.

4. The Final Skepticism

Natural History of Religion, Part 15

Though the stupidity of men, barbarous and uninstructed, be so great, that they may not see a sovereign Author in the more obvious works of nature to which they are so much familiarized; yet it scarcely seems possible, that any one of good understanding should reject that idea, when once it is suggested to him. A purpose, an intention, a design, is evident in every thing; and when our comprehension is so far enlarged as to contemplate the first rise of this visible system, we must adopt, with the strongest conviction, the idea of some intelligent cause or author. The uniform maxims, too, which prevail throughout the whole frame of the universe, naturally, if not necessarily, lead us to conceive this intelligence as single and undivided, where the prejudices of education oppose not so reasonable a theory. Even the contrarieties of nature, by discovering themselves every where, become proofs of some consistent plan, and establish one single purpose or intention, however inexplicable and incomprehensible.

Good and ill are universally intermingled and confounded; happiness and misery, wisdom and folly, virtue and vice. Nothing is pure and entirely of a piece. All advantages are attended with disadvantages. An universal compensation prevails in all conditions of being and existence. And it is not possible for us, by our most chimerical wishes, to form the idea of a station or situation altogether desirable. The draughts of life, according to the poet's fiction, are always mixed from the vessels on each hand of Jupiter: Or if any cup be presented altogether pure, it is drawn only, as the same poet tells us, from the left-handed vessel.

The more exquisite any good is, of which a small specimen is afforded us, the sharper is the evil allied to it; and few exceptions are found to this uniform law of nature. The most sprightly wit borders on madness; the highest effusions of joy produce the deepest melancholy; the most ravishing pleasures are attended with the most cruel lassitude and disgust; the most flattering hopes make way for the severest disappointments. And, in general, no course of life has such safety (for happiness is not to be dreamed of) as the temperate and moderate, which maintains, as far as possible, a mediocrity, and a kind of insensibility, in every thing.

As the good, the great, the sublime, the ravishing, are found eminently in the genuine principles of theism; it may be expected, from the analogy of nature, that the base, the absurd, the mean, the terrifying, will be equally discovered in religious fictions and chimeras.

The universal propensity to believe in invisible, intelligent power, if not an original instinct, being at least a general attendant of human nature, may be considered as a kind of mark or stamp, which the Divine workman has set upon his work; and nothing surely can more dignify mankind, than to be thus selected from all other parts of the creation, and to bear the image or impression of the universal Creator. But consult this image as it appears in the popular religions of the world. How is the Deity disfigured in our representations of him! What caprice, absurdity, and immorality are attributed to him! How much is he degraded even below the character which we should naturally, in common life, ascribe to a man of sense and virtue!

What a noble privilege is it of human reason to attain the knowledge of the Supreme Being; and, from the visible works of nature, be enabled to infer so sublime a principle as its supreme Creator? But turn the reverse of the medal. Survey most nations and most ages. Examine the religious principles which have, in fact, prevailed in the world. You will scarcely be persuaded that they are any thing but sick men's dreams: Or perhaps will regard them more as the playsome whimsies of monkeys in human shape, than the serious, positive, dogmatical asseverations of a being, who dignifies himself with the name of rational.

Hear the verbal protestations of all men: Nothing so certain as their religious tenets. Examine their lives: You will scarcely think that they repose the smallest confidence in them.

The greatest and truest zeal gives us no security against hypocrisy: The most open impiety is attended with a secret dread and compunction.

No theological absurdities so glaring that they have not sometimes been embraced by men of the greatest and most cultivated understanding. No religious precepts so rigorous that they have not been adopted by the most voluptuous and most abandoned of men.

Ignorance is the mother of devotion; a maxim that is proverbial, and confirmed by general experience. Look out for a people entirely destitute of religion: If you find them at all, be assured that they are but few degrees removed from brutes.

What so pure as some of the morals included in some theological system? What so corrupt as some of the practices to which these systems give rise?

The comfortable views, exhibited by the belief of futurity, are ravishing and delightful. But how quickly vanished on the appearance of its terrors, which keep a more firm and durable possession of the human mind!

The whole is a riddle, an enigma, an inexplicable mystery. Doubt, uncertainty, suspense of judgment, appear the only result of our most accurate scrutiny concerning this subject. But such is the frailty of human reason, and such the irresistible contagion of opinion, that even this deliberate doubt could scarcely be upheld; did we not enlarge our view, and opposing one species of superstition to another, set them a-quarrelling; while we ourselves, during their fury and contention, happily make our escape into the calm, though obscure, regions of philosophy.

8

BARON D'HOLBACH ON MAN'S INCOHERENT IDEA OF AN IMAGINARY GOD

> Do any gods exist in the heavens? They do not! If any man does not wish to believe this ancient folly, let him look and examine for himself.
>
> *Euripides, c. 480–406* B.C.,
> *Bellerophon, fragment 286*

Biographical Note

Born of German parents, Paul Heinrich Dietrich (1723–1789) came to Paris in 1749 and remained in France for the rest of his life. He inherited the title Baron D'Holbach from his uncle in 1753. He was associated with the younger *philosophes*, particularly Diderot. From an early familiarity with the physical sciences he progressed first to an unremitting hostility to institutional religion in any form and to Roman Catholicism in particular, and then to the first complete avowal of atheism published in modern Europe, *The System of Nature* (1770). Although D'Holbach wrote voluminously, almost all of his works were secretly conveyed to Holland or England, printed, and then smuggled back into France for clandestine sale under a variety of assumed names. To this day it is not always certain whether a given anticlerical or antireligious work of the period should be attributed to D'Holbach or not, but among his undoubted works are: *Christianity Unveiled* (1761), *The Religious Disease* (1768), *System of Nature* (1770), and *Common Sense or Natural Ideas Opposed to Supernatural* (1772). There is a certain irony in the final distribution of things. D'Holbach, the real but largely unrecognized atheist, was buried in sacred ground in Paris. Voltaire, the deist who had *opposed* the anonymous author of the *System of Nature* (in the article "God" in the *Philosophical Dictionary* and elsewhere), was interred in unholy ground outside the city.

Philosophical Note

The *System of Nature* is, as Voltaire observed, inclined to repetition, declamation, and lack of profundity. There are, moreover, very few ideas in it which go beyond updated versions of classical materialism combined with ideas culled from Hobbes, Hume, Collins, or the general anticlericalism of the *philosophes*. But what makes D'Holbach's work very special is his total, unremitting, and eloquent avowal of materialistic atheism. It is indeed a system of natural atheism — an argued attempt to see the world as a whole, and humanity's place in it, and the structure of society, as a coherent totality without supernatural input. The *System* was an anonymous scandal, but it had the success of a scandal, and after its circulation, full unbelief is a discussable position for the first time in Christian Europe.

The *System of Nature* is a work amounting to about 350 closely printed pages. It attempts (like Lucretius) to cover many aspects of the physical world as well as dealing with issues such as human immortality, the proofs for the existence of God, and the relation between morality and religion. The extracts are taken from Volume II, mostly from Chapter II "Of the Confused and Contradictory Ideas of Theology," but with a final section from Chapter VIII. Both chapters take up Hobbes' thesis that we can have no conception of God. But D'Holbach goes further. We have no coherent idea of God *and* this supposed God is imaginary. The subheadings are supplied. The notes are in the original but were added by Diderot.

1. Man's Incoherent Idea of an Imaginary God

From *The System of Nature*, Volume II, Chapter 2

GOD: A METAPHYSICAL PHANTOM   Man always entertains the idea, that what he is not in a condition to conceive, is much more noble, much more respectable, than that which he has the capacity to comprehend: he imagines that his God, like tyrants, does not wish to be examined too closely.

These prejudices in man for the marvelous, appear to have been the source that gave birth to those wonderful, unintelligible qualities with which theology clothed the sovereign of the world. The invincible ignorance of the human mind, whose fears reduced him to despair, engendered those obscure, vague notions, with which he decorated his God. He believed he could never displease him, provided he rendered him incommensurable, impossible to be compared with any thing of which he had a knowledge; either with that which was most sublime, or that which possessed the greatest magnitude. From hence came the multitude of negative attributes with which engenious dreamers have successively embellished their phantom God, to the end that they might more surely form a being distinguished from all others, or which possessed nothing in common with that which the human mind had the faculty of being acquainted with.

The theological metaphysical attributes, were in fact nothing but pure negations of the qualities found in man, or in those beings of which he has a knowledge. By these attributes their God was supposed exempted from every thing which they considered weakness or imperfection in him, or in the beings by whom he is surrounded. To say that God is infinite, as has been shown, is only to affirm, that unlike man, or the beings with whom he is acquainted, he is not circumscribed by the limits of space; this however, is what man can never in any manner comprehend, because he is himself finite.*

When it is said that God is eternal, it signifies he has not had, like man or like every thing that exists, a beginning, and that he will never have an end; to say he is immutable, is to say that unlike man or every thing which he sees, God is not subject to change: to say he is immaterial, is to advance, that his substance or essence is of a nature not conceivable by a man, but which must from that very circumstance be totally different from every thing of which he has cognizance.

It is from the confused collection of these negative qualities, that has resulted the theological God; the metaphysical whole of which it is impossible for man to form to himself any correct idea. In this abstract being every thing is infinity — immensity — spirituality — omniscience —order — wisdom — intelligence — omnipotence. In combining these vague terms, or these modifications, the priests believed they formed something; they extended these qualities by thought, and they imagined they made a God, whilst they only composed a chimera. They imagined that these perfections or these qualities must be suitable to this God, because they were not suitable to any thing of which they had a knowledge; they believed that an incomprehensible being must have inconceivable qualities. These were the materials of which theology availed itself to compose the inexplicable phantom before which they commanded the human race to bend the knee.

Nevertheless, a being so vague, so impossible to be conceived, so incapable of definition, so far removed from every thing of which man could have any knowledge, was but little calculated to fix his restless views; his mind requires to be arrested by qualities which he is capacitated to ascertain — of which he is in a condition to form a judgment.

---

*Hobbes, in his *Leviathan*, says: "Whatsoever we imagine, is finite. Therefore there is no idea, or conception of any thing we call infinite. No man can have in his mind an image of infinite magnitude, nor conceive infinite swiftness, infinite time, infinite force, or infinite power. When we say any thing is infinite, we signify only, that we are not able to conceive the ends and bound of the thing named, having no conception of the thing, but of our own inability." Sherlock says: "The word infinite is only a negation, which signifies that which has neither end, nor limits, nor extent, and, consequently, that which has no positive and determinate nature, and is therefore nothing"; he adds, "that nothing but custom has caused this word to be adopted, which without that, would appear devoid of sense, and a contradiction."

Thus after it had subtilized this metaphysical God, after it had rendered him so different in idea, from every thing that acts upon the senses, theology found itself under the necessity of again assimilating him to man, from whom it had so far removed him: it therefore again made him human by the moral qualities which is assigned him; it felt that without this it would not be able to persuade mankind there could possibly exist any relation between him and the vague, ethereal, fugitive, incommensurable being they are called upon to adore. They perceived that this marvellous God was only calculated to exercise the imagination of some few thinkers, whose minds were accustomed to labor upon chimerical subjects, or to take words for realities; in short it found, that for the greater number of the material children of the earth it was necessary to have a God more analogous to themselves, more sensible, more known to them.

In consequence the Divinity was reclothed with human qualities. Theology never felt the incompatibility of these qualities with a being it had made essentially different from man, who consequently could neither have his properties, nor be modified like himself. It did not see that a God who was immaterial, destitute of corporeal organs, was neither able to think nor to act as material beings, whose peculiar organizations render them susceptible of the qualities, the feelings, the will, the virtues, that are found in them. The necessity it felt to assimilate God to his worshippers, to make an affinity between them, made it pass over without consideration these palpable contradictions, and thus theology obstinately continued to unite those incompatible qualities, that discrepance of character, which the human mind attempted in vain either to conceive or to reconcile. According to it, a pure spirit was the mover of the material world; an immense being was enabled to occupy space, without however excluding nature; an immutable deity was the cause of those continual changes operated in the world: an omnipotent being did not prevent those evils which were displeasing to him; the source of order submitted to confusion: in short, the wonderful properties of this theological being every moment contradicted themselves.

THE "JUST" GOD   In order to justify this God from the evils that the human species experiences, the theist is reduced to the necessity of calling them punishments inflicted by a *just* God for the transgressions of man. If so, man has the power to make his God suffer. To offend presupposes relations between the one who offends and another who is offended; but what relations can exist between the infinite being who has created the world and feeble mortals? To offend any one is to diminish the sum of his happiness; it is to afflict him, to deprive him of something, to make him experience a painful sensation. How is it possible man can operate on the well-being of the omnipotent sovereign of nature, whose happiness is unalterable? How can the physical actions of a material substance have any influence over an immaterial substance, devoid of parts, having no point of contact? How can a corporeal being make an incorporeal being experience incommodious sensations? On the other hand, *justice*, according to the only ideas man can ever form of it, supposes a permanent disposition to render to each what is due to him; the theologian will not admit that God owes any thing to man; he insists that the benefits he bestows are all the gratuitous effects of his own goodness; that he has the right to dispose of the work of his hands according to his own pleasure; to plunge it if he please into the abyss of misery. But it is easy to see, that according to man's idea of justice, this does not even contain the shadow of it; that it is, in fact, the mode of action adopted by what he calls the most frightful tyrants. How then can he be induced to call God just who acts after this manner? Indeed, while he sees innocence suffering, virtue in tears, crime triumphant, vice recompensed, and at the same time is told the being whom theology has invented is the author, he will never be able to acknowledge them to have *justice*.* But, says the theist, these evils are transient; they will only last for a time: very well, but then your God is unjust, at least for a time. It is for their good that he chastises his friends. But if he is good, how can he consent to let them suffer even for a time? If he knows every thing why reprove his favorites from whom he has nothing to fear? If he is really omnipotent, why not spare them these transitory pains, and procure them at once a durable and permanent felicity? If his power cannot be shaken, why make himself uneasy at the vain conspiracies they would form against him?

[Some declamatory paragraphs are here omitted.]

◦ They will, however, reply to these difficulties, that goodness, wisdom, and justice, are, in God, qualities so eminent, or have such little similarity to ours, that they have no relation with these qualities when found in men. But I shall answer, how shall I form to myself ideas of these divine perfections, if they bear no resemblance to those of the virtues which I find in my fellow-creatures, or to the dispositions which I feel in myself? If the justice of God is not that of men; if it operates in that mode which men call injustice, if his goodness, his clemency, and his wisdom do not manifest themselves by such signs that we are able to recognize them; if all his divine qualities are contrary to received ideas; if in theology all the human actions are obscured or overthrown, how

---

Dies deficiet si velim numerare quibus bonis male evenerit; nec minus si commemorem quibus malis optime. Cicer. *de Nat. Deor.* lib. iii. If a virtuous king possessed the ring of Gyges, that is to say, had the faculty of rendering himself invisible, would he not make use of it to remedy abuses to reward the good, to prevent the conspiracies of the wicked, to make order and happiness reign throughout his states? God is an invisible and all-powerful monarch, nevertheless his states are the theater of crime, of confusion: he remedies nothing.

can mortals like myself pretend to announce them, to have a knowledge of them, or to explain them to others? Can theology give to the mind the ineffable boon of conceiving that which no man is in a capacity to comprehend? Can it procure to its agents the marvelous faculty of having precise ideas of a God composed of so many contradictory qualities? In short, is the theologian himself a God?

They silence us by saying, that God himself has spoken, that he has made himself known to men. But when, where, and to whom has he spoken? Where are these divine oracles? A hundred voices raise themselves in the same moment, a hundred hands show them to me in absurd and discordant collections: I run them over, and through the whole I find that the *God of wisdom* has spoken an obscure, insidious, and irrational language. I see that the *God of goodness* has been cruel and sanguinary; that the *God of justice* has been unjust and partial, has ordered iniquity; that the *God of mercies* destines the most hideous punishments to the unhappy victims of his anger. Besides, obstacles present themselves when men attempt to verify the pretended relations of a Divinity, who, in two countries, has never literally holden the same language; who has spoken in so many places, at so many times, and always so variously, that he appears every where to have shown himself only with the determined design of throwing the human mind into the strangest perplexity.

[Some declamatory paragraphs are here omitted.]

In short, theologians invest their God with the incommunicable privilege of acting contrary to all the laws of nature and of reason, whilst it is upon his reason, his justice, his wisdom and his fidelity in the fulfilling his pretended engagements, that they are willing to establish the worship which we owe him, and the duties of morality. What an ocean of contradictions! A being who can do every thing, and who owes nothing to any one, who, in his eternal decrees, can elect or reject, predestinate to happiness or to misery, who has the right of making men the playthings of his caprice, and to afflict them without reason, who could go so far as even to destroy and annihilate the universe, is he not a tyrant or a demon? Is there any thing more frightful than the immediate consequences to be drawn from these revolting ideas given to us of their God, by those who tell us to love him, to serve him, to imitate him, and to obey his orders? Would it not be a thousand times better to depend upon blind matter, upon a nature destitute of intelligence, upon chance, or upon nothing, upon a God of stone or of wood, than upon a God who is laying snares for men, inviting them to sin, and permitting them to commit those crimes which he could prevent, to the end that he may have the barbarous pleasure of punishing them without measure, without utility to himself, without correction to them, and without their example serving to reclaim others? A gloomy terror must necessarily result from the idea of such a being; his power will wrest from us much servile homage; we shall call him good to flatter him or to disarm his malice; but, without overturning the essence of things, such a God will never be able to make himself beloved by us, when we shall reflect that he owes us nothing, that he has the right of being unjust, that he has the power to punish his creatures for making a bad use of the liberty which he grants them, or for not having had that grace which he has been pleased to refuse them.

THE INCOMPATIBLE ATTRIBUTES OF GOD   However, admitting for a moment that God possesses all the human virtues in an infinite degree of perfection, we shall presently be obliged to acknowledge that he cannot connect them with those metaphysical, theological, and negative attributes, of which we have already spoken. If God is a spirit, how can he act like man, who is a corporeal being? A pure spirit sees nothing; it neither hears our prayers nor our cries, it cannot be conceived to have compassion for our miseries, being destitute of those organs by which the sentiments of pity can be excited in us. He is not *immutable*, if his disposition can change: he is not *infinite*, if the totality of nature, without being him, can exist conjointly with him; he is not *omnipotent*, if he permits, or if he does not prevent disorder in the world: he is not *omnipresent*, if he is not in the man who sins, or if he leaves at the moment in which he commits the sin. Thus, in whatever manner we consider this God, the human qualities which they assign him, necessarily destroy each other; and these same qualities cannot, in any possible manner, combine themselves with the supernatural attributes given him by theology.

REVELATION   With respect to the pretended *revelation* of the will of God, far from being a proof of his goodness, or of his commiseration for men, it would only be a proof of his malice. Indeed, all revelation supposes the Divinity guilty of leaving the human species, during a considerable time, unacquainted with truths the most important to their happiness. This revelation, made to a smaller number of chosen men, would moreover show a partiality in this being, an unjust predilection but little compatible with the goodness of the common Father of the human race. This revelation destroys also the divine immutability, since, by it, God would have permitted at one time, that men should be ignorant of his will, and at another time, that they should be instructed in it. This granted, all revelation is contrary to the notions which they give us of the justice or of the goodness of a God, who they tell us is immutable, and who, without having occasion to reveal himself, or to make himself known to them by miracles, could easily instruct and convince men, and inspire them with those ideas, which he desires; in short, dispose of their minds and of their hearts. What if we should examine in detail all those pretended revelations, which they assure us have been made to mortals? We shall see that God only retails fables unworthy of a wise being; acts in them, in a manner contrary to the natural notions of equity; announces enigmas and oracles impossible to be comprehended; paints himself under traits incompatible with his infinite perfections; exacts puerilities which degrade him in the eyes of reason, deranges the order which he has established in nature, to convince creatures, whom he will never cause to adopt those ideas, those sentiments, and that conduct, with which he would inspire them. In short, we shall find, that God has never manifested himself, but to announce inexplicable mysteries, unintelligible doctrines, ridiculous practices; to throw the human mind into fear, distrust, perplexity, and above all, to furnish a never-failing source of dispute to mortals.*

2. The First Concern of Man is Man

From *The System of Nature,* Volume II, Chapter 8

If we cannot cure nations of their inveterate prejudices, let us endeavour, at least, to prevent them from again falling into those excesses into which religion has so frequently hurried them; let men form to themselves chimeras; let them think of them as they will, provided their reveries do not make them forget they are men, and that a sociable being is not made to resemble ferocious animals. Let us balance the fictitious interests of heaven, by the sensible interests of the earth. Let sovereigns, and the people, at length acknowledge that the advantages resulting from truth, from justice, from good laws, from a rational education, and from a human and peaceable morality, are much more solid than those which they so vainly expect from their Divinities: let them feel that benefits so real and so precious ought not to be sacrificed to uncertain hopes, so frequently contradicted by experience. In order to convince themselves, let every rational man consider the numberless crimes which the name of God has caused upon the earth; let them study his frightful history, and that of his odious ministers, who have everywhere fanned the spirit of madness, discord, and fury. Let princes, and subjects at least, sometimes learn to resist the passions of these pretended interpreters of the Divinity, especially when they shall command them in his name to be inhuman, intolerant,

---

*It is evident that all revelation, which is not clear, or which teaches *mysteries,* cannot be the work of a wise and intelligent being: as soon as he speaks, we ought to presume, it is for the purpose of being understood by those to whom he manifests himself. To speak so as not to be understood, only shows folly or want of good faith. It is, then, very clear, that all things which the priesthood have called *mysteries,* are inventions, made to throw a thick veil over their own peculiar contradictions, and their own peculiar ignorance of the Divinity. But they think to solve all difficulties by saying *it is a mystery;* taking care, however, that men should know nothing of that pretended science, of which they have made themselves the depositaries.

and barbarous; to stifle the cries of nature, the voice of equity, the remonstrances of reason, and to shut their eyes to the interests of society.

Feeble mortals! How long will your imagination, so active and so prompt to seize on the marvellous, continue to seek out of the universe, pretexts to make you injurious to yourselves, and to the beings with whom ye live in society? Wherefore do ye not follow in peace the simple and easy route which your nature has marked out for ye? Wherefore strew with thorns the road of life? Wherefore multiply those sorrows to which your destiny exposes ye? What advantages can ye expect from a Divinity which the united efforts of the whole human species have not been able to make you acquainted with? Be ignorant, then, of that which the human mind is not formed to comprehend; abandon your chimeras; occupy yourselves with truth; learn the art of living happy; perfect your morals, your governments, and your laws; look to education, to agriculture, and to the sciences that are truly useful; labor with ardor; oblige nature by your industry to become propitious to ye, and the Gods will not be able to oppose any thing to your felicity. Leave to idle thinkers, and to useless enthusiasts, the unfruitful labor of fathoming depths from which ye ought to divert your attention: enjoy the benefits attached to your present existence; augment the number of them; never throw yourselves forward beyond your sphere. If you must have chimeras, permit your fellow-creatures to have theirs also; and do not cut the throats of your brethren, when they cannot rave in your own manner. If ye will have Gods, let your imagination give birth to them; but do not suffer these imaginary beings so far to intoxicate ye as to make ye mistake that which ye owe to those real beings with whom ye live. If ye will have unintelligible systems, if ye cannot be contented without marvelous doctrines, if the infirmities of your nature require an invisible crutch, adopt such as may suit with your humor; select those which you may think most calculated to support your tottering frame, do not insist on your neighbors making the same choice with yourself: but do not suffer these imaginary theories to infuriate your mind: always remember that, among the duties you owe to the *real* beings with whom ye are associated, the foremost, the most consequential, the most immediate, is a reasonable indulgence for the foibles of others.

9

THOMAS PAINE ON THE REBELLION OF REASON AND MORALITY AGAINST THE BIBLICAL REVELATION

Monarch of Gods and Demons, and all Spirits
But One, who throng those bright and rolling worlds
Which Thou and I alone of living things
Behold with sleepless eyes! Regard this Earth
Made multitudinous with thy slaves, whom thou
Requitest for knee-worship, prayer, and praise,
And toil, and hecatombs of broken hearts,
With fear and self-contempt and barren hope.

Shelley, Prometheus Unbound, 1818

Biographical Note

Thomas Paine (1737–1809) was born in Norfolk, England, and died in the United States. His parents were small-town tradespeople, and his own career, as an excise official, was uneventful until his dismissal in 1774 for what we would now call trade or labor union activity. In that year he went to the American colonies, where his first influential pamphlet was published: "Common Sense," an appeal for American independence. In this publication Paine argued that independence rather than redress of grievances should be the objective of the war, that the longer this was delayed the harder it would be to achieve, and that independence was the only thing that would make union in the form of "a continental charter" possible. Not content with being on the winning side in the ensuing conflict, Paine returned to Europe to promote his designs for a new type of iron bridge. Caught up in the events of the French Revolution, he wrote and published *The Rights of Man* (1791/92), the celebrated plea for government by democracy and in accordance with reason. As a result he was honored (if that is the right word) with election to the French National Convention, only to be arrested a year later for arguing in defense of the ex-king. Paine had not intended to have his thoughts about religion published until "a more advanced period of life." Evidently fearing that the advanced period had arrived, he had the manuscript of Part I of *The Age of Reason* smuggled out of Paris. It was published in 1794. But Paine was not executed. He was released and had to suffer the opprobrium caused by the violence of his ill-timed attack on Christianity. Disenchanted with Napoleon's France and by now regarded as a traitor in England, he returned to the United States in 1802 where he was befriended by Thomas Jefferson but reviled by the religious establishment. Paine died in obscurity in New York.

Philosophical Note

Paine was not an atheist. He emphatically identified himself as a believing deist for whom "the word of God is the creation we behold." His variety of unbelief in *The Age of Reason* is his unrelenting enmity to all the claims of biblical revelation and to the theological fictions and moral tyranny it had begot. The work was hugely influential and its very success now makes its polemic somewhat dated. Moreover, Paine's lack of a formal education shows. He is garrulous. He jumps about from topic to topic as any association of ideas takes him. He is impatient and angry, and on occasions merely silly. But he was effective. The following extracts are all taken from the beginning of Part I.

Against the Biblical Revelation
From *The Age of Reason*, Part I

Every national Church or religion has established itself by pretending some special mission from God, communicated to certain individuals. The Jews have their Moses; the Christians their Jesus Christ, their apostles and saints; and the Turks their Mahomet; as if the way to God was not open to every man alike.

Each of those Churches show certain books which they call *revelation*, or the word of God. The Jews say that their word of God was given by God to Moses face to face; the Christians say that their word of God came by divine inspiration; and the Turks say that their word of God (the Koran) was brought by an angel from heaven. Each of those Churches accuses the other of unbelief; and, for my own part, I disbelieve them all.

As it is necessary to affix right ideas to words, I will, before I proceed further into the subject, offer some observations on the word *revelation*. Revelation, when applied to religion, means something communicated *immediately* from God to man.

No one will deny or dispute the power of the Almighty to make such a communication if he pleases. But admitting, for the sake of a case, that something has been revealed to a certain person, and not revealed to any other person, it is revelation to that person only. When he tells it to a second person, a second to a third, a third to a fourth, and so on, it ceases to be a revelation to all those persons. It is revelation to the first person only, and *hearsay* to every other; and consequently they are not obliged to believe it.

It is a contradiction in terms and ideas to call anything a revelation that comes to us at second hand, either verbally or in writing. Revelation is necessarily limited to the first communication. After this it is only an account of something which that person says was a revelation to him; and though he may find himself obliged to believe it, it cannot be incumbent on me to believe it in the same manner, for it was not a revelation made to *me*, and I have only his word for it that it was made to him.

When Moses told the children of Israel that he received the two tables of the Commandments from the hand of God, they were not obliged to believe him, because they had no other authority for it than his telling them so; and I have no other authority for it than some historian telling me so. The Commandments carry no internal evidence of divinity with them. They contain some good moral precepts, such as any man qualified to be a law-giver or a legislator could produce himself without having recourse to supernatural intervention.*

When I am told that the Koran was written in heaven, and brought to Mahomet by an angel, the account comes too near the same kind of hearsay evidence, and second-hand authority as the former. I did not see the angel myself, and therefore I have a right not to believe it.

When also I am told that a woman, called the Virgin Mary, said, or gave out, that she was with child without any cohabitation with a man, and that her betrothed husband, Joseph, said that an angel told him so, I have a right to believe them or not; such a circumstance required a much stronger evidence than their bare word for it; but we have not even this, for neither Joseph nor Mary wrote any such matter themselves. It is only reported by others that *they said so.* It is hearsay upon hearsay, and I do not choose to rest my belief upon such evidence.

It is, however, not difficult to account for the credit that was given to the story of Jesus Christ being the son of God. He was born when the heathen mythology had still some fashion and repute in the world, and that mythology had prepared the people for the belief of such a story. Almost all the extraordinary men that lived under the heathen mythology were reputed to be the sons of some of their gods. It was not a new thing at that time to believe a man to have been celestially begotten; the intercourse of gods with women was then a matter of familiar opinion. Their Jupiter, according to their accounts, had cohabited with hundreds; the story, therefore, had nothing in it either new, wonderful,

---

*It is, however necessary to except the declaration which says that God *visits the sins of the fathers upon the children.* It is contrary to every principle of moral justice.

or obscene; it was conformable to the opinions that then prevailed among the people called Gentiles, or mythologists, and it was those people only that believed it. The Jews who had kept strictly to the belief of one God and no more, and who had always rejected the heathen mythology, never credited the story.

It is curious to observe how the theory of what is called the Christian Church sprung out of the tail of the heathen mythology. A direct incorporation took place in the first instance, by making the reputed founder to be celestially begotten. The trinity of gods that then followed was no other than a reduction of the former plurality, which was about twenty or thirty thousand. The statue of Mary succeeded the statue of Diana of Ephesus. The deification of heroes changed into the canonisation of saints. The mythologists had gods for everything: the Christian mythologists had saints for everything. The Church became as crowded with the one as the Pantheon had been with the other; and Rome was the place of both. The Christian theory is little else than the idolatry of the ancient mythologists, accommodated to the purposes of power and revenue; and it yet remains to reason and philosophy to abolish the amphibious fraud.

Nothing that is here said can apply, even with the most distant disrespect, to the *real* character of Jesus Christ. He was a virtuous and an amiable man. The morality that he preached and practised was of the most benevolent kind, and, though similar systems of morality had been preached by Confucius, and by some of the Greek philosophers, many years before; by the Quakers since, and by many good men in all ages; it has not been exceeded by any.

Jesus Christ wrote no account of himself, of his birth, parentage, or anything else. Not a line of what is called the New Testament is of his own writing. The history of him is altogether the work of other people; and as to the account given of his resurrection and ascension, it was the necessary counterpart to the story of his birth. His historians, having brought him into the world in a supernatural manner, were obliged to take him out again in the same manner, or the first part of the story must have fallen to the ground.

The wretched contrivance with which this latter part is told exceeds everything that went before it. The first part — that of the miraculous conception — was not a thing that admitted of publicity; and therefore the tellers of this part of the story had this advantage — that, though they might not be credited, they could not be detected. They could not be expected to prove it, because it was not one of those things that admitted of proof, and it was impossible that the person of whom it was told could prove it himself.

But the resurrection of a dead person from the grave, and his ascension through the air, is a thing very different as to the evidence it admits of to the invisible conception of a child in the womb. The resurrection and ascension, supposing them to have taken place, admitted of public and ocular demonstration, like that of the ascension of a balloon or the sun at noonday, to all Jerusalem at least. A thing which everybody is required to believe requires that the proof and evidence of it should be equal to all, and universal; and, as the public visibility of this last related act was the only evidence that could give sanction to the former part, the whole of it falls to the ground, because that evidence never was given. Instead of this, a small number of persons — not more than eight or nine — are introduced as proxies for the whole world, to say they *saw* it, and all the rest of the world are called upon to believe it. But it appears that Thomas did not believe the resurrection; and, as they say, would not believe without having ocular and manual demonstration himself. *So neither will I:* and the reason is equally as good for me and every other person and for Thomas.

It is in vain to attempt to palliate or disguise this matter. The story, so far as relates to the supernatural part, has every mark of fraud and imposition stamped upon the face of it. Who were the authors of it is as impossible for us to know as it is for us to be assured that the books in which the account is related were written by the persons whose names they bear. The best surviving evidence we now have respecting this affair is the Jews. They are regularly descended from the people who lived in the times, this resurrection and ascension is said to have happened, and they say *it is not true.* It has long appeared to me a strange inconsistency to cite the Jews as a proof of the truth of the story. It is just the same as if a man were to say: "I will prove the truth of what I have told you by producing the people who say it is false."

That such a person as Jesus Christ existed, and that he was crucified —which was the mode of execution at that day — are historical relations strictly within the limits of probability. He preached most excellent morality, and the equality of man; but he preached also against the corruptions and avarice of the Jewish priests, and this brought upon him the hatred and vengeance of the whole order of priesthood. The accusation which those priests brought against him was that of sedition and conspiracy against the Roman Government, to which the Jews were then subject and tributary; and it is not improbable that the Roman Government might have some secret apprehension of the effects of his doctrine as well as the Jewish priests; neither is it improbable that Jesus Christ had in contemplation the delivery of the Jewish nation from the bondage of the Romans. Between the two, however, this virtuous reformer and revolutionist lost his life.

[A number of pages criticizing the Old Testament — "the Bible" in Paine's usage — are here omitted.]

Thus much for the Bible; I now go on to the book called the New

Testament. The *new* Testament! — that is, the *new* will, as if there could be two wills of the Creator.

Had it been the object or the intention of Jesus Christ to establish a new religion, he would undoubtedly have written the system himself, or *procured it to be* written in his lifetime. But there is no publication extant authenticated with his name. All the books called the New Testament were written after his death. He was a Jew by birth and by profession, and he was the son of God in like manner that every other person is; for the Creator is the Father of All.

This first four books, called Matthew, Mark, Luke, and John, do not give a history of the life of Jesus Christ, but only detached anecdotes of him. It appears from these books that the whole time of his being a preacher was not more than eighteen months; and it was only during this short time that those men became acquainted with him. They make mention of him at the age of twelve years, sitting, they say, among the Jewish doctors, asking and answering them questions. As this was several years before their acquaintance with him began, it is most probable they had this anecdote from his parents. From this time there is no account of him for about sixteen years. Where he lived or how he employed himself during this interval is not known. Most probably he was working at his father's trade, which was that of a carpenter. It does not appear that he had any school education, and the probability is that he could not write, for his parents were extremely poor, as appears from their not being able to pay for a bed when he was born.

It is somewhat curious that the three persons whose names are the most universally recorded were of very obscure parentage. Moses was a foundling, Jesus Christ was born in a stable, and Mahomet was a mule-driver. The first and the last of these men were founders of different systems of religion; but Jesus Christ founded no new system. He called men to the practice of moral virtues and the belief of one God. The great trait in his character is philanthropy.

The manner in which he was apprehended shows that he was not much known at that time; and it shows also that the meetings he then held with his followers were in secret, and that he had given over, or suspended, preaching publicly. Judas could not otherways betray him than by giving information where he was, and pointing him out to the officers that went to arrest him; and the reason for employing and paying Judas to do this could arise only from the causes already mentioned, that of his not being much known, and living concealed.

The idea of his concealment not only agrees very ill with his reputed divinity, but associates with it something of pusillanimity; and his being betrayed, or, in other words, his being apprehended on the information of one of his followers, shows that he did not intend to be apprehended, and consequently that he did not intend to be crucified.

The Christian mythologists tell us that Christ died for the sins of the world, and that he came on *purpose to die.* Would it not then have been the same if he died of a fever, or of the small-pox, or of old age, or of anything else?

The declaratory sentence which, they say, was passed upon Adam in case he ate of the apple was not that *thou shalt surely be crucified,* but *thou shalt surely die.* The sentence was death, and not the *manner of dying.* Crucifixion, therefore, or any other particular manner of dying, made no part of the sentence that Adam was to suffer, and consequently, even upon their own tactics, it could make no part in the sentence that Christ was to suffer in the room of Adam. A fever would have done as well as a cross, if there was any occasion of either.

This sentence of death which, they tell us, was thus passed upon Adam, must either have meant dying naturally — that is, ceasing to live — or have meant what these mythologists call damnation; and, consequently, the act of dying on the part of Jesus Christ must, according to their system, apply as a prevention to one or other of these two *things* happening to Adam and to us.

That it does not prevent our dying is evident, because we all die; and if their accounts of longevity be true, men die faster since the crucifixion than before; and with respect to the second explanation (including with it the *natural death* of Jesus Christ as a substitute for the *eternal death or damnation* of all mankind), it is impertinently representing the Creator as coming off or revoking the sentence by a pun or a quibble upon the word *death.* The manufacturer of quibbles, St. Paul, if he wrote the books that bear his name, has helped this quibble on by making another quibble upon the word *Adam.* He makes there to be two Adams: the one who sins in fact and suffers by proxy; the other who sins by proxy and suffers in fact. A religion this interlaced with quibble, subterfuge, and pun, has a tendency to instruct its professors in the practice of these arts. They acquire the habit without being aware of the cause.

If Jesus Christ was the being which those mythologists tell us he was, and that he came into this world to *suffer,* which is a word they sometimes use instead of *to die,* the only real suffering he could have endured would have been *to live.* His existence here was a state of exilement or transportation from heaven, and the way back to his original country was to die. In fine, everything in this strange system is the reverse of what it pretends to be. It is the reverse of truth, and I become so tired with examining into its inconsistencies and absurdities that I hasten to the conclusion of it, in order to proceed to something better.

How much or what parts of the books called the New Testament were written by the persons whose names they bear is what we can know nothing of, neither are we certain in what language they were originally written. The matters they now contain may be classed under two heads: anecdote and epistolary correspondence.

The four books already mentioned — Matthew, Mark, Luke, and John — are altogether anecdotal. They relate events after they had taken place. They tell what Jesus Christ did and said, and what others did and said to him; and in several instances they relate the same event differently. Revelation is necessarily out of the question with respect to those books; not only because of the disagreement of the writers, but because revelation cannot be applied to the relating of facts by the persons who saw them done, nor to the relating or recording of any discourse or conversations by those who heard it. The book called the Acts of the Apostles — an anonymous work — belongs also to the anecdotal part.

All the other parts of the New Testament, except the book of enigmas called the Revelation, are a collection of letters under the name of epistles, and the forgery of letters under the name of epistles; and the forgery of letters has been such a common practice in the world that the probability is at least equal whether they are genuine or forged. One thing, however, is much less equivocal, which is that out of the matters contained in those books, together with the assistance of some old stories, the Church has set up a system of religion very contradictory to the character of the person whose name it bears. It has set up a religion of pomp and of revenue in pretended imitation of a person whose life was humility and poverty.

The invention of purgatory, and of the releasing of souls therefrom by prayers bought of the Church with money; the selling of pardons, dispensations, and indulgences are revenue laws, without bearing that name or carrying that appearance.

But the case, nevertheless, is that those things derive their origin from the proxyism of the crucifixion, and the theory deduced therefrom, which was that one person could stand in the place of another, and could perform meritorious services for him. The probability, therefore, is, that the whole theory or doctrine of what is called the redemption (which is said to have been accomplished by the act of one person in the room of another) as originally fabricated on purpose to bring forward and build all those secondary and pecuniary redemptions, upon; and that the passages in the books upon which the idea of the theory of redemption is built have been manufactured and fabricated for that purpose. Why are we to give this Church credit, when she tells us that those books are genuine in every part, any more than we give her credit for everything else she has told us, or for the miracles she says she has performed? That she *could* fabricate writings is certain, because she could write; and the composition of the writings in question is of that kind that anybody might do it; and that she *did* fabricate them is not more inconsistent with probability than that she should tell us, as she has done, that she could, and did, work miracles.

Since then no external evidence can, at this long distance of time, be produced to prove whether the Church fabricated the doctrine called redemption or not (for such evidence, whether for or against, would be subject to the same suspicion of being fabricated); the case can only be referred to the internal evidence which the thing carries of itself, and this affords a very strong presumption of its being a fabrication. For the internal evidence is that the theory or doctrine of redemption has for its basis an idea of pecuniary justice, and not that of moral justice.

If I owe a person money, and cannot pay him, and he threatens to put me in prison, another person can take the debt upon himself and pay it for me. But if I have committed a crime, every circumstance of the case is changed. Moral justice cannot take the innocent for the guilty, even if the innocent would offer itself. To suppose justice to do this is to destroy the principle of its existence, which is the thing itself. It is then no longer justice. It is indiscriminate revenge.

This single reflection will show that the doctrine of redemption is founded on a mere pecuniary idea corresponding to that of a debt which another person might pay; and as this pecuniary idea corresponds again with the system of second redemptions obtained through the means of money given to the Church for pardons, the probability is that the same persons fabricated both the one and the other of those theories, and that, in truth, there is no such thing as redemption; that it is fabulous, and that man stands in the same relative condition with his Maker he ever did stand since man existed; and that it is his greatest consolation to think so.

Let him believe this, and he will live more confidently and morally than by any other system. It is by his being taught to contemplate himself as an outcast, as a beggar, as a mumper, as one thrown, as it were, on a dunghill, at an immense distance from his Creator, and who must make his approaches by creeping and cringing to intermediate beings, that he conceives either a contemptuous disregard for everything under the name of religion, or becomes indifferent, or turns what he calls devout. In the latter case he consumes his life in grief, or the affectation of it. His prayers are reproaches. His humility is ingratitude. He calls himself a worm, and the fertile earth a dunghill, and all the blessings of life by the thankless name of vanities. He despises the choicest gift of God to man — the GIFT OF REASON; and, having endeavoured to force upon himself the belief of a system against which reason revolts, he ungratefully calls it *human reason*, as if man could give reason to himself.

[Some paragraphs are here omitted.]

As to the Christian system of faith, it appears to me as a species of Atheism; a sort of religious denial of God. It professes to believe in a man rather than in God. It is a compound made up chiefly of manism with but little Deism, and is near to Atheism as twilight is to darkness. It introduces between man and his Maker an opaque body which it calls a redeemer; as the moon introduces her opaque self between the earth and the sun, and it produces by this means a religious or an irreligious eclipse of light. It has put the whole orbit of reason into shade.

The effect of this obscurity has been that of turning everything upside down, and representing it in reverse; and among the revolutions it has thus magically produced, it has made a revolution in Theology.

That which is now called natural philosophy, embracing the whole circle of science, of which astronomy occupies the chief place, is the study of the works of God, and of the power and wisdom of God in his works, and is the true theology.

As to the theology that is now studied in its place, it is the study of human opinions and of human fancies *concerning* God. It is not the study of God himself in the works that he has made, but in the works or writings that man has made; and it is not among the least of the mischiefs that the Christian system has done to the world, that it has abandoned the original and beautiful system of theology, like a beautiful innocent, to distress and reproach, to make room for the hag of superstition.

10

ELIHU PALMER ON THE IMMORAL TEACHING OF JESUS BAR-JOSEPH

Whatever you wish that men would do to you, do so to them.

Matthew 7:12

You serpents, you brood of vipers, how are you to escape being sentenced to hell?

Matthew 23:33

Biographical Note

Palmer (1764–1806) was the first and one of the most radical unbelievers native to the New World. He was born in Connecticut and studied various reformed theologies before rejecting Christianity. He then read for the bar but was struck blind in 1793 by the yellow fever which killed his first wife at the same time. The remainder of his life was passed in writing and in lecturing to various small deistic or freethinking groups in the Hudson River area. He died in 1806, having befriended Thomas Paine on his return to America. He was the author of a number of published addresses and of one book: *Principles of Nature*, 1802.

Philosophical Note

Baron D'Holbach, with whose *System of Nature* Palmer was familiar, had inveighed against the bigotry and cruelty of religious morality (especially in its Old Testament form). Paine had inveighed against the morality of Christianity while excepting its founder from censure. Palmer takes matters one stage further. The actual moral *teachings* of Jesus bar-Joseph are corrupt and his conduct a bad (or impossible) moral example. It is scarcely necessary to remark that Palmer's ideas were not acceptable to the vast majority of those who heard about them (although his book went through twelve editions in the United States and England before 1830) and are still not generally accepted today. But Palmer's book did serve to open up the *possibility* of a discussion about the moral worth of what people take to be Jesus' own teaching; a discussion studiously avoided by most previous writers. The extract that follows is taken from Chapter XI: "That the Immorality of the Christian Religion Proves that it is not of Divine Origin." For more recent developments of the same theme, see the Bibliography at the end of this book.

The Immoral Teaching of Jesus bar-Joseph

From *Principles of Nature*, Chapter 11

In the New Testament, many principles are advanced inconsistent with moral truth, destructive of the peace of society, and subversive of the best interests of the human race. Some of these ruinous and immoral sentiments must be noticed, and made the subject of useful comment. *The gospel of Jesus Christ* is announced to a wicked world, as a great and important blessing; but an examination of this system will shew that it is calculated to annihilate every thing valuable in human existence; to create endless wars among the nations of the earth; to destroy domestic peace and tranquillity; discourage industry, and arrest the energetic progress of the human faculties in their career of beneficial improvement. In proof of these assertions, the following passages are quoted: (Luke, chap. xiv. verse 26) "If any man come to me, and hate not his father, and mother, and wife, and children, and brethren, and sisters, yea, and his own life, he cannot be my disciple." In the gospel of St. Matthew we are commanded to love our enemies. By what strange perversion of moral sentiment is it, that we are commanded in one place to hate our nearest relations, and in another to exercise a tender and affectionate regard to our implacable enemies? . . .

The above passage is always inconsistent with that part of the decalogue which says, *Honour thy father and thy mother;* for surely we cannot hate and honour them at the same time. It is also expressly contradictory to the mold and benevolent temper so frequently exhibited in the Epistles of John. *If any man say that he is in the light and hateth his brother, he is in darkness, even until now.* If the above passage in Luke be true, the condition on which we are to become the disciples of Christ, is that of hating our brother, and all our relations: while in the writings of John, love is absolutely necessary to the idea of true religion. How these opposite declarations can stand together, it is difficult to conceive. Christian fanaticism is able, perhaps, to reconcile them; but reason sees in them nothing but inconsistency, and the heated *zeal* of an incorrect and disordered imagination.

Another passage of most destructive immorality, is in Matthew's Gospel (chap. x. ver. 35.) *Think not that I am come to send peace on earth; I come not to send peace but a sword. For I am come to set a man at variance against his father, and the daughter against her mother, and the daughter-in-law against her mother-in-law, and a man's foes shall be of his own household.* If this was really the object of Christ's mission, no man was ever sent upon a more bloody and baneful expedition. This is carrying the sword of war into the hearts of nations, and sowing the seeds of private animosity in the bosom of domestic life. It is inconsistent with the goodness of God, that he should have been the author of a religion which has annihilated rational peace, and subverted the foundation of social and domestic tranquillity. This same dreadful idea is expressed in other parts of the New Testament, and furnishes an immutable ground of decision against the moral principle and divinity of this religion.

But not content with spreading far and wide the baleful effects of public and private calamity, this revealed system has positively enjoined, what, if reduced to practice, would bring upon the world universal starvation, and cause the human race to become extinct. (See Matthew, chap. vi.) *Therefore I say unto you, take no thought for your life, what ye shall eat or what ye shall drink; nor yet for your body what ye shall put on. Is not the life more than meat, and the body than raiment? Behold the fowls of the air; for they sow not, neither do they reap, nor gather into barns, yet your heavenly Father feedeth them. Are ye not much better than they? Which of you by taking thought, can add one cubit unto his stature? And why take ye thought for raiment? Consider the lilies of the field how they grow; they toil not, neither do they spin; And yet I say unto you that even Solomon in all his glory, was not arrayed like one of these. Therefore take no thought saying, what shall we eat; or what shall we drink, or wherewithal shall we be clothed?* If these directions were followed, the corporeal and mental industry of man would be destroyed, and famine, ignorance, and misery would be the necessary consequence. It is in vain that we are told that these passages do not mean what they express; if, when we are told that we ought to love our enemies, it is meant that we should *not* love them; and when we are told that we ought to hate our nearest relations, it is meant that we should *not* hate them; if when we are told that we ought to take no thought for the morrow, it is meant that we *should* take thought. If such be the explanatory methods by which the injurious force of these passages is to be done away, there is an end to all confidence in language, and the religion of Jesus is better calculated for deception than instruction.

The writings of Paul, that heated and fanatic zealot in the Christian faith, are equally noxious to the cause of moral virtue, and are calculated to annihilate the most virtuous efforts of every individual. *It is not of him that willeth nor of him that runneth; not of works lest any man should boast; of ourselves we can do nothing;* together with a hundred other passages of a similar nature, which go directly to suppress all the elevated exertions of the human faculties, and if literally followed, would turn man from intelligent activity, to a state of brutal indolence. It is extremely destructive to the moral happiness of mankind to teach them the want of powers, or the inadequacy of those they possess; because that fact is otherwise, because it is a solemn truth that the powers of man are competent to provide for his happiness; they are equal to the exigencies of existence. It is superstition that has made him a fool, it is religious tyranny that has enslaved his mind, perverted his faculties, and tarnished the glory of his intellectual energies. Christianity has taught him two awful and destructive lessons; first, that he is incapacitated for the performance of moral actions; and secondly in case he *should* perform them, they would add no merit or superior excellence to his character; that his best righteousness is like filthy rags which God would treat with marked abhorrence.

The repetition of such discouraging impressions must necessarily work an effect remarkably injurious to the virtuous activity of the human race. It is in conformity to this immoral instruction, that we see fanatic Christians every where boasting of their own inability, and doing violence to that internal sentiment which would otherwise constantly impel them to the performance of acts of justice, benevolence, and universal charity. In addition to the pointed declarations of the *holy scriptures* against the power and practice of morality, the inventors and promoters of the Christian religion have set up various kinds of doctrines, which diminish the motives to good actions and lead the uninstructive mind to repose confidence in something foreign from its own exertions and merit, such as atonement, baptism, faith, sacramental suppers, oblations, and ablutions, together with many other idle ceremonies and wild vagaries of a distempered and fanatic brain.

The idea that Jesus the son of Mary died for the sins of the world, and that henceforth moral virtue can have no saving efficacy, is among the most destructive conceptions by which the moral world has been insulted and perverted. The supernatural grace of God, which Christians for so many ages have been in search of, has hitherto eluded the grasp of all rational and philosophic men; and to those who pretend to be acquainted with this celestial gift, it has been at times more trouble than profit: since innumerable doubts have been created concerning its reality and modes of operation in the human heart.

The cursory survey that has been taken of the immoral precepts and principles contained *in the Old and New Testament*, clearly proves that these books are not of divine origin. The God of the Jews and Christians, according to their own description, is a changeable, passionate, angry, unjust, and revengeful being; infuriate in his wrath, capricious in his conduct, and destitute, in many respects, of those sublime and immutable properties which really belong to the Preserver of the universe. The characters spoken of in the scriptures, as the favourites of heaven, such as Moses, Joshua, David, Solomon, Jesus, and Paul, are none of them good moral characters; it is not probable, therefore, that they were selected by the Creator as the organs of celestial communication. In the *Old Testament*, national and individual justice is disregarded, and God is made the accomplice of crimes which human nature abhors. The maxims of the *New Testament* are a perversion of all correct principles in a code of moral virtue. The whole system is calculated to take man out of himself, to destroy his confidence in his own energies, to debase his faculties, vitiate his social affections, and brutalize the most useful qualities of human existence. The highest dignity of the human race consists in the practice of an exalted virtue, in the exercise of a fine sympathetic benevolence, and in reciprocating our feelings and affections, in promoting the justice and order of society, in relieving the unfortunate and supporting the cause of truth, in diminishing evil and augmenting good; in short, in promoting universally the science, the virtue, and happiness of the world. There is, however, no possibility of faithfully performing these duties while under the shackles of Jewish and Christian superstition. The remedy consists in a return to nature, and in elevating our views and conceptions above those theological absurdities which have degraded man to a level with the beast, and taught him to respect his civil and ecclesiastical tyrants as beings of a higher order, or celestial messengers from a vindictive and revengeful God.

11

PERCY BYSSHE SHELLEY AGAINST REVELATION AND DEISM

> Philosophy has no end in view save truth:
> faith . . . looks for nothing but obedience and
> piety. Again, philosophy is based on axioms which
> must be sought from nature alone: faith is based
> on history and language, and must be sought for
> only in scripture and revelation.
>
> *Spinoza*

Biographical Note

Percy Bysshe Shelley was born in 1792 at the dawn of the French Revolution, and it was the explosion of ideas—political, literary, and philosophical—then released that formed the driving forces for his tempestuous life. He was brought up as a conventional Anglican, but at some time while he was at Eton College (1804–1810) he adopted the intellectual position of deism: that is, rejecting biblical revelation but affirming the arguments for a god's existence. However, the arguments did not long satisfy him and he was sent down from Oxford in 1811 for publishing the brief pamphlet "The Necessity of Atheism." For the next eleven years he lived as rebel, propagandist, political idealist, and, above all, poet. Shelley was drowned at sea on July 8, 1822, when his boat overturned during a storm as he was returning from a visit to Byron.

Philosophical Note

The universally known romantic poet might seem an unlikely source for a major philosophical contribution to the literature of unbelief, but Shelley's *A Refutation of Deism* is a work of this nature. It was printed and circulated privately in 1814 (there were very few copies), and reveals the author's remarkable command both of ideas and sources— biblical, classical, and modern. As far as can be determined, it has never before been printed in a serious philosophical context, but it is a most powerful epitome of unbelief. It combines a rejection of the Judeo-

Christian revelation on the grounds of its immoral character and suspect historicity with a rejection of the arguments for the existence of God; and it does all this in the familiar, coded way in which the position of its author — unbelief — can at the end be inferred only as a probability. In the first half of the Dialogue, Theosophus attacks the grounds and reasons of the Christian revelation and then, having explicitly rejected Christianity, briefly affirms the typical arguments for the existence of God. (Shelley calls these arguments *deism*, but they are also an integral part of traditional *theism*.) In the second half Eusebes mounts a Hume-based rejection of these arguments and then points out that this leaves Christianity as the only alternative to atheism. The Dialogue is reproduced in full except for Shelley's extensive footnote quotations from the Bible. These are in illustration of his arguments.

Against Revelation and Deism
The Dialogue: *A Refutation of Deism*, 1814

PREFACE   The object of the following Dialogue is to prove that the system of Deism is untenable. It is attempted to shew that there is no alternative between Atheism and Christianity; that the evidences of the Being of a God are to be deduced from no other principles than those of Divine Revelation.

The Author endeavours to shew how much the cause of natural and revealed Religion has suffered from the mode of defence adopted by Theosophistical Christians. How far he will accomplish what he proposed to himself, in the composition of this Dialogue, the world will finally determine.

The mode of printing this little work may appear too expensive, either for its merits or its length. However inimical this practice confessedly is, to the general diffusion of knowledge, yet it was adopted in this instance with a view of excluding the multitude from the abuse of a mode of reasoning, liable to misconstruction on account of its novelty.

Eusebes and Theosophus

EUSEBES   Theosophus, I have long regretted and observed the strange infatuation which has blinded your understanding. It is not without acute uneasiness that I have beheld the progress of your audacious scepticism trample on the most venerable institutions of our forefathers, until it has rejected the salvation which the only begotten Son of God deigned to proffer in person to a guilty and unbelieving world. To this excess, then, has the pride of the human understanding at length arrived? To measure itself with Omniscience! To scan the intentions of Inscrutability!

You can have reflected but superficially on this awful and important subject. The love of paradox, an affectation of singularity, or the pride of reason has seduced you to the barren and gloomy paths of infidelity. Surely you have hardened yourself against the truth with a spirit of coldness and cavil.

Have you been wholly inattentive to the accumulated evidence which the Deity has been pleased to attach to the revelation of his will? The antient books in which the advent of the Messiah was predicted, the miracles by which its truth has been so conspicuously confirmed, the martyrs who have undergone every variety of torment in attestation of its veracity? You seem to require mathematical demonstration in a case which admits of no more than strong moral probability. Surely the merit of that faith which we are required to repose in our Redeemer would be thus entirely done away. Where is the difficulty of according credit to that which is perfectly plain and evident? How is he entitled to a recompense who believes what he cannot disbelieve?

When there is satisfactory evidence that the witnesses of the Christian miracles passed their lives in labours, dangers, and sufferings, and consented severally to be racked, burned, and strangled, in testimony of the truth of their account, will it be asserted that they were actuated by a disinterested desire of deceiving others? That they were hypocrites for no end but to teach the purest doctrine that ever enlightened the world, and martyrs without any prospect of emolument or fame? The sophist, who gravely advances an opinion thus absurd, certainly sins with gratuitous and indefensible pertinacity.

The history of Christianity is itself the most indisputable proof of those miracles by which its origin was sanctioned to the world. It is itself one great miracle. A few humble men established it in the face of an opposing universe. In less than fifty years an astonishing multitude was converted, as Suetonius, Pliny, Tacitus, and Lucian attest; and shortly afterwards thousands who had boldly overturned the altars, slain the priests and burned the temples of Paganism, were loud in demanding the recompense of martyrdom from the hands of the infuriated heathens. Not until three centuries after the coming of the Messiah did his holy religion incorporate itself with the institutions of the Roman Empire, and derive support from the visible arm of fleshly strength. Thus long without any assistance but that of its Omnipotent author, Christianity prevailed in defiance of incredible persecutions, and drew fresh vigour from circumstances the most desperate and unpromising. By what process of sophistry can a rational being persuade himself to reject a religion, the original propagation of which is an event wholly unparalleled in the sphere of human experience?

The morality of the Christian religion is as original and sublime, as its miracles and mysteries are unlike all other portents. A patient acquiescence in injuries and violence; a passive submission to the will of sovereigns; a disregard of those ties by which the feelings of humanity have ever been bound to this unimportant world; humility and faith, are doctrines neither similar nor comparable to those of any other system. Friendship, patriotism, and magnanimity; the heart that is quick in sensibility, the hand that is inflexible in execution; genius, learning and courage, are qualities which have engaged the admiration of mankind, but which we are taught by Christianity to consider as splendid and delusive vices.

I know not why a Theist should feel himself more inclined to distrust the historians of Jesus Christ than those of Alexander the Great. What do the tidings of redemption contain which render them peculiarly obnoxious to discredit? It will not be disputed that a revelation of the Divine will is a benefit to mankind. It will not be asserted that even under the Christian revelation, we have too clear a solution of the vast enigma of the Universe, too satisfactory a justification of the attributes of God. When we call to mind the profound ignorance in which, with the exception of the Jews, the philosophers of antiquity were plunged; when we recollect that men, eminent for dazzling talents and fallacious virtues, Epicurus, Democritus, Pliny, Lucretius, Euripides, and innumerable others, dared publicly to avow their faith in Atheism with impunity, and that the Theists, Anaxagoras, Pythagoras and Plato, vainly endeavoured by that human reason, which is truly incommensurate to so vast a purpose, to establish among philosophers the belief in one Almighty God, the creator and preserver of the world; when we recollect that the multitude were grossly and ridiculously idolatrous, and that the magistrates, if not Atheists, regarded the being of a God in the light of an abstruse and uninteresting speculation; when we add to these considerations a remembrance of the wars and the oppressions, which about the time of the advent of the Messiah, desolated the human race, is it not more credible that the Deity actually interposed to check the rapid progress of human deterioration, than that he permitted a specious and pestilent imposture to seduce mankind into the labyrinth of a deadlier superstition? Surely the Deity has not created man immortal, and left him for ever in ignorance of his glorious destination. If the Christian Religion is false, I see not upon what foundation our belief in a moral governor of the universe, or our hopes of immortality can rest.

Thus then the plain reason of the case, and the suffrage of the civilized world, conspire with the more indisputable suggestions of faith, to render impregnable that system which has been so vainly and so wantonly assailed. Suppose, however, it were admitted that the conclusions of human reason and the lessons of worldly virtue should be found, in the detail, incongruous with Divine Revelation; by the dictates of which would it become us to abide? Not by that which errs whenever it is employed, but by that which is incapable of error: not by the ephemeral systems of vain philosophy, but by the word of God, which shall endure for ever.

Reflect, O Theosophus, that if the religion you reject be true, you are justly excluded from the benefits which result from a belief in its efficiency to salvation. Be not regardless, therefore, I entreat you, of the curses so emphatically heaped upon infidels by the inspired organs of the will of God: the fire which is never quenched, the worm that never dies. I dare not think that the God in whom I trust for salvation, would terrify his creatures with menaces of punishment which he does not intend to inflict. The ingratitude of incredulity is, perhaps, the only sin to which the Almighty cannot extend his mercy without compromising his justice. How can the human heart endure, without despair, the mere conception of so tremendous an alternative? Return, I entreat you, to that tower of strength which securely overlooks the chaos of the conflicting opinions of men. Return to that God who is your creator and preserver, by whom alone you are defended from the ceaseless wiles of your eternal enemy. Are human institutions so faultless that the principle upon which they are founded may strive with the voice of God? Know that faith is superior to reason, in as much as the creature is surpassed by the Creator; and that whensoever they are incompatible, the suggestions of the latter, not those of the former, are to be questioned.

Permit me to exhibit in their genuine deformity the errors which are seducing you to destruction. State to me with candour the train of sophisms by which the evil spirit has deluded your understanding. Confess the secret motives of your disbelief; suffer me to administer a remedy to your intellectual disease. I fear not the contagion of such revolting sentiments: I fear only lest patience should desert me before you have finished the detail of your presumptuous credulity.

Against Revelation

THEOSOPHUS   I am not only prepared to confess but to vindicate my sentiments. I cannot refrain, however, from premising, that in this controversy I labour under a disadvantage from which you are exempt. You believe that incredulity is immoral, and regard him as an object of suspicion and distrust whose creed is incongruous with your own. But truth is the perception of the agreement or disagreement of ideas. I can no more conceive that a man who perceives the disagreement of any ideas should be persuaded of their agreement, than that he should overcome a physical impossibility. The reasonableness or the folly of the articles of our creed is therefore no legitimate object of merit or demerit; our opinions depend not on the will, but on the understanding.

If I am in error (and the wisest of us may not presume to deem himself secure from all illusion) that error is the consequence of the prejudices by which I am prevented, of the ignorance by which I am incapacitated from forming a correct estimation of the subject. Remove those prejudices, dispel that ignorance, make truth apparent, and fear not the obstacles that remain to be encountered. But do not repeat to me those terrible and frequent curses, by whose intolerance and cruelty I have so often been disgusted in the perusal of your sacred books. Do not tell me that the All-Merciful will punish me for the conclusions of that reason by which he has thought fit to distinguish me from the beasts that perish. Above all, refrain from urging considerations drawn from reason, to degrade that which you are thereby compelled to acknowledge as the ultimate arbiter of the dispute. Answer my objections as I engage to answer your assertions, point by point, word by word.

You believe that the only and ever-present God begot a Son whom he sent to reform the world, and to propitiate its sins; you believe that a book, called the Bible, contains a true account of this event, together with an infinity of miracles and prophecies which preceded it from the creation of the world. Your opinion that these circumstances really happened appears to me, from some considerations which I will proceed to state, destitute of rational foundation.

To expose all the inconsistency, immorality and false pretensions which I perceive in the Bible, demands a minuteness of criticism at least as voluminous as itself. I shall confine myself, therefore, to the confronting of your tenets with those primitive and general principles which are the basis of all moral reasoning.

In creating the Universe, God certainly proposed to himself the happiness of his creatures. It is just, therefore, to conclude that he left no means unemployed, which did not involve an impossibility, to accomplish this design. In fixing a residence for this image of his own Majesty, he was doubtless careful that every occasion of detriment, every opportunity of evil, should be removed. He was aware of the extent of his powers, he foresaw the consequences of his conduct, and doubtless modelled his being consentaneously with the world of which he was to be the inhabitant, and the circumstances which were destined to surround him.

The account given by the Bible has but a faint concordance with the surmises of reason concerning this event.

According to this book, God created Satan, who, instigated by the impulses of his nature, contended with the Omnipotent for the throne of Heaven. After a contest for the empire, in which God was victorious, Satan was thrust into a pit of burning sulphur. On man's creation, God placed within his reach a tree whose fruit he forbade him to taste, on pain of death; permitting Satan, at the same time, to employ all his artifice to persuade this innocent and wondering creature to transgress the fatal prohibition.

The first man yielded to this temptation; and to satisfy Divine Justice the whole of his posterity must have been eternally burned in hell, if God had not sent his only Son on earth, to save those few whose salvation had been foreseen and determined before the creation of the world.

God is here represented as creating man with certain passions and powers, surrounding him with certain circumstances, and then condemning him to everlasting torments because he acted as omniscience had foreseen, and was such as omnipotence had made him. For to assert that the Creator is the author of all good, and the creature the author of all evil, is to assert that one man makes a straight line and a crooked one, and that another makes the incongruity.

Barbarous and uncivilized nations have uniformly adored, under various names, a God of which themselves were the model: revengeful, blood-thirsty, grovelling and capricious. The idol of a savage is a demon that delights in carnage. The steam of slaughter, the dissonance of groans, the flames of a desolated land, are the offerings which he deems acceptable, and his innumerable votaries throughout the world have made it a point of duty to worship him to his taste. The Phenicians, the Druids and the Mexicans have immolated hundreds at the shrines of their divinity, and the high and holy name of God has been in all ages the watchword of the most unsparing massacres, the sanction of the most atrocious perfidies.

But I appeal to your candor, O Eusebes, if there exists a record of such grovelling absurdities and enormities so atrocious, a picture of the Deity so characteristic of a demon as that which the sacred writings of the Jews contain. I demand of you, whether as a conscientious Theist you can reconcile the conduct which is attributed to the God of the Jews with your conceptions of the purity and benevolence of the divine nature.

The loathsome and minute obscenities to which the inspired writers perpetually descend, the filthy observances which God is described as personally instituting, the total disregard of truth and contempt of the first principles of morality, manifested on the most public occasions by the chosen favourites of Heaven, might corrupt, were they not so flagitious as to disgust.

When the chief of this obscure and brutal horde of assassins asserts that the God of the Universe was enclosed in a box of shittim wood, "two feet long and three feet wide," and brought home in a new cart, I smile at the impertinence of so shallow an imposture. But it is blasphemy of a more hideous and unexampled nature to maintain that the Almighty God expressly commanded Moses to invade an unoffending nation; and, on account of the difference of their worship, utterly to destroy every human being it contained, to murder every infant and unarmed man in cold blood, to massacre the captives, to rip up the matrons, and to retain the maidens alone for concubinage and violation.

[See Exodus, 32:26; Numbers, 31: 7 – 18.] At the very time that philosophers of the most enterprising benevolence were founding in Greece those institutions which have rendered it the wonder and luminary of the world, am I required to believe that the weak and wicked king of an obscure and barbarous nation, a murderer, a traitor and a tyrant, was the man after God's own heart? A wretch, at the thought of whose unparalleled enormities the sternest soul must sicken in dismay! An unnatural monster, who sawed his fellow beings in sunder, harrowed them to fragments under harrows of iron, chopped them to pieces with axes, and burned them in brick-kilns, because they bowed before a different, and less bloody idol than his own. It is surely no perverse conclusion of an infatuated understanding that the God of the Jews is not the benevolent author of this beautiful world.

The conduct of the Deity in the promulgation of the Gospel, appears not to the eye of reason more compatible with his immutability and omnipotence than the history of his actions under the law accords with his benevolence.

You assert that the human race merited eternal reprobation because their common father had transgressed the divine command, and that the crucifixion of the Son of God was the only sacrifice of sufficient efficacy to satisfy eternal justice. But it is no less inconsistent with justice and subversive of morality that millions should be responsible for a crime which they had no share in committing, than that, if they had really committed it, the crucifixion of an innocent being could absolve them from moral turpitude. *Ferretne ulla civitas latorem istiusmodi legis, ut condemnaretur filius, aut nepos, si pater aut avus deliquisset?* Certainly this is a mode of legislation peculiar to a state of savageness and anarchy; this is the irrefragable logic of tyranny and imposture.

The supposition that God has ever supernaturally revealed his will to man at any other period than the original creation of the human race, necessarily involves a compromise of his benevolence. It assumes that he withheld from mankind a benefit which it was in his power to confer. That he suffered his creatures to remain in ignorance of truths essential to their happiness and salvation. That during the lapse of innumerable ages, every individual of the human race had perished without redemption, from an universal stain which the Deity at length descended in person to erase. That the good and wise of all ages, involved in one common fate with the ignorant and wicked, have been tainted by involuntary and inevitable error which torments infinite in duration may not avail to expiate.

In vain will you assure me with amiable inconsistency that the mercy of God will be extended to the virtuous, and that the vicious will alone be punished. The foundation of the Christian Religion is manifestly compromised by a concession of this nature. A subterfuge thus palpable plainly annihilates the necessity of the incarnation of God for the redemption of the human race, and represents the descent of the Messiah as a gratuitous display of Deity, solely adapted to perplex, to terrify and to embroil mankind.

It is sufficiently evident that an omniscient being never conceived the design of reforming the world by Christianity. Omniscience would surely have foreseen the inefficacy of that system, which experience demonstrates not only to have been utterly impotent in restraining, but to have been most active in exhaling the malevolent propensities of men. During the period which elapsed between the removal of the seat of empire to Constantinople in 328, and its capture by the Turks in 1453, what salutary influence did Christianity exercise upon that world which it was intended to enlighten? Never before was Europe the theatre of such ceaseless and sanguinary wars; never were the people so brutalized by ignorance and debased by slavery.

I will admit that one prediction of Jesus Christ has been indisputably fulfilled. *I come not to bring peace upon earth, but a sword.* Christianity indeed has equalled Judaism in the atrocities, and exceeded it in the extent of its desolation. Eleven millions of men, women, and children, have been killed in battle, butchered in their sleep, burned to death at public festivals of sacrifice, poisoned, tortured, assassinated, and pillaged in the spirit of the Religion of Peace, and for the glory of the most merciful God.

In vain will you tell me that these terrible effects flow not from Christianity, but from the abuse of it. No such excuse will avail to palliate the enormities of a religion pretended to be divine. A limited intelligence is only so far responsible for the effects of its agency as it foresaw, or might have foreseen them; but Omniscience is manifestly chargeable with all the consequences of its conduct. Christianity itself declares that the worth of the tree is to be determined by the quality of its fruit. The extermination of infidels; the mutual persecutions of hostile sects; the midnight massacres and slow burning of thousands, because their creed contained either more or less than the orthodox standard, of which Christianity has been the immediate occasion; and the invariable opposition which philosophy has ever encountered from the spirit of revealed religion, plainly show that a very slight portion of sagacity was sufficient to have estimated at its true value the advantages of that belief to which some Theists are unaccountably attached.

You lay great stress upon the originality of the Christian system of morals. If this claim be just, either your religion must be false, or the Deity has willed that opposite modes of conduct should be pursued by mankind at different times, under the same circumstances; which is absurd.

The doctrine of acquiescing in the most insolent despotism; of praying for and loving our enemies; of faith and humility, appears to fix the perfection of the human character in that abjectness and credulity which priests and tyrants of all ages have found sufficiently convenient for their purposes. It is evident that a whole nation of Christians (could such an anomaly maintain itself a day) would become, like cattle, the property of the first occupier. It is evident that ten highwaymen would suffice to subjugate the world if it were composed of slaves who dared not to resist oppression.

The apathy to love and friendship, recommended by your creed, would, if attainable, not be less pernicious. This enthusiasm of anti-social misanthropy, if it were an actual rule of conduct, and not the speculation of a few interested persons, would speedily annihilate the human race. A total abstinence from sexual intercourse is not perhaps enjoined, but is strenuously recommended, and was actually practised to a frightful extent by the primitive Christians. [See I Cor. 7.]

The penalties inflicted by that monster Constantine, the first Christian Emperor, on the pleasures of unlicensed love, are so iniquitously severe, that no modern legislator could have affixed them to the most atrocious crimes. This cold-blooded and hypocritical ruffian cut his son's throat, strangled his wife, murdered his father-in-law and his brother-in-law, and maintained at his court a set of blood-thirsty and bigoted Christian Priests, one of whom was sufficient to excite the one half of the world to massacre the other.

I am willing to admit that some few axioms of morality, which Christianity has borrowed from the philosophers of Greece and India, dictate, in an unconnected state, rules of conduct worthy of regard; but the purest and most elevated lessons of morality must remain nugatory, the most probable inducements to virtue must fail of their effect, so long as the slightest weight is attached to that dogma which is the vital essence of revealed religion.

Belief is set up as the criterion of merit or demerit; a man is to be judged not by the purity of his intentions but by the orthodoxy of his creed; an assent to certain propositions, is to outweigh in the balance of Christianity the most generous and elevated virtue.

But the intensity of belief, like that of every other passion, is precisely proportioned to the degrees of excitement. A graduated scale, on which should be marked the capabilities of propositions to approach to the test of the senses, would be a just measure of the belief which ought to be attached to them: and but for the influence of prejudice or ignorance this invariably *is* the measure of belief. That is believed which is apprehended to be true, nor can the mind by any exertion avoid attaching credit to an opinion attended with overwhelming evidence. Belief is not an act of volition, nor can it be regulated by the mind: it is manifestly incapable therefore of either merit or criminality. The system which assumes a false criterion of moral virtue, must be as pernicious as it is absurd. Above all, it cannot be divine, as it is impossible that the Creator of the human mind should be ignorant of its primary powers.

The degree of evidence afforded by miracles and prophecies in favor of the Christian Religion is lastly to be considered.

Evidence of a more imposing and irresistible nature is required in proportion to the remoteness of any event from the sphere of our experience. Every case of miracles is a contest of opposite improbabilities, whether it is more contrary to experience that a miracle should be true, or that the story on which it is supported should be false: whether the immutable laws of this harmonious world should have undergone violation, or that some obscure Greeks and Jews should have conspired to fabricate a tale of wonder.

The actual appearance of a departed spirit would be a circumstance truly unusual and portentous; but the accumulated testimony of twelve old women that a spirit had appeared is neither unprecedented nor miraculous.

It seems less credible that the God whose immensity is uncircumscribed by space, should have committed adultery with a carpenter's wife, than that some bold knaves or insane dupes had deceived the credulous multitude. We have perpetual and mournful experience of the latter: the former is yet under dispute. History affords us innumerable examples of the possibility of the one: Philosophy has in all ages protested against the probability of the other.

Every superstition can produce its dupes, its miracles, and its mysteries; each is prepared to justify its peculiar tenets by an equal assemblage of portents, prophecies and martyrdoms.

Prophecies, however circumstantial, are liable to the same objection as direct miracles: it is more agreeable to experience that the historical evidence of the prediction really having preceded the event pretended to be foretold should be false, or that a lucky conjuncture of events should have justified the conjecture of the prophet, than that God should communicate to a man the discernment of future events. I defy you to produce more than one instance of prophecy in the Bible, wherein the inspired writer speaks so as to be understood, wherein his prediction has not been so unintelligible and obscure as to have been itself the subject of controversy among Christians.

That one prediction which I except is certainly most explicit and circumstantial. It is the only one of this nature which the Bible contains. Jesus himself here predicts his own arrival in the clouds to consummate a period of supernatural desolation, before the generation which he addressed should pass away. [See Matthew, 24.] Eighteen hundred years have past, and no such event is pretended to have happened. This single plain prophecy, thus conspicuously false, may serve as a criterion of those which are more vague and indirect, and which apply in an hundred senses to an hundred things.

Either the pretended predictions in the Bible were meant to be understood, or they were not. If they were, why is there any dispute concerning them: if they were not, wherefore were they written at all? But the God of Christianity spoke to mankind in parables, that seeing they might not see, and hearing they might not understand.

The Gospels contain internal evidence that they were not written by eye-witnesses of the event which they pretend to record. The Gospel of St. Matthew was plainly not written until some time after the taking of Jerusalem, that is, at least forty years after the execution of Jesus Christ: for he makes Jesus say that *upon you may come all the righteous blood shed upon the earth, from the blood of righteous Abel unto the blood of Zacharias son of Barachias whom ye slew between the altar and the temple.* [See Matthew, 2.] Now Zacharias, son of Barachias, was assassinated between the altar and the temple by a faction of zealots, during the siege of Jerusalem. [Josephus]

You assert that the design of the instances of supernatural interposition which the Gospel records was to convince mankind that Jesus Christ was truly the expected Redeemer. But it is as impossible that any human sophistry should frustrate the manifestation of Omnipotence, as that Omniscience should fail to select the most efficient means of accomplishing its design. Eighteen centuries have passed and the tenth part of the human race have a blind and mechanical belief in that Redeemer, without a complete reliance on the merits of whom, their lot is fixed in everlasting misery: surely if the Christian system be thus dreadfully important its Omnipotent author would have rendered it incapable of those abuses from which it has never been exempt, and to which it is subject in common with all human institutions, he would not have left it a matter of ceaseless cavil or complete indifference to the immense majority of mankind. Surely some more conspicuous evidences of its authenticity would have been afforded than driving out devils, drowning pigs, curing blind men, animating a dead body, and turning water into wine. Some theatre worthier of the transcendent event, than Judea, would have been chosen, some historians more adapted by their accomplishments and their genius to record the incarnation of the immutable God. The humane society restores drowned persons; every empiric can cure every disease; drowning pigs is no very difficult matter, and driving out devils was far from being an original or an unusual occupation in Judea. Do not recite these stale absurdities as proofs of the Divine origin of Christianity.

If the Almighty has spoken, would not the Universe have been convinced? If he had judged the knowledge of his will to have been more important than any other science to mankind, would he not have rendered it more evident and more clear?

Now, O Eusebes, have I enumerated the general grounds of my disbelief of the Christian Religion.—I could have collated its Sacred

Writings with the Brahminical record of the early ages of the world, and identified its institutions with the antient worship of the Sun. I might have entered into an elaborate comparison of the innumerable discordances which exist between the inspired historians of the same event. Enough however has been said to vindicate me from the charge of groundless and infatuated scepticism. I trust therefore to your candour for the consideration, and to your logic for the refutation, of my arguments.

EUSEBES   I will not dissemble, O Theosophus, the difficulty of solving your general objections to Christianity, on the grounds of human reason. I did not assist at the councils of the Almighty when he determined to extend his mercy to mankind, nor can I venture to affirm that it exceeded the limits of his power to have afforded a more conspicuous or universal manifestation of his will.

But this is a difficulty which attends Christianity in common with the belief in the being and attributes of God. This whole scheme of things might have been, according to our partial conceptions, infinitely more admirable and perfect. Poisons, earthquakes, disease, war, famine and venomous serpents; slavery and persecution are the consequences of certain causes, which according to human judgment might well have been dispensed with in arranging the economy of the globe.

Is this the reasoning which the Theist will choose to employ? Will he impose limitations on that Deity whom he professes to regard with so profound a veneration? Will he place his God between the horns of a logical dilemma which shall restrict the fulness either of his power or his bounty?

Certainly he will prefer to resign his objections to Christianity, than pursue the reasoning upon which they are found, to the dreadful conclusions of cold and dreary Atheism.

I confess that Christianity appears not unattended with difficulty to the understanding which approaches it with a determination to judge its mysteries by reason. I will even confess that the discourse, which you have just delivered, ought to unsettle any candid mind engaged in a similar attempt. The children of this world are wiser in their generation than the children of light.

But if I succeed in convincing you that reason conducts to conclusions destructive of morality, happiness, and the hope of futurity, and inconsistent with the very existence of human society, I trust that you will no longer confide in a director so dangerous and faithless.

I require you to declare, O Theosophus, whether you would embrace Christianity or Atheism, if no other systems of belief shall be found to stand the touchstone of enquiry.

I do not hesitate to prefer the Christian system, or indeed any system of religion, however rude and gross, to Atheism. Here we truly sympathize; nor do I blame, however I may feel inclined to pity, the man who in his zeal to escape this gloomy faith, should plunge into the most abject superstition.

The Atheist is a monster among men. Inducements, which are omnipotent over the conduct of others, are impotent for him. His private judgment is his criterion of right and wrong. He dreads no judge but his own conscience, he fears no hell but the loss of his self-esteem. He is not to be restrained by punishments, for death is divested of its terror, and whatever enters into his heart to conceive, that will he not scruple to execute. *Iste non timet omnia providentem et cogitantem, et animadvertentem, et omnia ad se pertinere putantem, curiosum et plenum negotii Deum.*

This dark and terrible doctrine was surely the abortion of some blind speculator's brain; some strange and hideous perversion of intellect, some portentous distortion of reason. There can surely be no metaphysician sufficiently bigoted to his own system to look upon this harmonious world, and dispute the necessity of intelligence; to contemplate the design and deny the designer; to enjoy the spectacle of this beautiful Universe and not feel himself instinctively persuaded to gratitude and adoration. What arguments of the slightest plausibility can be adduced to support a doctrine rejected alike by the instinct of the savage and the reason of the sage?

I readily engage, with you, to reject reason as a faithless guide, if you can demonstrate that it conducts to Atheism. So little, however, do I mistrust the dictates of reason, concerning a supreme Being, that I promise, in the event of your success, to subscribe the wildest and most monstrous creed which you can devise. I will call credulity, faith; reason, impiety; the dictates of the understanding shall be the temptations of the Devil, and the wildest dreams of the imagination, the infallible inspirations of Grace.

EUSEBES   Let me request you then to state, concisely, the grounds of your belief in the being of a God. In my reply I shall endeavour to controvert your reasoning, and shall hold myself acquitted by my zeal for the Christian religion, of the blasphemies which I must utter in the progress of my discourse.

THEOSOPHUS   I will readily state the grounds of my belief in the being of a God. You can only have remained ignorant of the obvious proofs of this important truth, from a superstitious reliance upon the evidence afforded by a revealed religion. The reasoning lies within an extremely narrow compass; *quicquid enim nos vel meliores vel beatiores facturum est, aut in aperto, aut in proximo posuit natura.*

From every design we justly infer a designer. If we examine the structure of a watch, we shall readily confess the existence of a watchmaker. No work of man could possibly have existed from all eternity. From the contemplation of any product of human art, we conclude that there was an artificer who arranged its several parts. In like manner, from the marks of design and contrivance exhibited in the Universe, we are necessitated to infer a designer, a contriver. If the parts of the Universe have been designed, contrived, and adapted, the existence of a God is manifest.

But design is sufficiently apparent. The wonderful adaptation of substances which act to those which are acted upon; of the eye to light, and of light to the eye; of the ear to sound, and of sound to the ear; of every object of sensation to the sense which it impresses prove that neither blind chance, nor undistinguishing necessity has brought them into being. The adaptation of certain animals to certain climates, the relation borne to each other by animals and vegetables, and by different tribes of animals; the relation, lastly, between man and the circumstances of his external situation are so many demonstrations of Deity.

All is order, design, and harmony, so far as we can descry the tendency of things, and every new enlargement of our views, every new display of the material world, affords a new illustration of the power, the wisdom and the benevolence of God.

The existence of God has never been the topic of popular dispute. There is a tendency to devotion, a thirst for reliance on supernatural aid inherent in the human mind. Scarcely any people, however barbarous, have been discovered, who do not acknowledge with reverence and awe the supernatural causes of the natural effects which they experience. They worship, it is true, the vilest and most inanimate substances, but they firmly confide in the holiness and power of these symbols, and thus own their connexion with what they can neither see nor perceive.

If there is motion in the Universe, there is a God. The power of beginning motion is no less an attribute of mind than sensation or thought. Wherever motion exists it is evident that mind has operated. The phenomena of the Universe indicate the agency of powers which cannot belong to inert matter.

Every thing which begins to exist must have a cause: every combination, conspiring to an end, implies intelligence.

Against Deism

EUSEBES Design must be proved before a designer can be inferred. The matter in controversy is the existence of design in the Universe, and it is not permitted to assume the contested premises and thence infer the matter in dispute. Insidiously to employ the words contrivance, design, and adaptation before these circumstances are made apparent in the Universe, thence justly inferring a contriver, is a popular sophism against which it behoves us to be watchful.

To assert that motion is an attribute of mind, that matter is inert, that every combination is the result of intelligence is also an assumption of the matter in dispute.

Why do we admit design in any machine of human contrivance? Simply because innumerable instances of machines having been contrived by human art are present to our mind, because we are acquainted with persons who could construct such machines; but if, having no previous knowledge of any artificial contrivance, we had accidentally found a watch upon the ground, we should have been justified in concluding that it was a thing of Nature, that it was a combination of matter with whose cause we were unacquainted, and that any attempt to account for the origin of its existence would be equally presumptuous and unsatisfactory.

The analogy which you attempt to establish between the contrivances of human art, and the various existences of the Universe, is inadmissible. We attribute these effects to human intelligence, because we know beforehand that human intelligence is capable of producing them. Take away this knowledge, and the grounds of our reasoning will be destroyed. Our entire ignorance, therefore, of the Divine Nature leaves this analogy defective in its most essential point of comparison.

What consideration remains to be urged in support of the creation of the Universe by a supreme Being? Its admirable fitness for the production of certain effects, that wonderful consent of all its parts, that universal harmony by whose changeless laws innumerable systems of worlds perform their stated revolutions, and the blood is driven through the veins of the minutest animalcule that sports in the corruption of an insect's lymph: on this account did the Universe require an intelligent Creator, because it exists producing invariable effects, and inasmuch as it is admirably organised for the production of these effects, so the more did it require a creative intelligence.

Thus have we arrived at the substance of your assertion, "That whatever exists, producing certain effects, stands in need of a Creator, and the more conspicuous is its fitness for the production of these effects, the more certain will be our conclusion that it would not have existed from eternity, but must have derived its origin from an intelligent creator."

In what respect then do these arguments apply to the Universe, and not apply to God? From the fitness of the Universe to its end you infer the necessity of an intelligent Creator. But if the fitness of the Universe, to produce certain effects, be thus conspicuous and evident, how much more exquisite fitness to his end must exist in the Author of this Universe? If we find great difficulty from its admirable arrangement in conceiving that the Universe has existed from all eternity, and to resolve this difficulty suppose a Creator, how much more clearly must we perceive the necessity of this very Creator's creation whose perfections comprehend an arrangement far more accurate and just.

The belief of an infinity of creative and created Gods, each more eminently requiring an intelligent author of his being than the foregoing, is a direct consequence of the premises which you have stated. The assumption that the Universe is a design, leads to a conclusion that there are an infinity of creative and created Gods, which is absurd. It is impossible indeed to prescribe limits to learned error, when Philosophy relinquishes experience and feeling for speculation.

Until it is clearly proved that the Universe was created, we may reasonably suppose that it has endured from all eternity. In a case where two propositions are diametrically opposite, the mind believes that which is less incomprehensible: it is easier to suppose that the Universe has existed from all eternity, than to conceive an eternal being capable of creating it. If the mind sinks beneath the weight of one, is it an alleviation to increase the intolerability of the burthen?

A man knows, not only that he now is, but that there was a time when he did not exist; consequently there must have been a cause. But we can only infer, from effects, causes exactly adequate to those effects. There certainly is a generative power which is effected by particular instruments; we cannot prove that it is inherent in these instruments, nor is the contrary hypothesis capable of demonstration. We admit that the generative power is incomprehensible, but to suppose that the same effects are produced by an eternal Omnipotent and Omniscient Being, leaves the cause in the same obscurity, but renders it more incomprehensible.

We can only infer from effects causes exactly adequate to those effects. An infinite number of effects demand an infinite number of causes, nor is the philosopher justified in supposing a greater connexion or unity in the latter, than is perceptible in the former. The same energy cannot be at once the cause of the serpent and the sheep; of the blight by which the harvest is destroyed, and the sunshine by which it is matured; of the ferocious propensities by which man becomes a victim to himself, and of the accurate judgment by which his institutions are improved. The spirit of our accurate and exact philosophy is outraged by conclusions which contradict each other so glaringly.

The greatest, equally with the smallest motions of the Universe, are subjected to the rigid necessity of inevitable laws. These laws are the unknown causes of the known effects perceivable in the Universe. Their effects are the boundaries of our knowledge, their names the expressions of our ignorance. To suppose some existence beyond, or above them, is to invent a second and superfluous hypothesis to account for what has already been accounted for by the laws of motion and the properties of matter. I admit that the nature of these laws is incomprehensible, but the hypothesis of a Deity adds a gratuitous difficulty, which so far from alleviating those which it is adduced to explain, requires new hypotheses for the elucidation of its own inherent contradictions.

The laws of attraction and repulsion, desire and aversion, suffice to account for every phenomenon of the moral and physical world. A precise knowledge of the properties of any object, is alone requisite to determine its manner of action. Let the mathematician be acquainted with the weight and volume of a cannon ball, together with the degree of velocity and inclination with which it is impelled, and he will accurately delineate the course it must describe, and determine the force with which it will strike an object at a given distance. Let the influencing motive, present to the mind of any person be given, and the knowledge of his consequent conduct will result. Let the bulk and velocity of a comet be discovered, and the astronomer, by the accurate estimation of the equal and contrary actions of the centripetal and centrifugal forces, will justly predict the period of its return.

The anomalous motions of the heavenly bodies, their unequal velocities and frequent aberrations, are corrected by that gravitation by which they are caused. The illustrious Laplace has shewn that the approach of the Moon to the Earth, and the Earth to the Sun, is only a secular equation of a very long period, which has its maximum and minimum. The system of the Universe then is upheld solely by physical powers. The necessity of matter is the ruler of the world. It is vain philosophy which supposes more causes than are exactly adequate to explain the phenomena of things. *Hypotheses non fingo: quicquid enim ex phænomenis non deducitur, hypothesis vocanda est; et hypotheses vel metaphysicæ, vel physicae, vel qualitatum occultarum, seu mechanicae, in philosophiâ locum non habent.*

You assert that the construction of the animal machine, the fitness of certain animals to certain situations, the connexion between the organs of perception and that which is perceived; the relation between everything which exists, and that which tends to preserve it in its existence, imply design. It is manifest that if the eye could not see, nor the stomach digest, the human frame could not preserve its present mode of existence. It is equally certain, however, that the elements of its composition, if they did not exist in one form, must exist in another; and that the combinations which they would form, must so long as they endured, derive support for their peculiar mode of being from their fitness to the circumstances of their situation.

It by no means follows, that because a being exists, performing certain functions, he was fitted by another being to the performance of these functions. So rash a conclusion would conduct, as I have before shewn, to an absurdity; and it becomes infinitely more unwarrantable from the consideration that the known laws of matter and motion, suffice to unravel, even in the present imperfect state of moral and physical science, the majority of those difficulties which the hypothesis of a Deity was invented to explain.

Doubtless no disposition of inert matter, or matter deprived of qualities, could ever have composed an animal, a tree, or even a stone. But matter deprived of qualities, is an abstraction, concerning which it is impossible to form an idea. Matter, such as we behold it, is not inert. It is infinitely active and subtile. Light, electricity, and magnetism are fluids not surpassed by thought itself in tenuity and activity: like thought they are sometimes the cause and sometimes the effect of motion; and, distinct as they are from every other class of substances with which we are acquainted, seem to possess equal claims with thought to the unmeaning distinction of immateriality.

The laws of motion and the properties of matter suffice to account for every phenomenon, or combination of phenomena exhibited in the Universe. That certain animals exist in certain climates, results from the consentaneity of their frames to the circumstances of their situation: let these circumstances be altered to a sufficient degree, and the elements of their composition must exist in some new combination no less resulting than the former from those inevitable laws by which the Universe is governed.

It is the necessary consequence of the organization of man, that his stomach should digest his food: it inevitably results also from his gluttonous and unnatural appetite for the flesh of animals that his frame be diseased and his vigor impaired; but in neither of these cases is adaptation of means to end to be perceived. Unnatural diet, and the habits consequent upon its use are the means, and every complication of frightful disease is the end, but to assert that these means were adapted to this end by the Creator of the world, or that human caprice can avail to traverse the precautions of Omnipotence, is absurd. These are the consequences of the properties of organized matter; and it is a strange perversion of the understanding to argue that a certain sheep was created to be butchered and devoured by a certain individual of the human species, when the conformation of the latter, as is manifest to the most superficial student of comparative anatomy, classes him with those animals who feed on fruits and vegetables.

The means by which the existence of an animal is sustained requires a designer in no greater degree than the existence itself of the animal. If it exists, there must be means to support its existence. In a world where *omne mutatur nihil interit*, no organized being can exist without a continual separation of that substance which is incessantly exhausted, nor can this separation take place otherwise than by the invariable laws which result from the relations of matter. We are incapacitated only by our ignorance from referring every phenomenon, however unusual, minute or complex, to the laws of motion and the properties of matter; and it is an egregious offence against the first principles of reason to suppose an immaterial creator of the world, *in quo omnia moventur sed sine mutuâ passione:* which is equally a superfluous hypothesis in the mechanical philosophy of Newton, and a useless excrescence on the inductive logic of Bacon.

What then is this harmony, this order which you maintain to have required for its establishment, what it needs not for its maintenance, the agency of a supernatural intelligence? Inasmuch as the order visible in the Universe requires one cause, so does the disorder whose operation is not less clearly apparent, demand another. Order and disorder are no more than modifications of our own perceptions of the relations which subsist between ourselves and external objects, and if we are justified in inferring the operation of a benevolent power from the advantages attendant on the former, the evils of the latter bear equal testimony to the activity of a malignant principle, no less pertinacious in inducing evil out of good, than the other is unremitting in procuring good from evil.

If we permit our imagination to traverse the obscure regions of possibility, we may doubtless imagine, according to the complexion of our minds, that disorder may have a relative tendency to unmingled good, or order be relatively replete with exquisite and subtile evil. To neither of these conclusions, which are equally presumptuous and unfounded, will it become the philosopher to assent. Order and disorder are expressions denoting our perceptions of what is injurious or beneficial to ourselves, or to the beings in whose welfare we are compelled to sympathize by the similarity of their conformation to our own.

A beautiful antelope panting under the fangs of a tiger, a defenceless ox, groaning beneath the butcher's axe, is a spectacle which instantly awakens compassion in a virtuous and unvitiated breast. Many there are, however, sufficiently hardened to the rebukes of justice and the precepts of humanity, as to regard the deliberate butchery of thousands of their species, as a theme of exultation and a source of honour, and to consider any failure in these remorseless enterprises as a defect in the system of things. The criteria of order and disorder are as various as those beings from whose opinions and feelings they result.

Populous cities are destroyed by earthquakes, and desolated by pestilence. Ambition is everywhere devoting its millions to incalculable calamity. Superstition, in a thousand shapes, is employed in brutalizing and degrading the human species, and fitting it to endure without a murmur the oppression of its innumerable tyrants. All this is abstractedly neither good nor evil, because good and evil are words employed to designate that peculiar state of our own perceptions, resulting from the encounter of any object calculated to produce pleasure or pain. Exclude the idea of relation, and the words good and evil are deprived of import.

Earthquakes are injurious to the cities which they destroy, beneficial to those whose commerce was injured by their prosperity, and indifferent to others which are too remote to be affected by their influence. Famine is good to the corn-merchant, evil to the poor, and indifferent to those whose fortunes can at all times command a superfluity. Ambition is evil to the restless bosom it inhabits, to the innumerable victims who are dragged by its ruthless thirst for infamy to expire in every variety of anguish, to the inhabitants of the country it depopulates, and to the human race whose improvement it retards; it is indifferent with regard to the system of the Universe, and is good only to the vultures and the jackalls that track the conqueror's career, and to the worms who feast in security on the desolation of his progress. It is manifest that we cannot reason with respect to the universal system from that which only exists in relation to our own perceptions.

You allege some considerations in favor of a Deity from the universality of a belief in his existence.

The superstitions of the savage, and the religion of civilized Europe appear to you to conspire to prove a first cause. I maintain that it is from the evidence of revelation alone that this belief derives the slightest countenance.

That credulity should be gross in proportion to the ignorance of the mind which it enslaves, is in strict consistency with the principles of human nature. The idiot, the child, and the savage, agree in attributing their own passions and propensities to the inanimate substances by which they are either benefited or injured. The former become Gods and the latter Demons; hence prayers and sacrifices, by the means of which the rude Theologian imagines that he may confirm the benevolence of the one, or mitigate the malignity of the other. He has averted the wrath of a powerful enemy by supplications and submission; he has secured the assistance of his neighbour by offerings; he has felt his own anger subside before the entreaties of a vanquished foe, and has cherished gratitude for the kindness of another. Therefore does he believe that the elements will listen to his vows. He is capable of love and hatred towards his fellow beings, and is variously impelled by those principles to benefit or injure them. The source of his error is sufficiently obvious. When the winds, the waves and the atmosphere, act in such a manner as to thwart or forward his designs, he attributes to them the same propensities of whose existence within himself he is conscious when he is instigated by benefits to kindness, or by injuries to revenge. The bigot of the woods can form no conception of beings possessed of properties differing from his own: it requires, indeed, a mind considerably tinctured with science, and enlarged by cultivation to contemplate itself, not as the centre and model of the Universe, but as one of the infinitely various multitude of beings of which it is actually composed.

There is no attribute of God which is not either borrowed from the passions and powers of the human mind, or which is not a negation. Omniscience, Omnipotence, Omnipresence, Infinity, Immutability, Incomprehensibility, and Immateriality, are all words which designate properties and powers peculiar to organised beings, with the addition of negations, by which the idea of limitation is excluded.*

That the frequency of a belief in God (for it is not universal) should

*See Le Système de la Nature: this book is one of the most eloquent vindications of Atheism.

be any argument in its favour, none to whom the innumerable mistakes of men are familiar, will assert. It is among men of genius and science that Atheism alone is found, but among these alone is cherished an hostility to those errors, with which the illiterate and vulgar are infected.

How small is the proportion of those who really believe in God, to the thousands who are prevented by their occupations from ever bestowing a serious thought upon the subject, and the millions who worship butterflies, bones, feathers, monkeys, calabashes and serpents. The word God, like other abstractions, signifies the agreement of certain propositions, rather than the presence of any idea. If we found our belief in the existence of God on the universal consent of mankind, we are duped by the most palpable of sophisms. The word God cannot mean at the same time an ape, a snake, a bone, a calabash, a Trinity, and a Unity. Nor can that belief be accounted universal against which men of powerful intellect and spotless virtue have in every age protested. *Non pudet igitur physicum, id est speculatorem venatoremque naturae, ex animis consuctudine imbutis petere testimonium veritatis?*

Hume has shewn, to the satisfaction of all philosophers, that the only idea which we can form of causation is derivable from the constant conjunction of objects, and the consequent inference of one from the other. We denominate that phenomenon the cause of another which we observe with the fewest exceptions to precede its occurrence. Hence it would be inadmissible to deduce the being of a God from the existence of the Universe; even if this mode of reasoning did not conduct to the monstrous conclusion of an infinity of creative and created Gods, each more eminently requiring a Creator than its predecessor.

If Power be an attribute of existing substance, substance could not have derived its origin from power. One thing cannot be at the same time the cause and the effect of another. — The word power expresses the capability of any thing to be or act. The human mind never hesitates to annex the idea of power to any object of its experience. To deny that power is the attribute of being, is to deny that being can be. If power be an attribute of substance, the hypothesis of a God is a superfluous and unwarrantable assumption.

Intelligence is that attribute of the Deity, which you hold to be most apparent in the Universe. Intelligence is only known to us as a mode of animal being. We cannot conceive intelligence distinct from sensation and perception, which are attributes to organized bodies. To assert that God is intelligent, is to assert that he has ideas; and Locke has proved that ideas result from sensation. Sensation can exist only in an organized body, an organised body is necessarily limited both in extent and operation. The God of the rational Theosophist is a vast and wise animal.

You have laid it down as a maxim that the power of beginning motion is an attribute of mind as much as thought and sensation.

Mind cannot create, it can only perceive. Mind is the recipient of impressions made on the organs of sense,and without the action of external objects we should not only be deprived of all knowledge of the existence of mind, but totally incapable of the knowledge of any thing. It is evident, therefore, that mind deserves to be considered as the effect, rather than the cause of motion. The ideas which suggest themselves too are prompted by the circumstances of our situation, these are the elements of thought, and from the various combinations of these our feelings, opinions, and volitions inevitably result.

That which is infinite necessarily includes that which is finite. The distinction therefore between the Universe, and that by which the Universe is upheld, is manifestly erroneous. To devise the word God, that you may express a certain portion of the universal system, can answer no good purpose in philosophy: In the language of reason, the words God and Universe are synonymous. *Omnia enim per Dei potentiam facta sunt, imo, quia naturae potentia nulla est nisi ipsa Dei potentia, artem est nos catemus Dei potentiam non intelligere quatenus causas naturales ignoramus; adeoque stultè ad eandam Dei potentiam recurritur quando rei alieujus, causam naturalem, sive est, ipsam Dei potentiam ignoramus.* *

Thus from the principles of that reason to which you so rashly appealed as the ultimate arbiter of our dispute, have I shewn that the popular arguments in favour of the being of a God are totally destitute of colour. I have shewn the absurdity of attributing intelligence to the cause of those effects which we perceive in the Universe, and the fallacy which lurks in the argument from design. I have shewn that order is no more than a peculiar manner of contemplating the operation of necessary agents, that mind is the effect, not the cause of motion, that power is the attribute, not the origin of Being. I have proved that we can have no evidence of the existence of a God from the principles of reason.

You will have observed, from the zeal with which I have urged arguments so revolting to my genuine sentiments, and conducted to a conclusion in direct contradiction to that faith which every good man must eternally preserve, how little I am inclined to sympathise with those of my religion who have pretended to prove the existence of God by the unassisted light of reason. I confess that the necessity of a revelation has been compromised by treacherous friends to Christianity, who have maintained that the sublime mysteries of the being of a God and the immortality of the soul are discoverable from other sources than itself.

I have proved that on the principles of that philosophy to which Epicurus, Lord Bacon, Newton, Locke and Hume were addicted, the existence of God is a chimera.

*Spinosa. *Tractus Theologico-Politicus*, chap. i.

The Christian Religion then, alone, affords indisputable assurance that the world was created by the power, and is preserved by the Providence of an Almighty God, who, in justice has appointed a future life for the punishment of the vicious and the remuneration of the virtuous.

Now, O Theosophus, I call upon you to decide between Atheism and Christianity; to declare whether you will pursue your principles to the destruction of the bonds of civilized society, or wear the easy yoke of that religion which proclaims "peace upon earth, good-will to all men."

THEOSOPHUS   I am not prepared at present, I confess, to reply clearly to your unexpected arguments. I assure you that no considerations, however specious, should seduce me to deny the existence of my Creator.

I am willing to promise that if, after mature deliberation, the arguments which you have advanced in favour of Atheism should appear incontrovertible, I will endeavour to adopt so much of the Christian scheme as is consistent with my persuasion of the goodness, unity, and majesty of God.

12

ARTHUR SCHOPENHAUER ON RELIGION AS THE METAPHYSIC OF THE PEOPLE

It is putting too great a respect on the Vulgar,
and on their Superstitions, to pique one self on
sincerity with regard to them. Did ever one make
it a point of honour to speak truth to children or
madmen?

Hume, in a letter of 1764

On account of the intellectual limitation of the
masses, religion adequately satisfies man's
ineradicable metaphysical need, and takes the
place of pure philosophical truth which is
limitlessly difficult, and perhaps ultimately
impossible to attain.

Schopenhauer in 1851

Biographical Note

Arthur Schopenhauer was born in Danzig in 1788. After a childhood
spent variously in France, England, Switzerland, and Austria, he un-
derwent a wide-ranging academic education in the Universities of Göt-
tingen and Berlin. In 1819 he published *The World as Will and Idea* in
which his main contribution to philosophy was developed. The work
was not the success its author expected, and his own opposition to the
dominant Hegelianism (he seems to have regarded Hegel as a philosophical charlatan) retarded his teaching career in the University of
Berlin. Nevertheless other publications — on free will, the foundation
of ethics, and the will in nature — appeared in the 1830s and 1840s. In
1851 in Berlin he published two volumes of essays with the somewhat
unnerving title *Parerga and Paralipomena*: "Stray yet systematically
arranged thoughts on a variety of subjects." The work at last brought
some measure of fame to "the philosopher of pessimism." Schopenhauer died in Frankfurt in 1860. Much of his work was published in
English translations during the late nineteenth century, including the
section on religion from *Parerga and Paralipomena*, part of which is
reproduced here.

Philosophical Note

Schopenhauer does not have a vast amount to say about religion, but what he does say indicates a new perspective on the subject. In his own person he believed neither in God nor in immorality. But the burning personal and political hostility to the tyranny of religion, and the revolutionary anticlericalism of Voltaire, D'Holbach, Paine, and others leading up to and involved with the French Revolution is missing in his work. Schopenhauer, like Marx and Feuerbach and Freud and many others in the nineteenth century, accepts religion as a normal, perhaps an almost ineradicable phenomenon of human life and society, and asks why this is so. Religion to Schopenhauer is superfluous to the enforcement of morality and it is not *true* in any but a "flowery or allegorical" sense. But religion is *needed* by ordinary people to give direction and form to their lives. The philosophical person may transcend religion, but he or she should not expect others to do so.

Schopenhauer's style is pungent and memorable, and his thought leads one clearly and enticingly on. The problem is to know where to stop reading in a short extract. The following section is taken from Chapter 15, "On Religion: A Dialogue" from *Parerga and Paralipomena*. The whole Dialogue is about seventy pages long. Its balance and undogmatic play of ideas perhaps indicates the influence of Hume, of whose *Dialogues concerning Natural Religion* Schopenhauer thought very highly.

Religion as the Metaphysic of the People
From *Parerga and Paralipomena*, Chapter 15

Demopheles. Between ourselves, my dear fellow, I don't care about the way you sometimes have of exhibiting your talent for philosophy; you make religion a subject for sarcastic remarks, and even for open ridicule. Everyone thinks his religion sacred, and therefore you ought to respect it.

Philalethes. That doesn't follow! I don't see why, because other people are simpletons, I should have any regard for a pack of lies. I respect truth everywhere, and so I can't respect what is opposed to it. My maxim is *Vigeat veritas et pereat mundus*, like the lawyers' *Fiat justitia et pereat mundus*. Every profession ought to have an analogous device.

Demopheles. Then I suppose doctors should say *Fiant pilulae et pereat mundus*, — there wouldn't be much difficulty about that!

Philalethes. Heaven forbid! You must take everything *cum grano salis*.

Demopheles. Exactly; that's why I want you to take religion *cum grano salis*. I want you to see that you must meet the requirements of the people according to the measure of their comprehension. Where you have masses of people, of crude susceptibilities and clumsy intelligence, sordid in their pursuits and sunk in drudgery, religion provides the only means of proclaiming and making them feel the high import of life. For the average man takes an interest, primarily, in nothing but what will satisfy his physical needs and hankerings, and beyond this, give him a little amusement and pastime. Founders of religion and philosophers come into the world to rouse him from his stupor and point to the lofty meaning of existence; philosophers for the few, the emancipated, founders of religion for the many, for humanity at large. For, as your friend Plato has said, the multitude can't be philosophers, and you shouldn't forget that. Religion is the metaphysics of the masses; by all means let them keep it: let it therefore command external respect, for to discredit it is to take it away. Just as they have popular poetry, and the popular wisdom of proverbs, so they must have popular metaphysics too: for mankind absolutely needs *an interpretation of life*; and this, again must be suited to popular comprehension. Consequently, this interpretation is always an allegorical investiture of the truth: and in practical life and in its effects on the feelings, that is to say, as a rule of action and as a comfort and consolation in suffering and death, it accomplishes perhaps just as much as the truth itself could achieve if we possessed it. Don't take offence at its unkempt, grotesque and apparently absurd form; for with your education and learning, you have no idea of the round about ways by which people in their crude state have to receive their knowledge of deep truths. The various religions are only various forms in which the truth, which taken by itself is above their comprehension, is grasped and realised by the masses; and truth becomes inseparable from these forms. Therefore, my dear sir, don't take it amiss if I say that to make a mockery of these forms is both shallow and unjust.

Philalethes. But isn't it every bit as shallow and unjust to demand that there shall be no other system of metaphysics but this one, cut out as it is to suit the requirements and comprehension of the masses? that its doctrines shall be the limit of human speculation, the standard of all thought, so that the metaphysics of the few, the emancipated, as you call them, must be devoted only to confirming, strengthening, and explaining the metaphysics of the masses? that the highest powers of human intelligence shall remain unused and undeveloped, even be nipped in the bud, in order that their activity may not thwart the popular metaphysics? And isn't this just the very claim which religion sets up? Isn't it a little too much to have tolerance and delicate forbearance preached by what is intolerance and cruelty itself? Think of the heretical tribunals, inquisitions, religious wars, crusades, Socrates' cup of poison, Bruno's and Vanini's death in the flames! Is all this to-day quite a thing of the past? How can genuine philosophical effort, sincere search after truth, the noblest calling of the noblest men, be let and hindered more completely than by a conventional system of metaphysics enjoying a State monopoly, the principles of which are impressed into every head in earliest youth so earnestly, so deeply, and so firmly, that, unless the mind is miraculously elastic, they remain indelible. In this way the groundwork of all healthy reason is once for all deranged; that is to say, the capacity for original thought and unbiased judgment, which is weak enough in itself, is, in regard to those subjects to which it might be applied, for ever paralysed and ruined.

Demopheles. Which means, I suppose, that people have arrived at a conviction which they won't give up in order to embrace yours instead.

Philalethes. Ah! if it were only a conviction based on insight. Then one could bring arguments to bear, and the battle would be fought with equal weapons. But religions admittedly appeal, not to conviction as the result of argument, but to belief as demanded by revelation. And as the capacity for believing is strongest in childhood, special care is taken to make sure of this tender age. This has much more to do with the doctrines of belief taking root than threats and reports of miracles. If, in early childhood, certain fundamental views and doctrines are paraded with unusual solemnity, and an air of the greatest earnestness never before visible in anything else; if, at the same time, the possibility of a doubt about them be completely passed over, or touched upon only to indicate that doubt is the first step to eternal perdition, the resulting impression will be so deep that, as a rule, that is, in almost every case, doubt about them will be almost as impossible as doubt about one's own existence. Hardly one in ten thousand will have the strength of mind to ask himself seriously and earnestly — is that true? To call such as can do it strong minds, *esprits forts*, is a description apter than is generally supposed. But for the ordinary mind there is nothing so absurd or revolting but what, if inculcated in that way, the strongest belief in it will strike root. If, for example, the killing of a heretic or infidel were essential to the future salvation of his soul, almost everyone would make it the chief event of his life, and in dying would draw consolation and strength from the remembrance that he had succeeded. As a matter of fact, almost every Spaniard in days gone by used to look upon an *auto da fe* as the most pious of all acts and one most agreeable to God. A parallel to this may be found in the way in which the Thugs (a religious sect in India, suppressed a short time ago by the English, who executed numbers of them) express their sense of religion and their veneration for the goddess Kali; they take every opportunity of murdering their friends and travelling companions, with the object of getting possession of their goods, and in the serious conviction that they are thereby doing a praiseworthy action, conductive to their eternal welfare.* The power

---

*Cf. Illustrations of the history and practice of the Thugs, London, 1837; also the *Edinburgh Review*, Oct.–Jan., 1836–7.

of religious dogma, when incalculated early, is such as to stifle conscience, compassion and finally every feeling of humanity. But if you want to see with your own eyes and close at hand what timely inoculation of belief will accomplish, look at the English. Here is a nation favoured before all others by nature; endowed, more than all others, with discernment, intelligence, power of judgment, strength of character; look at them, abased and made ridiculous, beyond all others, by their stupid ecclesiastical superstition, which appears amongst their other abilities like a fixed idea or monomania. For this they have to thank the circumstance that education is in the hands of the clergy, whose endeavour it is to impress all the articles of belief, at the earliest age, in a way that amounts to a kind of paralysis of the brain; this in its turn expresses itself all their life in an idiotic bigotry, which makes otherwise most sensible and intelligent people amongst them degrade themselves so that one can't make head or tail of them. If you consider how essential to such a masterpiece is inoculation in the tender age of childhood, the missionary system appears no longer only as the acme of human importunity, arrogance and impertinence, but also as an absurdity, if it doesn't confine itself to nations which are still in their infancy, like Caffirs, Hottentots, South Sea Islanders, etc. Amongst these races it is successful; but in India the Brahmans treat the discourses of the missionaries with contemptuous smiles of approbation, or simply shrug their shoulders. And one may say generally that the proselytising efforts of the missionaries in India, in spite of the most advantageous facilities, are, as a rule, a failure. An authentic report in Vol. XXI. of the *Asiatic Journal* (1826) states that after so many years of missionary activity not more than three hundred living converts were to be found in the whole of India, where the population of the English possessions alone comes to one hundred and fifteen millions; and at the same time it is admitted that the Christian converts are distinguished for their extreme immorality. Three hundred venal and bribed souls out of so many millions! There is no evidence that things have gone better with Christianity in India since then, in spite of the fact that the missionaries are now trying, contrary to stipulation and in schools exclusively designed for secular English instruction, to work upon the children's minds as they please, in order to smuggle in Christianity; against which the Hindoos are most jealously on their guard.

As I have said, childhood is the time to sow the seeds of belief, and not manhood; more especially where an earlier faith has taken root. An acquired conviction such as is feigned by adults is, as a rule, only the mask for some kind of personal interest. And it is the feeling that this is almost bound to be the case which makes a man who has changed his religion in mature years an object of contempt to most people everywhere; who thus show that they look upon religion, not as a matter of reasoned conviction, but merely as a belief inoculated in childhood, before any test can be applied. And that they are right in their view of religion is also obvious from the way in which not only the masses, who are blindly credulous, but also the clergy of every religion, who, as such, have faithfully and zealously studied its sources, foundations, dogmas and disputed points, cleave as a body to the religion of their particular country; consequently for a minister of one religion or confession to go over to another is the rarest thing in the world. The Catholic clergy, for example, are fully convinced of the truth of all the tenets of their Church, and so are the Protestant clergy of theirs, and both defend the principles of their creeds with like zeal. And yet the conviction is governed merely by the country native to each; to the South German ecclesiastic the truth of the Catholic dogma is quite obvious, to the North German, the Protestant. If, then, these convictions are based on objective reasons, the reasons must be climatic, and thrive, like plants, some only here, some only there. The convictions of those who are thus locally convinced are taken on trust and believed by the masses everywhere.

Demopheles. Well, no harm is done, and it doesn't make any real difference. As a fact, Protestantism is more suited to the north, Catholicism to the south.

Philalethes. So it seems. Still I take a higher standpoint, and keep in view a more important object, the progress, namely, of the knowledge of truth among mankind. And from this point of view, it is a terrible thing that, wherever a man is born, certain propositions are inculcated in him in earliest youth, and he is assured that he may never have any doubts about them, under penalty of thereby forfeiting eternal salvation; propositions, I mean, which affect the foundation of all our other knowledge and accordingly determine for ever, and, if they are false, distort for ever, the point of view from which our knowledge starts; and as, further, the corollaries of these propositions touch the entire system of our intellectual attainments at every point, the whole of human knowledge is thoroughly adulterated by them. Evidence of this is afforded by every literature; the most striking by that of the Middle Age, but in a too considerable degree by that of the fifteenth and sixteenth centuries. Look at even the first minds of all those epochs; how paralysed they are by false fundamental positions like these; how, more especially, all insight into the true constitution and working of Nature is, as it were, blocked up. During the whole of the Christian period Theism presents a solid barrier to all intellectual effort, and chiefly to philosophy, arresting or stunting all progress. For the scientific men of these ages God, devil, angels, demons hid the whole of nature; no enquiry was followed to the end, nothing ever thoroughly examined; everything which went beyond the most obvious causal nexus was immediately set down to those personalities. *"It was at once explained by a reference to God, angels or demons,"* as Pomponatius expressed himself when the matter was being discussed, *"and philosophers at any rate have nothing analogous."* There is, to be sure, a suspicion of irony in this statement of Pomponatius, as his perfidy in other matters is known; still, he is only giving expression to the general way of thinking of his age. And if, on the other hand, any one possessed the rare quality of an elastic mind, which alone could burst the bonds, his writings and he himself with them were burnt; as happened to Bruno and Vanini. How completely an ordinary mind is paralyzed by that early preparation in metaphysics is seen in the most vivid way and on its most ridiculous side, whenever it undertakes to criticise the doctrines of an alien creed. The efforts of the ordinary man are generally found to be directed to a careful exhibition of the incongruity of its dogmas with those of his own belief: he is at great pains to show that not only do they not say, but certainly do not mean, the same thing; and with that he thinks, in his simplicity, that he has demonstrated the falsehood of the alien creed. The efforts of the ordinary man are generally found to be the two may be right; his own articles of belief he looks upon as *a priori* true and certain principles.

Demopheles. So that's your higher point of view! I assure you there is a higher still. *First live, then philosophise* is a maxim of more comprehensive import than appears at first sight. The first thing to do is to control the raw and evil dispositions of the masses, so as to keep them from pushing injustice to extremes, and from committing cruel, violent and disgraceful acts. If you were to wait until they had recognised and grasped the truth, you would undoubtedly come too late; and truth, supposing that it had been found, would surpass their powers of comprehension. In any case an allegorical investiture of it, a parable or myth, is all that would be of any service to them. As Kant said, there must be a public standard of Right and Virtue; it must always flutter high overhead. It is a matter of indifference what heraldic figures are inscribed on it, so long as they signify what is meant. Such an allegorical representation of truth is always and everywhere, for humanity at large, a serviceable substitute for a truth to which it can never attain, for a philosophy which it can never grasp; let alone the fact that it is daily changing its shape, and has in no form as yet met with general acceptance. Practical aims, then, my good Philalethes, are in every respect superior to theoretical.

Philalethes. What you say is very like the ancient advice of Timæus of Locrus, the Pythagorean, *stop the mind with falsehood if you can't speed it with truth.* I almost suspect that your plan is the one which is so much in vogue just now, that you want to impress upon us that

> The hour is nigh
> When we may feast in quiet.

You recommend us, in fact, to take timely precautions, so that the waves of the discontented raging masses mayn't disturb us at table. But the whole point of view is as false as it is now-a-days popular and commended; and so I make haste to enter a protest against it. It is *false* that state, justice, law cannot be upheld without the assistance of religion and its dogmas; and that justice and public order need religion as a necessary complement, if legislative enactments are to be carried out. It is *false*, were it repeated a hundred times! An effective and striking argument to the contrary is afforded by the ancients, especially the Greeks. They had nothing at all of what we understand by religion. They had no sacred documents, no dogma to be learned and its acceptance furthered by everyone, its principles to be inculcated early on the young. Just as little was moral doctrine preached by the ministers of religion, nor did the priests trouble themselves about morality or about what the people did or left undone. Not at all. The duty of the priests was confined to temple-ceremonial, prayers, hymns, sacrifices, processions, lustrations and the like, the object of which was anything but the moral improvement of the individual. What was called religion consisted, more especially in the cities, in giving temples here and there to some of the gods of the greater tribes, in which the worship described was carried on as a state matter, and was consequently, in fact, an affair of police. No one, except the functionaries performing, was in any way compelled to attend, or even to believe in it. In the whole of antiquity there is no trace of any obligation to believe in any particular dogma. Merely in the case of an open denial of the existence of the gods, or any other reviling of them, a penalty was imposed, and that on account of the insult offered to the state, which served those gods: beyond this it was free to everyone to think of them what he pleased. If anyone wanted to gain the favour of those gods privately, by prayer or sacrifice, it was open to him to do so at his own expense and at his own risk; if he didn't do it, no one made any objection, least of all the state. In the case of the Romans everyone had his own Lares and Penates at home; these were, however, in reality, only the venerated busts of ancestors. Of the immortality of the soul and a life beyond the grave, the ancients had no firm, clear or, least of all, dogmatically fixed idea, but very loose, fluctuating, indefinite and problematical notions, everyone in his own way: and the ideas about the gods were just as varying, individual and vague. There was therefore really no *religion*, in our sense of the word, amongst the ancients. But did anarchy and lawlessness prevail amongst them on that account? Is not law and civil order, rather, so much their work, that it still forms the foundation of our own? Was there not complete protection for property, even though it consisted for the most part of slaves? And did not this state of things last for more than a thousand years? So that I can't recognize, I must even protest against the practical aims and the necessity of religion in the sense

indicated by you, and so popular now-a-days, that is, as an indispensable foundation of all legislative arrangements. For, if you take that
point of view, the pure and sacred endeavor after truth will, to say the
least, appear quixotic, and even criminal, if it ventures, in its feeling of
justice, to denounce the authoritative creed as a usurper who has taken
possession of the throne of truth and maintained his position by keeping up the deception.

Demopheles. But religion is not opposed to truth; it itself teaches
truth. And as the range of its activity is not a narrow lecture room, but
the world and humanity at large, religion must conform to the requirements and comprehension of an audience so numerous and so mixed.
Religion must not let truth appear in its naked form; or, to use a medical
simile, it must not exhibit it pure, but must employ a mythical vehicle, a
medium, as it were. You can also compare truth in this respect to
certain chemical stuffs which in themselves are gaseous, but which for
medicinal uses, as also for preservation or transmission, must be bound
to a stable, solid base, because they would otherwise volatilize. Chlo-
rine gas, for example, is for all purposes applied only in the form of
chlorides. But if truth, pure, abstract and free from all mythical alloy, is
always to remain unattainable, even by philosophers, it might be compared to fluorine, which cannot even be isolated, but must always
appear in combination with other elements. Or, to take a less scientific
simile, truth, which is inexpressible except by means of myth and
allegory, is like water, which can be carried about only in vessels; a
philosopher who insists on obtaining it pure is like water, which can be
carried about only in vessels; a philosopher who insists on obtaining it
pure is like a man who breaks the jug in order to get the water by itself.
This is, perhaps, an exact analogy. At any rate, religion is truth allegori-
cally and mythically expressed, and so rendered attainable and digest-
ible by mankind in general. Mankind couldn't possibly take it pure and
unmixed, just as we can't breathe pure oxygen; we require an addition
of four times its bulk in nitrogen. In plain language, the profound
meaning, the high aim of life, can only be unfolded and presented to
the masses symbolically, because they are incapable of grasping it in its
true signification. Philosophy, on the other hand, should be like the
Eleusinian mysteries, for the few, the élite.

Philalethes. I understand. It comes, in short, to truth wearing the
garment of falsehood. But in doing so it enters on a fatal alliance. What
a dangerous weapon is put into the hands of those who are authorised
to employ falsehood as the vehicle of truth! If it is as you say, I fear the
damage caused by the falsehood will be greater than any advantage the
truth could ever produce. Of course, if the allegory were admitted to
be such, I should raise no objection; but with the admission it would
rob itself of all respect, and consequently, of all utility. The allegory
must, therefore, put in a claim to be true in the proper sense of the

word, and maintain the claim; while, at the most, it is true only in an allegorical sense. Here lies the irreparable mischief, the permanent evil; and this is why religion has always been and will always be in conflict with the noble endeavour after pure truth.

Demopheles. Oh no! that danger is guarded against. If religion mayn't exactly confess its allegorical nature, it gives sufficient indication of it.

Philalethes. How so?

Demopheles. In its mysteries. "Mystery," is in reality only a technical theological term for religious allegory. All religions have their mysteries. Properly speaking, a mystery is a dogma which is plainly absurd, but which, nevertheless, conceals in itself a lofty truth, and one which by itself would be completely incomprehensible to the ordinary understanding of the raw multitude. The multitude accepts it in this disguise on trust, and believes it, without being led astray by the absurdity of it, which even to its intelligence is obvious; and in this way it participates in the kernel of the matter so far as it is possible for it to do so. To explain what I mean, I may add that even in philosophy an attempt has been made to make use of a mystery. Pascal, for example, who was at once a pietist, a mathematician, and a philosopher, says in this threefold capacity: *God is everywhere centre and nowhere periphery.* Malebranche has also the just remark: *Liberty is a mystery.* One could go a step further and maintain that in religions everything is mystery. For to impart truth, in the proper sense of the word, to the multitude in its raw state is absolutely impossible; all that can fall to its lot is to be enlightened by a mythological reflection of it. Naked truth is out of place before the eyes of the profane vulgar; it can only make its appearance thickly veiled. Hence, it is unreasonable to require of a religion that it shall be true in the proper sense of the word; and this, I may observe in passing, is now-a-days the absurd contention of Rationalists and Supernaturalists alike. Both start from the position that religion must be the real truth; and while the former demonstrate that it is not the truth, the latter obstinately maintain that it is; or rather, the former dress up and arrange the allegorical element in such a way, that, in the proper sense of the word, it could be true, but would be, in that case, a platitude; while the latter wish to maintain that it is true in the proper sense of the word, without any further dressing; a belief, which, as we ought to know, is only to be enforced by inquisitions and the stake. As a fact, however, myth and allegory really form the proper element of religion; and under this indispensable condition, which is imposed by the intellectual limitation of the multitude, religion provides a sufficient satisfaction for those metaphysical requirements of mankind which are indestructible. It takes the place of that pure philosophical truth which is infinitely difficult and perhaps never attainable.

Philalethes. Ah! just as a wooden leg takes the place of a natural one; it supplies what is lacking, barely does duty for it, claims to be regarded as a natural leg, and is more or less artfully put together. The only difference is that, whilst a natural leg as a rule preceded the wooden one, religion has everywhere got the start of philosophy.

Demopheles. That may be, but still for a man who hasn't a natural leg, a wooden one is of great service. You must bear in mind that the metaphysical needs of mankind absolutely require satisfaction, because the horizon of man's thoughts must have a background and not remain unbounded. Man has, as a rule, no faculty for weighing reasons and discriminating between what is false and what is true; and besides, the labour which nature and the needs of nature impose upon him, leaves him no time for such inquiries, or for the education which they presuppose. In his case, therefore, it is no use talking of a reasoned conviction; he has to fall back on belief and authority. If a really true philosophy were to take the place of religion, nine-tenths at least of mankind would have to receive it on authority; that is to say, it too would be a matter of faith, for Plato's dictum, that the multitude can't be philosophers, will always remain true. Authority, however, is an affair of time and circumstance alone, and so it can't be bestowed on that which has only reason in its favor; it must accordingly be allowed to nothing but what has acquired it in the course of history, even if it is only an allegorical representation of truth. Truth in this form, supported by authority, appeals first of all to those elements in the human constitution which are strictly metaphysical, that is to say, to the need man feels of a theory in regard to the riddle of existence which forces itself upon his notice, a need arising from the consciousness that behind the physical in the world there is a metaphysical, something permanent as the foundation of constant change. Then it appeals to the will, to the fears and hopes of mortal beings living in constant struggle; for whom accordingly, religion creates gods and demons whom they can cry to, appease and win over. Finally, it appeals to that moral consciousness which is undeniably present in man, lends to it that corroboration and support without which it would not easily maintain itself in the struggle against so many temptations. It is just from this side that religion affords an inexhaustible source of consolation and comfort in the innumerable trials of life, a comfort which does not leave men in death, but rather then only unfolds its full efficacy. So religion may be compared to one who takes a blind man by the hand and leads him, because he is unable to see for himself, whose concern it is to reach his destination, not to look at everything by the way.

Philalethes. That is certainly the strong point of religion. If it is a fraud, it is a pious fraud; that is undeniable. But this makes priests something between deceivers and teachers of morality: they daren't teach the real truth, as you have quite rightly explained, even if they knew it, which is not the case. A true philosophy, then, can always exist, but not a true religion; true, I mean, in the proper understanding of the word, not merely in that flowery or allegorical sense which you have described; a sense in which all religions would be true, only in various degrees. It is quite in keeping with the inextricable mixture of weal and woe, honesty and deceit, good and evil, nobility and baseness, which is the average characteristic of the world everywhere, that the most important, the most lofty, the most sacred truths can make their appearance only in combination with a lie, can even borrow strength from a lie as from something that works more powerfully on mankind; and, as revelation, must be ushered in by a lie. This might indeed be regarded as the *cachet* of the moral world. However, we won't give up the hope that mankind will eventually reach a point of maturity and education at which it can on the one side produce, and on the other receive, the true philosophy. *Simplex sigillum veri*: the naked truth must be so simple and intelligible that it can be imparted to all in its true form, without any admixture of myth and fable, without disguising it in the form of *religion*.

Demopheles. You've no notion how stupid most people are.

Philalethes. I am only expressing a hope which I can't give up. If it were fulfilled, truth in its simple and intelligible form would of course drive religion from the place it has so long occupied as its representative, and by that very means kept open for it. The time would have come when religion would have carried out her object and completed her course: the race she had brought to years of discretion she could dismiss, and herself depart in peace: that would be the *euthanasia* of religion. But as long as she lives, she has two faces, one of truth, one of fraud. According as you look at one or the other, you will bear her favour or ill-will. Religion must be regarded as a necessary evil, its necessity resting on the pitiful imbecility of the great majority of mankind, incapable of grasping the truth, and therefore requiring, in their pressing need, something to take its place.

13

LUDWIG FEUERBACH ON GOD AS MAN'S PROJECTION OF HIMSELF

> If oxen and horses had hands or could draw with
> hands and create representations like those made
> by men, the gods of oxen would be like oxen and
> horses would draw pictures of gods like horses,
> and each species would make its gods in
> accordance with the form each species possesses.
>
> *Xenophanes, c. 540* B.C.

Biographical Note

Ludwig Feuerbach (1804–1872) received an extensive education in the natural sciences, theology, philosophy, and history at Erlangen, Heidelberg, and Berlin universities. His first publication was *Thoughts on Death and Immortality* (1830), which denied personal immortality and reargued the old Epicurean thesis that the *stuff* of the body survives but is recycled in the eternal processes of the universe. Having little taste and less aptitude for teaching, Feuerbach had the good fortune to be dismissed from Erlangen in 1832 for publishing a pamphlet that criticized Christianity as inhumane. For the next twenty-eight years he was to all intents and purposes an intellectual revolutionary living on private means: at rural ease, reclined on the comfort of and supported by the money from his wife's porcelain factory. His most influential work, *The Essence of Christianity*, was published in 1841. It was translated into English by George Eliot, and it is from her 1854 translation that the following extract is taken. After the failure of his wife's factory in 1860, Feuerbach was supported by the charity of friends and by earnings from his ponderous books. He died of a stroke in 1872.

Philosophical Note

Feuerbach is aggressively atheistic and materialistic. His account of religion is of something that is projected by humanity onto the cosmos at large as an idealized and objectivized image of humanity. He does

147

not concern himself with the objective or external truth of religion as Cicero, Hume, and D'Holbach, for example, had done. There is merely a phenomenon to be explained. Feuerbach's explanation is of the *nothing but* variety — "the divine being is nothing else than . . ." — a reductionist technique also evident in the works of Marx and Freud, both of whom were influenced by Feuerbach. Feuerbach argues repetitively and in a rush. His style is urgent and assertive. The following extract is from the preliminary chapter to Part I of *The Essence of Christianity*.

God as Man's Projection of Himself
From *The Essence of Christianity*, preliminary chapter

In the perceptions of the senses, consciousness of the object is distinguishable from consciousness of self; but in religion, consciousness of the object and self-consciousness coincide. The object of the senses is out of man, the religious object is within him, and therefore as little forsakes him as his self-consciousness or his conscience; it is the intimate, the closest object. "God," says Augustine, for example, "is nearer, more related to us, and therefore more easily known by us, than sensible, corporeal things." The object of the senses is in itself indifferent — independent of the disposition or of the judgment; but the object of religion is a selected object; the most excellent, the first, the supreme being; it essentially presupposes a critical judgment, a discrimination between the divine and the nondivine, between that which is worthy of adoration and that which is not worthy. And here may be applied, without any limitation, the propositions: the object of any subject is nothing else than the subject's own nature taken objectively. Such as are a man's thoughts and dispositions, such is his God; so much worth as a man has, so much and no more has his God. Consciousness of God is self-consciousness, knowledge of God is self-knowledge. By his God thou knowest the man, and by the man his God; the two are identical. Whatever is God to a man, that is his heart and soul; and conversely, God is the manifested inward nature, the expressed self of a man, — religion the solemn unveiling of a man's hidden treasures, the revelation of his intimate thoughts, the open confession of his love-secrets.

But when religion — consciousness of God — is designated as the self-consciousness of man, this is not to be understood as affirming that the religious man is directly aware of this identity; for, on the contrary, ignorance of it is fundamental to the peculiar nature of religion. To preclude this misconception, it is better to say, religion is man's earliest and also indirect form of self-knowledge. Hence, religion everywhere precedes philosophy, as in the history of the race, so also in that of the individual. Man first of all sees his nature as if *out of* himself, before he finds it in himself. His own nature is in the first instance contemplated by him as that of another being. Religion is the childlike condition of humanity; but the child sees his nature — man — out of himself; in childhood a man is an object to himself, under the form of another man. Hence the historical progress of religion consists in this: that what by an earlier religion was regarded as objective, is now recognised as subjective; that is, what was formerly contemplated and worshipped as God is now perceived to be something *human*. What was at first religion becomes at a later period idolatry; man is seen to have adored his own nature. Man has given objectivity to himself, but has not recognised the object as his own nature: a later religion takes this forward step; every advance in religion is therefore a deeper self-knowledge. But every particular religion, while it pronounces its predecessors idolatrous, excepts itself — and necessarily so, otherwise it would no longer be religion — from the fate, the common nature of all religions: it imputes only to other religions what is the fault, if fault it be, of religion in general. Because it has a different object, a different tenor, because it has transcended the ideas of preceding religions, it erroneously supposes itself exalted above the necessary eternal laws which constitute the essence of religion — it fancies its object, its ideas, to be superhuman. But the essence of religion, thus hidden from the religious, is evident to the thinker, by whom religion is viewed objectively, which it cannot be by its votaries. And it is our task to show that the antithesis of divine and human is altogether illusory, that it is nothing else than the antithesis between the human nature in general and the human individual; that, consequently, the object and contents of the Christian religion are altogether human.

˙ Religion, at least the Christian, is the relation of man to himself, or more correctly to his own nature (*i.e.*, his subjective nature); but a relation to it, viewed as a nature apart from his own. The divine being is nothing else than the human being, or, rather, the human nature purified, freed from the limits of the individual man, made objective — *i.e.*, contemplated and revered as another, a distinct being. All the attributes of the divine nature are, therefore, attributes of the human nature.

In relation to the attributes, the predicates, of the Divine Being, this is admitted without hesitation, but by no means in relation to the subject of these predicates. The negation of the subject is held to be irreligion, nay, atheism; though not so the negation of the predicates. But that which has no predicates or qualities, has no effect upon me; that which has no effect upon me has no existence for me. To deny all the qualities of a being is equivalent to denying the being himself. A being without qualities is one which cannot become an object to the mind, and such a being is virtually non-existent. Where man deprives God of all qualities, God is no longer anything more to him than a negative being. To the truly religious man, God is not a being without qualities, because to him he is a positive, real being. The theory that God cannot be defined, and consequently cannot be known by man, is therefore the offspring of recent times, a product of modern unbelief.

As reason is and can be pronounced finite only where man regards sensual enjoyment, or religious emotion, or aesthetic contemplation, or moral sentiment, as the absolute, the true; so the proposition that God is unknowable or undefinable, can only be enunciated and become fixed as a dogma, where this object has no longer any interest for the intellect; where the real, the positive, alone has any hold on man, where the real alone has for him the significance of the essential, of the absolute, divine object, but where at the same time, in contradiction with this purely worldly tendency, there yet exist some old remains of religiousness. On the ground that God is unknowable, man excuses himself to what is yet remaining of his religious conscience for his forgetfulness of God, his absorption in the world: he denies God practically by his conduct, — the world has possession of all his thoughts and inclinations, — but he does not deny him theoretically, he does not attack his existence; he lets that rest. But this existence does not affect or incommode him; it is a merely negative existence, an existence without existence, a self-contradictory existence, — a state of being which, as to its effects, is not distinguishable from non-being. The denial of determinate, positive predicates concerning the divine nature is nothing else than a denial of religion, with, however, an appearance of religion in its favor, so that it is not recognised as a denial; it is simply a subtle, disguised atheism. The alleged religious horror of limiting God by positive predicates is only the irreligious wish to know nothing more of God, to banish God from the mind. Dread of limitation is dread of existence. All real existence, *i.e.*, all existence which is truly such, is qualitative, determinative existence. He who earnestly believes in the Divine existence is not shocked at the attributing even of gross sensuous qualities to God. He who dreads an existence that may give offense, who shrinks from the grossness of a positive predicate, may as well renounce existence altogether. A God who is injured by determinate qualities has not the courage and the strength to exist. Qualities are the fire, the vital breath, the oxygen, the salt of existence. An existence in general, an existence without qualities, is an insipidity, an absurdity. But there can be no more in God than is supplied by religion. Only where man loses his taste for religion, and thus religion itself becomes insipid, does the existence of God become an insipid existence — an existence without qualities.

There is, however, a still milder way of denying the divine predicates than the direct one just described. It is admitted that the predicates of the divine nature are finite, and, more particularly, human qualities, but their rejection is rejected; they are even taken under protection, because it is necessary to man to have a definite conception of God, and since he is man he can form no other than a human conception of him. In relation to God, it is said, these predicates are certainly without any objective validity; but to me, if he is to exist for me, he cannot appear otherwise than as he does appear to me, namely, as a being with attributes analogous to the human. But this distinction between what God is in himself, and what he is for me destroys the peace of religion, and is besides in itself an unfounded and untenable distinction. I cannot know whether God is something else in himself or for himself than he is for me; what he is to me is to me all that he is. For me, there lies in these predicates under which he exists for me, what he is in himself, his very nature; he is for me what he can alone ever be for me. The religious man finds perfect satisfaction in that which God is in relation to himself; of any other relation he knows nothing, for God is to him what he can alone be to man. In the distinction above stated, man takes a point of view above himself, *i.e.*, above his nature, the absolute measure of his being; but this transcendentalism is only an illusion; for I can make the distinction between the object as it is in itself, and the object as it is for me, only where an object can really appear otherwise to me, not where it appears to me such as the absolute measure of my nature determines it to appear — such as it must appear to me. It is true that I may have a merely subjective conception, *i.e.*, one which does not arise out of the general constitution of my species; but if my conception is determined by the constitution of my species, the distinction between what an object is in itself, and what it is for me ceases; for this conception is itself an absolute one. The measure of the species is the absolute measure, law, and criterion of man. And, indeed, religion has the conviction that its conceptions, its predicates of God, are such as every man ought to have, and must have, if he would have the true ones — that they are the conceptions necessary to human nature; nay, further, that they are objectively true, representing God as he is. To every religion the gods of *other* religions are only notions concerning God, but its own conception of god is to it God himself, the true God — God such as he is in himself. Religion is satisfied only with a complete Deity, a God without reservation; it will not have a mere phantasm of God; it demands God himself. Religion gives up its own existence when it gives up the nature of God; it is no longer a truth when it renounces the possession of the true God. Scepticism is the arch-enemy of religion; but the distinction between object and conception — between God as he is in himself, and God as he is for me — is a sceptical distinction, and therefore an irreligious one.

That which is to man the self-existent, the highest being, to which he can conceive nothing higher — that is to him the Divine Being. How then should he inquire concerning this being, what he is in himself? If God were an object to the bird, he would be a winged being: the bird knows nothing higher, nothing more blissful, than the winged condition. How ludicrous would it be if this bird pronounced: To me God appears as a bird, but what he is in himself I know not. To the bird the highest nature is the bird-nature; take from him the conception of this, and you take from him the conception of the highest being. How, then, could he ask whether God in himself were winged? To ask whether God is in himself what he is for me, is to ask whether God is God, is to lift oneself above one's God, to rise up against him.

Wherever, therefore, this idea, that the religious predicates are only anthropomorphisms, has taken possession of a man, there has doubt, has unbelief, obtained the mastery of faith. And it is only the inconsequence of faint-heartedness and intellectual imbecility which does not proceed from this idea to the formal negation of the predicates, and from thence to the negation of the subject to which they relate. If thou doubtest the objective truth of the predicates, thus must also doubt the objective truth of the subject whose predicates they are. If thy predicates are anthropomorphisms, the subject of them is an anthropomorphism too. If love, goodness, personality, &c., are human attributes, so also is the subject which thou presupposest, the existence of God, the belief that there is a God, an anthropomorphism — a presupposition purely human.

14

KARL MARX AND VLADIMIR LENIN ON RELIGION AS THE OPIUM OF THE PEOPLE

> It should be the duty of princes and heads of
> republics to uphold the foundations of the religion
> of their countries, for then it is easy to keep their
> people religious, and consequently well ordered
> and united. And therefore everything that tends to
> favor religion (even though it were believed to be
> false) should be received and made use of to
> strengthen it. And the wiser the rulers are and the
> better they understand the natural course of
> things, the more this should be done. In fact this
> was the practice (observed by politic men) which
> gave rise to belief in celebrated religious miracles
> —however false they may be.
>
> *Niccolò Machiavelli, The Prince, Chap. 18*

Biographical Note

At the risk of reproducing in a book concerned with unbelief something about as valuable as a ten-line entry on Jesus bar-Joseph and Paul of Tarsus in an encyclopedia of Christianity, I here offer the following biographical information about Karl Marx:

He was born in 1818 to a Jewish family living in the Rhineland. He studied at the Universities of Bonn and Berlin and submitted a doctoral thesis on Epicurus and Democritus at Jena in 1841. For a short time he was editor of a liberal newspaper in Cologne. A series of politically motivated expulsions moved him successively to Paris, Brussels, and back to Cologne before he finally settled in London in 1849. For the remainder of his life he enjoyed the freedom of capitalist England and the resources of the British Museum library to construct *Das Kapital* — the immense systematic view of history, society, and economics that was coherent enough, even in its unfinished form at his death in 1883, to provide the ideological basis of communism. *Das Kapital,* like the Bible, has perhaps been more deferred to than read, especially by the masses whose lot might be supposed to be its main concern.

Lenin (1870–1924), the father of modern Russia, was from his earliest student days at the University of Kazan the archetype of the modern revolutionary leader. He was expelled, took a correspondence course, was imprisoned, was exiled to Siberia, and then lived abroad writing and plotting revolution from 1900 to 1917. From 1917 until his death he headed the Bolshevik government of the Soviet Union. Arthur Ransome, the children's writer and journalist, who was in Moscow after Lenin's death, recorded the very significant observation that he felt himself to be present at the beginning of a new religion rather than at the death of a national hero.

Philosophical Note

Like Feuerbach, neither Marx nor Lenin is concerned with the possibility that religion (of any sort) might be *true* — even in the "flowry or allegorical" sense half sanctioned by Schopenhauer. There is thus no significant refutation of religious beliefs or arguments in their writings. Their brief accounts of religion (and their total rejection of it) are of a phenomenon that obstructs people's true evaluation of their own worth, and substitutes unattainable ideal goals for the real and attainable goals of the material world. Moreover the ideal goals of religion are fostered by the capitalist classes as a means of diverting the energies of the masses from the pursuit of material objectives that would disturb the *status quo*. For Marx and Lenin the overthrow of religion is thus both a condition of material progress for the masses and a consequence of it.

The following extracts comprehend most of the important points made by Marx and Lenin about religion. Neither man wrote extensively on the subject although both of their attitudes toward it have obviously been of overwhelming importance in the progress of unbelief in the modern world. The passages omitted in the sections by Marx are concerned with political or other issues.

The Opium of the People

1. Marx: foreword to his doctoral thesis *"The difference between the natural philosophy of Democritus and the natural philosophy of Epicurus,"* Berlin 1841.

The form of this treatise would be more strictly scientific, on the one hand, and less pedantic in some points, on the other, had it not been originally intended as a doctor's thesis. However, I am obliged through external causes to have it printed in its present form. Besides, I believe that in it I have solved a hitherto unsolved problem in the history of Greek philosophy.

Experts know that there are no preliminary works which could be useful in any way for the subject of this treatise. Up to this time there has been nothing but repetition of Cicero's and Plutarch's rigmarole. Gassendi, who freed Epicurus from the interdict laid on him by the Fathers of the Church and the whole of the Middle Ages — that age of materialized irrationalism — provides but one interesting point in his observations. He tries to conciliate his Catholic conscience with his heathen knowledge and Epicurus with the Church — an obviously futile effort. It is like throwing the habit of a Christian nun over the exuberant body of the Greek Lais. It is more a case of Gassendi learning philosophy from Epicurus than being able to teach us about Epicurus's philosophy.

This treatise should be considered as a precursor to a larger work in which I shall expound in detail the cycle of the Epicurean, stoic and sceptic philosophies in their connection with the whole of Greek speculation.[8] The shortcomings of this treatise as to form and the like will be remedied in that work.

Hegel, on the whole, correctly defined the general features of the above-mentioned systems. But in the admirably extensive and daring plan of his *History of Philosophy*, from which we can date all history of philosophy, it was impossible, for one thing, to go into details, and, for another, the great thinker's view of what he called speculation *par excellence* prevented him from acknowledging the higher importance of those systems for the history of Greek philosophy and for the Greek mind in general. These systems are the key to the true history of Greek philosophy. A more profound indication of their relation to Greek life is to be found in my friend Köppen's *Friedrich der Grosse und seine Widersacher (Frederick the Great and his Opponents).*

If a criticism of Plutarch's polemic against Epicurus's theology is added as an appendix, it is because that polemic is not unique, but is representative of an *espèce* in that it very aptly shows the attitude of theologizing reason to philosophy.

The criticism makes no mention of the falseness of Plutarch's standpoint in general when he cites philosophy before the forum of religion. On this point a passage from David Hume will do as well as any kind of discussion:

" 'Tis certainly a kind of indignity to philosophy, whose *sovereign authority* ought everywhere to be acknowledged, to oblige her on every occasion to make apologies for her conclusions, and justify herself to every particular art and science which may be offended at her. *This puts one in mind of a king arraigned for high treason against his subjects.*"[8]

As long as philosophy still has a drop of blood left in its world-conquering, absolutely free heart, it will not cease to call to its opponents with Epicurus:

"Not he who rejects the gods of the crowd is impious, but he who embraces the crowds opinion of the gods."

Philosophy makes no secret of it. Prometheus' admission "In sooth I hate all gods" (from *Prometheus Bound* by Aeschylus) is its own admission, its own motto against all gods, heavenly and earthly, who do not acknowledge the consciousness of man as the supreme divinity. There must be no god on a level with it.

And to the wretched March hares who exult over the apparent deterioration of philosophy's social position it again answers, as Prometheus did to Hermes, the messenger of the gods, "I shall never exchange my fetters for slavish servility. It is better to be chained to the rock than bound in the service of Zeus." Prometheus is the noblest of the saints and martyrs in the calendar of philosophy.

2. Marx: From the leading article to no. 179 of *Kölnische Zeitung*, 1842.

Just as the downfall of the ancient world was approaching there arose the *school of Alexandria*, which strove to prove by force "the eternal truth" of Greek mythology and its thorough agreement "with the data of scientific research." The Emperor Julian also belonged to that trend, which thought it would cause the new spirit of the times that was asserting itself to disappear if it kept its eyes closed so as not to see it. But let us keep to Mr. H.'s results! In the religious of antiquity "the faint notions of the divine were veiled in the deepest night of error" and could therefore not resist scientific research. With Christianity the situation is reversed, as any thinking machine will conclude. Indeed, Mr. H. says:

"The best conclusions of scientific research have so far served only to confirm the truths of the Christian religion."

Apart from the fact that every philosophy of the past without exception was accused by the theologians of apostasy, not excepting even the pious Malebranche and the inspired Jakob Böhme, that Leibniz was accused by the Brunswick peasants of being a *"Löwenix"* *(Glaubenichts* — one who believes in nothing) and by the Englishman Clarke and Newton's other followers of being an atheist; apart from the fact that Christianity, as the most capable and consistent of the Protestant theologians affirm, cannot agree with reason because "worldly" and "religious" reason contradict each other, which Tertullian classically expressed: *"verum est, quia absurdum est"*; apart from all this, how can the agreement of scientific research with religion be proved except by forcing research to resolve itself into religion by letting it follow its own course. The least we can say is that further compulsion is no proof.

If, of course, you acknowledge beforehand as scientific research only what conforms to your own view, it is not difficult for you to make prophecies; but then what advantage has your assertion over that of the Indian Brahmin who proves the holiness of the Vedas by reserving for himself alone the right to read it!

Yes, says H., "scientific research." But any research that contradicts Christianity "stops half-way" or "takes a wrong road." Can one make the argument easier for oneself?

Once scientific research 'has "*made clear*" to itself the content of what it has found, it will never clash with the truths of Christianity' but at the same time the state must ensure that this "*making clear*" is impossible, for research must never appeal to the powers of comprehension of the masses, i.e., must never become popular and clear *to itself.* Even if it is attacked by all the unscientific papers of the monarchy it must be modest and keep silence.

Christianity precludes the possibility of 'any new decadence,' but the police must be on its guard so that the philosophizing newspaper writers do not lead to decadence; it must keep an extremely strict guard. Error will be recognized as such of itself in the struggle with truth, without any need for suppression by external force; but the state must make the struggle of truth easier by depriving the champions of "error" not indeed of internal freedom, which it cannot take away from them, but of the possibility of that freedom, the possibility of existence.

Christianity is sure of victory, but according to Mr. H. it is not so sure of victory that it can scorn the help of the police.

3. Marx: from the Introduction to "Contribution to the Critique of Hegel's Philosophy of Right," 1844.

For Germany the *criticism of religion* is in the main complete, and criticism of religion is the premise of all criticism.

The *profane* existence of error is discredited after its heavenly *oratio pro aris et focis* has been rejected. Man, who looked for a superman in the fantastic reality of heaven and found nothing there but the *reflexion* of himself, will no longer be disposed to find but the *semblance* of himself, the non-human *[Unmensch]* where he seeks and must seek his true reality.

The basis of irreligious criticism is: *Man makes religion*, religion does not make man. In other words, religion is the self-consciousness and self-feeling of man who has either not yet found himself or has already lost himself again. But *man* is no abstract being squatting outside the world. Man is *the world of man*, the state, society. This state, this society, produce religion, *a reversed world-consciousness*, because they are *a reversed world.* Religion is the general theory of that world, its encyclopaedic compendium, its logic in a popular form, its spiritualistic *point d'honneur*, its enthusiasm, its moral sanction, its solemn completion, its universal ground for consolation and justification. It is *the fantastic realization* of the human essence because the *human essence* has no true reality. The struggle against religion is therefore mediately the fight against *the other world,* of which religion is the spiritual *aroma.*

Religious distress is at the same time the *expression* of real distress and the *protest* against real distress. Religion is the sigh of the oppressed creature, the heart of a heartless world, just as it is the spirit of a spiritless situation. It is the *opium* of the people.

The abolition of religion as the *illusory* happiness of the people is required for their *real* happiness. The demand to give up the illusions about its condition is the *demand to give up a condition which needs illusions.* The criticism of religion is therefore *in embryo the criticism of the vale of woe,* the *halo* of which is religion.

Criticism has plucked the imaginary flowers from the chain not so that man will wear the chain without any fantasy or consolation but so that he will shake off the chain and cull the living flower. The criticism of religion disillusions man to make him think and act and shape his reality like a man who has been disillusioned and has come to reason, so that he will revolve round himself and therefore round his true sun. Religion is only the illusory sun which revolves round man as long as he does not revolve round himself.

The task of history, therefore, once the *world beyond the truth* has disappeared, is to establish the *truth of this world.* The immediate *task of philosophy,* which is at the service of history, once the *saintly form* of human self-alienation has been unmasked, is to unmask self-alienation in its *unholy forms.* Thus the criticism of heaven turns into the criticism of the earth, the *criticism of religion* into the *criticism of right* and the *criticism of theology* into the *criticism of politics.* [About five pages dealing with the criticism of politics are here omitted.]

4. Lenin: The article "Socialism and Religion," from *Novaya Zhizn,* 16 December 1905.

Modern society is based entirely on the exploitation of the enormous masses of the working-class, by an insignificant minority of the population — the landowning and capitalist classes. This society is a slave society, for the "free" workers, who work all their lives for the benefit of capital, have a "right" only to so much of the means of existence as is essential to sustain them as slaves while producing profit for the capitalists — or in short sufficient to secure and perpetuate capitalist slavery.

This economic oppression of the workers gives rise inevitably to all forms of political oppression and social degradation: it renders the spiritual and moral life of the masses coarser and more sordid. The workers may acquire a greater or less degree of political freedom to fight for their economic emancipation, but so long as the domination of capital continues, no amount of freedom will rid them of destitution, unemployment and oppression.

Religion is one of the forms of spiritual oppression which everywhere weigh upon the masses who are crushed by continuous toil for others, by poverty and deprivation. The helplessness of all the exploited in their struggle against the exploiters inevitably generates a belief in a better life after death, even as the helplessness of the savage in his struggle with nature gives rise to a belief in gods, devils, miracles, etc.

Religion teaches those who toil in poverty all their lives to be resigned and patient in this world, and consoles them with the hope of reward in heaven. As for those who live upon the labor of others, religion teaches them to be "charitable" — thus providing a justification for exploitation and, as it were, also a cheap ticket to heaven likewise. "Religion is the opium of the people." Religion is a kind of spiritual intoxicant, in which the slaves of capital drown their humanity, and blunt their desire for a decent human existence.

But a slave who has become conscious of his slavery, and who has risen to the height of fighting for his emancipation, has half-ceased to be a slave. The class-conscious worker of to-day, brought up in the environment of a big factory, and enlightened by town life, rejects religious prejudices with contempt. He leaves heaven to the priests and bourgeois hypocrites. He fights for a better life for himself, here on earth. The modern proletariat ranges itself on the side of Socialism, which, with the help of science, is dispersing the fog of religion and is liberating the workers from their faith in a life after death, by rallying them to the present-day struggle for a better life here upon earth.

"Religion must be regarded as a private matter"; in these words the attitude of Socialists to religion is usually expressed. But we must define the meaning of these words precisely so as to avoid misunderstanding. We demand that religion be regarded as a private matter as far as the State is concerned, but under no circumstances can we regard it as a private matter in our own party.

The State must not concern itself with religion; religious societies must not be bound to the State. Everyone must be absolutely free to profess whatever religion he likes, or to profess No religion, i.e., to be an atheist, as every Socialist usually is. There must be no discrimination whatever in the rights of citizens on religious grounds. Even particulars concerning the religion of citizens on official documents must be completely done away with. No subsidies must be paid to the Established Church, and no grants from state funds made to church or religious societies. These must become independent of the State, voluntary associations of citizens of one faith.

Only the fulfillment of these demands can put an end to that shameful and accursed past when the Church was in feudal dependence on the State, and Russian citizens were in feudal dependence on the Established Church; when inquisitorial, medieval laws (which are still on our statute books and in our legal codes) were actively in force. These laws laid down penalties for the profession or nonprofession of a particular religion. They violated the conscience of the individual, and connected the distribution of official posts and revenues with the distribution of this or that state church intoxicant. Complete separation of Church and State — this must be the demand of the socialist proletariat to-day.

The Russian Revolution must enforce this demand, as a necessary installment of political freedom. The Russian Revolution is in fact in a particularly favorable position for doing this, since the disgusting political red tape of the feudal autocracy has stirred up discontent and indignation even among the clergy. Cowed and ignorant as the orthodox Russian clergy is, it has nevertheless been sufficiently aroused by the thunder of the collapsing mediaeval Russian regime to endorse the popular demand for liberty. The clergy joins in the protest against the tyranny of officialdom and rebels against the police inquisition forced on the "Servants of God."

Socialists must support this movement, and carry these demands of the honest and sincere clergy to their logical conclusion. Socialists must take them at their word when they talk about liberty, and demand that they completely sever all connection between religion and the police. We must say to them: "If you are sincere you must stand for a complete separation of the Church from the State, for a separation of the school from the church, and insist that religion be regarded entirely and unconditionally as a private matter. If you do not accept these consistent demands of liberty, it means that you are still a slave to inquisitorial traditions — it means that you are still hankering after government posts and the revenues attached to them, it means that you do not believe in the spiritual force of your weapon, and that you still wish to take bribes from the government. If this is so, the class-conscious Russian workers will declare ruthless war on you."

To the proletarian Socialist Party, however, religion is not a private matter. Our Party is a league of class-conscious, progressive fighters for the liberation of the working-class. Such a league cannot and must not be indifferent to ignorance or benightedness in the shape of religious beliefs. We demand the entire separation of the State from the Church, in order to disperse the fog of religion by purely intellectual and only intellectual weapons, by our press and oral persuasion. One of the objects of our organisation, the Russian Social-Democratic Labor Party, is precisely to fight against all religious deception of the workers. For us, the ideological struggle is not a private matter but one that concerns the whole Party, and the whole proletariat.

If so, why do we not declare in our programme that we are atheists? Why do we not debar Christians and believers in God from joining our Party?

The answer to this question reveals a very important difference between the bourgeois-democratic, and the Socialist-democratic attitude towards religion.

Our programme is entirely based on scientific — to be more precise —upon *materialist* philosophy. In explaining our programme therefore we must necessarily explain the actual historical and economic roots of religion. Our programme thus necessarily includes the propaganda of atheism. Further the publication of scientific literature (which up till now has been strictly forbidden and persecuted by the autocratic feudal government) must now form one of the items of our party work. We shall now, probably, have to follow the advice which, once upon a time, Engels gave to the German Socialists — to translate and spread among the masses the enlightening atheist literature of the Eighteenth century.

But we must under no circumstances allow ourselves to be side-tracked into a treatment of the religious question in the abstract — idealistically — as a matter of "reason" quite detached from the class struggle — a presentation often given by radical bourgeois democrats. It would be absurd to imagine in a society based upon the unlimited oppression and degradation of the working masses that it is possible to dispel religious prejudices by mere preaching. It would be bourgeois narrow-mindedness to lose sight of the fact that the religious oppression of humanity is only a product or reflex aspect of the economic oppression in society. No books, no preaching, can possibly enlighten the proletariat, unless it is enlightened by its own struggle against the dark forces of capitalism. A union in that genuinely revolutionary struggle of the oppressed class to set up a heaven on earth is more important to us than a unity in proletarian opinion about the imaginary paradise in the sky.

That is why we do not declare, and must not declare in our programme that we are "Atheists"; that is why we do not forbid and must not forbid proletarians who still cling to the remnants of old prejudices to come into closer contact with our Party. We shall always preach a scientific philosophy; we must fight against the inconsistencies of the "Christians"; but this does not mean that the religious question must be pushed into the foreground where it does not belong. We must not allow the forces waging a genuinely revolutionary economic and political struggle to be broken up for the sake of opinions and dreams that are of third-rate importance, which are rapidly losing all political significance, and which are being steadily relegated to the rubbish heap by the normal course of economic development.

The reactionary bourgeoisie, here as elsewhere, always takes pains to fan religious animosities in order to divert the attention of the masses away from those really important and fundamental questions, economic and political, which the Russian proletariat, by combining in the practice of a revolutionary struggle, is deciding. This reactionary tactic of splitting the proletarian forces, which to-day manifests itself mainly by Black-Hundred pogroms, may to-morrow, express itself in more subtle forms. We will in any case oppose to it a calm, sustained and patient advocacy of proletarian solidarity and scientific philosophy, which will avoid rousing secondary differences.

The revolutionary proletariat will see to it that religion does really become a private matter as far as the State is concerned. And then, under a regime cleaned of mediaeval mustiness, the proletariat will wage a great open struggle for the abolition of economic slavery, the real source of the religious deception of humanity.

5. Lenin: The article "The Attitude of the Workers' Party towards Religion," *Proletarii,* May 1909. (The first three pages of historical introduction are omitted.)

Marxism is materialism. As such it is as relentlessly opposed to Religion as was the materialism of the Encyclopaedists of the eighteenth century, or as was the materialism of Feuerbach. This is beyond doubt. But the dialectic materialism of Marx and Engels goes beyond the Encyclopaedists and Feuerbach; it applies the materialist philosophy to the field of history, to the field of social science. We must combat religion—this is the A.B.C. of *all* materialism, and consequently of Marxism. But Marxism is not materialism which stops at the A.B.C. Marxism goes further. It says: We must be able to combat religion, and in order to do this we must explain from the materialistic point of view why faith and religion are prevalent among the masses.

The fight against religion must not be limited nor reduced to abstract-ideological preaching. This struggle must be linked up with the concrete practical class movement; its aim must be to eliminate the social roots of religion. Why does religion retain its hold among the backward strata of the urban proletariat—among wide strata of the semi-proletariat and the masses of the peasantry? Because of the ignorance of the people!—answers the progressive bourgeoisie, the radical or bourgeois materialist. Hence—"Down with religion," "Long live Atheism," "The dissemination of Atheist views is our chief task!"

The Marxist says: "No, this is not true. Such a conception expresses the superficial limitations of bourgeois culture and the narrowness of its objective. It is shallow, and explains the roots of religion, not in a materialist, but in an idealistic fashion."

In modern capitalist countries the basis of religion is primarily *social.*

The roots of modern religion are deeply embedded in the social oppression of the working masses, and in their apparently complete helplessness before the blind forces of capitalism, which every day and every hour cause a thousand times more horrible suffering and torture for ordinary working folk than are caused by exceptional events such as war, earthquakes, etc. "Fear created the gods." Fear of the blind force of capital — blind because its action cannot be foreseen by the masses — a force which at every step in life threatens the worker and the small business man with "sudden," "unexpected," "accidental" destruction and ruin, bringing in their train beggary, pauperism, prostitution, and deaths from starvation — this is THE *tap-root* of modern religion which, first of all, and above all, the materialist must keep in mind, if he does not wish to remain stuck for ever in the infant school of materialism.

No amount of reading matter, however enlightening, will eradicate religion from those masses who are crushed by the grinding toil of capitalism and subjected to the blind destructive forces of capitalism, until these masses, themselves, learn to fight against the social facts from which religion arises in a united, disciplined, planned and conscious manner — until they learn to fight *against the rule of the capitalist in all its forms.*

Does this mean that educational books against religion are harmful or superfluous? No. Not at all. It means that the propagation of Atheism by the Social-Democracy must be *subordinated* to a more basic task — the development of the class struggle of the exploited masses against the exploiters.

Those who have not gone to the root of dialectical materialism (i.e., of the philosophy of Marx and Engels) may not be able to understand this; or, at least, not able to understand it at first. What! Subordinate ideological propaganda, the propagation of definite ideas? Subordinate the struggle against religion, the thousand-year-old enemy of culture and progress, to the class struggle, to the struggle for transient practical-economic and political aims?

This is one of the many current objections raised against Marxism which reveal a thorough misunderstanding of Marxist dialectics. The contradiction which so confuses those who raise these objections is the contradiction of life itself, i.e., it is a dialectical and not a verbal or an invented contradiction.

To draw a hard and fast line between the theoretical propagation of Atheism, between breaking down the religious beliefs of certain sections of the proletariat, and the effect, the development, the general implications of the class struggle of these sections, is to reason non-dialectically; to transform a variable, relative boundary into an absolute one. It is a forcible tearing asunder of that which is indissolubly connected in reality. For example, the proletariat of a given district in a given branch of industry can be divided, let us say, into a vanguard of fairly class-conscious Social-Democrats (who are, it stands to reason, atheists), and the rather backward mass which, still having ties with the villages and the peasantry, still believes in God, goes to church, or is even directly influenced by the priest. These constitute, let us assume, the Christian Workers' Union. Let us suppose, further, that the economic struggle in such a locality has resulted in a strike. A Marxist must place the success of the strike movement above all else, must definitely oppose the division of the workers in this struggle into atheists and Christians, must fight resolutely against such a division.

In such circumstances the preaching of atheism is superfluous and harmful — not from the narrow-minded consideration of not frightening the backward elements, or of losing votes at elections, etc., but from the point of view of the actual progress of the class struggle, which, in the conditions of modern capitalist society, will convert Christian workers to Social-Democracy, and to atheism a hundred times more effectively than any bald atheist sermons. To preach atheism at such a time, and in such circumstances, would only be playing *into the hands* of the Church and the priests, who would desire nothing more than to have the workers participating in the strike movement divided in accordance with their religious beliefs.

The Anarchist, who preaches war against God at all costs, actually helps the priests and bourgeoisie (as in fact the anarchists always do). The Marxist must be a materialist, i.e., an enemy of religion. But he must be a *dialectical* materialist, i.e., one who fights against religion not in the abstract, not by means of abstract, purely theoretical propaganda, equally suited to all times and to all places, but concretely, on the basis of the class struggle actually proceeding — a struggle which is educating the masses better than anything else could do. The Marxist must be able to judge the concrete situation as a whole. He must always be able to determine the boundary between anarchism and opportunism (this boundary is relative, mobile and ever-changing; but it exists), not to fall either into the abstract, wordy and in fact futile "revolutionism" of the Anarchist, or into the philistinism and opportunism of the petty bourgeois, or liberal intellectual, who shirks the fight against religion, forgets his tasks, reconciles himself to a belief in God, and who is guided, not by the interests of the class struggle, but by petty, mean calculations such as: not to offend, not to repel, not to frighten; and who is governed by the wise rule: "live and let live," etc., etc.

It is from this point of view that we must decide all particular questions concerning the attitude of Social-Democrats to religion. For example, the question often arises, is a priest eligible for membership of the Social-Democratic Party? Usually, this question is answered in the affirmative without any reservation and the experience of European Social-Democratic parties is cited. But this experience was the result not only of the application of the Marxist doctrine to the workers' movement, but, of the peculiar historical circumstances in Western

Europe. These conditions being absent in Russia (we will say more about these conditions later) an unqualified affirmative in this case is incorrect. We must not say once and for all, that under no circumstances can priests be allowed to join the Social-Democratic Party; but neither should we affirm categorically the opposite.

If a priest comes to co-operate with us in our work — if he conscientiously performs party work, and does not oppose the party programme — we can accept him into the ranks of Social-Democracy, for the contradictions between the spirit and principles of our programme and the religious convictions of the priest could, in these circumstances, be regarded as a matter in which he contradicts himself, as one which concerns him alone. A political party cannot examine its members to see if there are any contradictions between their philosophy and the Party programme. Of course, such a case would be rare exception, even in Western Europe; it is hardly possible in Russia. But if, for example, a priest joined the Social-Democratic Party, and made it his chief and almost exclusive business to propagate religious views, then, of course, the Party would have to expel him.

We must not only admit into the Social-Democratic Party all those workers who still retain faith in God, we must redouble our efforts to recruit them. We are absolutely opposed to the slightest affront to these workers' religious convictions. We recruit them in order to educate them in the spirit of our programme, and not in order to carry on an active struggle against religion. We allow freedom of opinion inside the Party, but within certain limits, determined by freedom of grouping. We are not obliged to associate with those who advocate views that have been repudiated by the majority of the Party.

Another example: Is it right, under all circumstances to censure members of the Social-Democratic Party for declaring that "Socialism is my religion," and for advocating views which correspond to such a declaration? No! This is undoubtedly a retreat from Marxism (and consequently from Socialism), but the significance of such a retreat, its specific gravity, so to say, may be different under different conditions. It is one thing if an agitator or someone addressing workers, speaks in this way in order to make himself better understood, as an introduction to his subject, in order to present his views in terminology to which the backward masses are more accustomed. It is quite another thing when a writer begins to preach "God-creating" or God-creating Socialism (in the spirit, for example, of our Lunacharsky and Co.). To pronounce censure in the first case would be mere quibbling, or even misplaced restriction of the freedom of the propagandist, on the freedom of "pedagogical" style; in the second case, censure by the party is necessary and obligatory. For the former, the statement "Socialism is my religion" is a step *from* religion to Socialism, for the latter it is a step from Socialism *to* religion.

Let us examine now the conditions which in the West gave rise to the opportunist interpretation of the thesis "religion is a private matter." Undoubtedly, this is due to the operation of those general causes which gave rise to opportunism generally, such as the sacrifice of the fundamental interests of the workers' movement for momentary advantages. The party of the proletariat demands *that the government* shall declare religion a private matter, but it does not for a moment regard the question of the fight against the opium of the people — the fight against religious superstition, etc. — as a private matter. The opportunists have so distorted the question as to make it appear that the Social-Democratic *Party* regards religion as a private matter.

Apart from the usual opportunistic distortion (which our Duma fraction entirely omitted to explain in their speeches during the debate on religion) there are the specific, historical conditions which give rise to-day, if one can so express oneself, to a considerable indifference among European Social-Democrats upon the question of religion. These conditions are of a twofold nature.

First, the fight against religion is the historical task of the revolutionary bourgeoisie, and in the West this task was, to a great extent, undertaken (or was being undertaken) by the bourgeois democracy in the epoch of *their* revolution — of their attack upon the feudalism left over from the Middle Ages. Both in France and in Germany there is a tradition of bourgeois struggle against religion, a struggle which was *begun* long before Socialism arose (for instance, the Encyclopaedists, Feuerbach). In Russia, because of the conditions of our bourgeois-democratic revolution, this task lies almost wholly on the shoulders of the working-class. Petty-bourgeois (populist) democracy did not do too much for us in this respect (as the new Black Hundred Cadets or Cadet Black Hundreds of "Vekh" think it did), *but much too little* in comparison with what was done in Europe.

On the other hand, the traditions of the bourgeois war on religion have given rise in Europe to a specifically bourgeois distortion of this struggle by Anarchism, one which the Marxists have explained long since and which repeatedly takes a standpoint identical with that of the bourgeoisie, in spite of the 'fury' with which it attacks that bourgeoisie. The anarchists and Blanquists in the Latin countries, Johan Most and Co. in Germany (incidentally Most was a pupil of Dühring), and the anarchists of the 'eighties in Austria carried revolutionary phraseology in the struggle against religion to a *ne plus ultra.* It is not surprising that the European Social-Democrats go astray, even farther than the anarchists. This is natural, and to some degree, forgivable; but we Russian Social-Democrats should not forget the specific historical conditions of the West.

Secondly, in the West *after* the national bourgeois revolutions had drawn to a close, *after* the introduction of more or less complete freedom of conscience, the question of the democratic struggle against religion had been forced into the background by the struggle which bourgeois democracy waged against Socialism to such an extent that the bourgeois governments deliberately tried to draw the attention of the masses away from Socialism by organizing a quasi-liberal "drive" against clericalism. Such was the character of the "Kulturkampf" in Germany and of the fight of the bourgeois republicans in France against clericalism. The present day "indifference" to the fight against religion, which is so widespread among Social-Democrats in the West, was preceded by bourgeois anti-clericalism, the purpose of which was to divert the attention of the masses of the workers from Socialism.

And this is quite understandable and legitimate, because Social-Democrats had to oppose bourgeois and Bismarckian anti-clericalism, with the tactics of *subordinating* the struggle against religion to the struggle for Socialism.

Conditions in Russia are quite different. The proletariat is the leader of our bourgeois-democratic revolution. Its Party must be the ideological leader in the struggle against every vestige of mediaevalism, including the old state religion, and against every attempt to revive it or to give it a different base, etc. Therefore, although Engels rebuked the German Social-Democrats rather mildly for their opportunism in substituting the *declaration* that religion is a private matter for Social-Democrats and the Social-Democratic Party — for the workers' party *demand* that the *State* shall declare religion a private matter — he would have rebuked the Russian opportunists who imitate this German distortion a *hundred times more sharply*.

Our faction acted quite correctly when it declared from the Duma tribunal that religion is the opium of the people, and in this way they created a precedent which should serve as the basis of all speeches delivered by Russian Social-Democrats on the question of religion. Should they have gone further and developed in greater detail their atheistic arguments? We think not. This might have incurred the danger of exaggerating the fight of the proletarian political party against religion; it might have led to the obliteration of the line of demarcation separating the. bourgeois from the Socialist fight against religion. The first thing the Social-Democratic fraction in the Black Hundred Duma had to do was done with honour.

The second, and perhaps the most important thing that had to be done from the Social-Democratic standpoint was to explain the class role of the Church and the clergy in supporting the Black Hundred government and the bourgeoisie in their fight against the working-class. This also was done with honor.

Thirdly, it was necessary to explain the true meaning of the postulate which the German opportunists advance, i.e., "Religion must be declared to be a private matter."

FRIEDRICH NIETZSCHE ON THE PATHOLOGY OF RELIGION AND THE DEATH OF GOD

Up to the present man has hardly cultivated sympathy at all. He has merely sympathy with pain, and sympathy with pain is not the highest form of sympathy. All sympathy is fine, but sympathy with suffering is the least fine mode. . . . One should sympathize with the entirety of life, not with life's sores and maladies merely, but with life's joy and beauty and energy and health and freedom. . . .

Upon the other hand, the terrible truth that pain is a mode through which man may realise himself exercised a wonderful fascination over the world. Shallow speakers and shallow thinkers in pulpits and on platforms often talk about the world's worship of pleasure, and whine against it, but it is rarely in the world's history that its ideal has been one of joy and beauty. The worship of pain has far more often dominated the world. Mediaevalism, with its saints and martyrs, its love of self-torture, its wild passion for wounding itself, its gashing with knives, and its whipping with rods—Mediaevalism is real Christianity and the mediaeval Christ is the real Christ. When the Renaissance dawned upon the world, and brought with it the new ideals of the beauty of life and the joy of living, men could not understand Christ. . . .

Christ had no message for the Renaissance, which was wonderful because it brought an ideal at variance with his, and to find the presentation of the real Christ we must go to mediaeval art. There, he is one maimed and marred; one who is not comely to look on, because Beauty is a joy; one who is not in fair raiment, because that may be a joy also: he is a beggar who has a marvelous soul; he is a leper whose soul is divine; he needs neither property nor health; he is a God realizing his perfection through pain.

Oscar Wilde, The Soul of Man under Socialism

Biographical Note

Friedrich Nietzsche was born in 1844 in Röcken in Prussia. When he was only four years old, his father became insane and died within a few months. As a consequence Nietzsche was brought up in a household comprising his mother, his father's mother, two maiden aunts, and his sister. Noticed even while at school as a child of errant genius, he attended Bonn and Leipzig universities before a brief period of military service in 1867–1868. This was terminated by a chest injury sustained while he was mounting a horse. In 1869 he was invited to take a professorial position at Basel University: an astounding gesture to a man of only twenty-five. In 1870 he volunteered as a medical orderly in the Franco-Prussian War, and caught both dysentery and diphtheria from wounded soldiers. He returned to Basel where he continued to write and teach until his retirement in 1879 on grounds of ill health. Between his retirement and the sudden onset of irreparable insanity in 1889, some of his greatest works were produced. He died in 1900.

Almost throughout his life Nietzsche suffered dreadful bodily ills. He had miserably bad eyesight, terrible migraine headaches and intestinal neuralgia, and the injuries and infections he had sustained in the Prussian army permanently augmented his ill health. His insanity in 1889 was *probably* the result of tertiary syphilis, although if it were, it seems certain that none of his doctors told him in advance that he had the disease. Moreover unless the disease was congenital, it must remain in doubt as to how or when he was infected since except for a possible single visit to a brothel while he was a student, which has been questioned by recent biographers, he had no known sexual relations with women (or with men either for that matter) despite having many friends in the ordinary society of life.

None of his published works is, however, adversely marked by any signs of his impending insanity. Indeed the brilliant style and incisive aphoristic wit of his works make them some of the most readable products of German nineteenth-century literature—and the most disturbing.

Philosophical Note

In Nietzsche's multitudinous works (the English edition of his works, Edinburgh and London 1909–1913, amounts to 18 volumes), his atheism is as real and evident as that of D'Holbach or Marx, but his perception of the outcome of atheism is incomparably more profound. D'Holbach had affirmed a scientific materialism that shared all its premises with Epicurus and he had almost nonchalantly assumed the moral progress of humanity and a return to the humanistic and individual ideals of

Epicurus himself. Marx had affirmed materialism coupled with a historical dialectic that carried with it this worldly, socioeconomic values which would supplant the idealistic diversions of religion in the impending Communist society. Nietzsche, on the other hand, saw that the death of God — the destruction of Christian ideological roots and old values in European society — would produce a vast trauma, a loss of values, which would take decades, perhaps centuries, to make good. But the end would be good; better than the contorted psychology and the resentment which Nietzsche perceived to be central to the religion of love.

Many of Nietzsche's works — and all those from which sections are taken here — are made up of separate articles or aphorisms varying in length from a single sentence to a few pages. This means that despite the scale of Nietzsche's writings, it is relatively easy to grasp some of his main thoughts from brief extracts. The sections that follow are taken from four works. The numbers indicate the paragraph or section in the original. The first collection is from *Human, All-too-Human* (1878) and is concerned mainly with the pathology of sin. The second is from *The Joyful Wisdom* (1882) and deals with Nietzsche's much-used metaphor of the death of God. The third is from *Beyond Good and Evil* (1886), and the last is from Nietzsche's most sustained critique of Christianity, *The Antichrist* (1895).

Nietzsche can be read in two ways, in large doses taken quickly so that the general accumulation and direction of his ideas are grasped, or slowly, a few articles at a time, so that his highly original perceptions can be thoroughly absorbed. I commend the latter method — always bearing in mind Nietzsche's own warning "And when you gaze long into the abyss the abyss also gazes into you."

1. *The Pathology of Saints and Sinners*
From *Human, All-too-Human*

113.

CHRISTIANITY AS ANTIQUITY. — When on a Sunday morning we hear the old bells ring out, we ask ourselves, "Is it possible! This is done on account of a Jew crucified two thousand years ago who said he was the Son of God. The proof of such an assertion is wanting." Certainly in our times the Christian religion is an antiquity that dates from very early ages, and the fact that its assertions are still believed, when otherwise all claims are subjected to such strict examination, is perhaps the oldest part of this heritage. A God who creates a son from a mortal woman; a sage who requires that man should no longer work, no longer judge, but should pay attention to the signs of the approaching end of the world; a justice that accepts an innocent being as a substitute in sacrifice; one who commands his disciples to drink his blood; prayers for miraculous intervention; sins committed against a God and atoned for through a God; the fear of a future to which death is the portal; the form of the cross in an age which no longer knows the signification and the shame of the cross, how terrible all this appears to us, as if risen from the grave of the ancient past! Is it credible that such things are still believed?

114.

WHAT IS UN-GREEK IN CHRISTIANITY. — The Greeks did not regard the Homeric gods as raised above them like masters, nor themselves as being under them like servants, as the Jews did. They only saw, as in a mirror, the most perfect examples of their own caste; an ideal, therefore, and not an opposite of their own nature. There is a feeling of relationship, a mutual interest arises, a kind of symmachy. Man thinks highly of himself when he gives himself such gods, and places himself in a relation like that of the lower nobility towards the higher; while the Italian nations hold a genuine peasant-faith, with perpetual fear of evil and mischievous powers and tormenting spirits. Wherever the Olympian gods retreated into the background, Greek life was more sombre and more anxious. Christianity, on the contrary, oppressed man and crushed him utterly, sinking him as if in deep mire; then into the feeling of absolute depravity it suddenly threw the light of divine mercy, so that the surprised man, dazzled by forgiveness, gave a cry of joy and for a moment believed that he bore all heaven within himself. All psychological feelings of Christianity work upon this unhealthy excess of sentiment, and upon the deep corruption of head and heart it necessitates; it desires to destroy, break, stupefy, confuse, — only one thing it does not desire, namely *moderation,* and therefore it is in the deepest sense barbaric, Asiatic, ignoble, and un-Greek.

115.

TO BE RELIGIOUS WITH ADVANTAGE. — There are sober and industrious people on whom religion is embroidered like a hem of higher humanity; these do well to remain religious, it beautifies them. All people who do not understand some kind of trade in weapons — tongue and pen included as weapons — become servile; for such the Christian religion is very useful, for then servility assumes the appearance of Christian virtues and is surprisingly beautiful. People to whom their daily life appears too empty and monotonous easily grow religious; this is comprehensible and excusable, only they have no right to demand religious sentiments from those whose daily life is not empty and monotonous.

116.

THE COMMONPLACE CHRISTIAN. — If Christianity were right, with its theories of an avenging God, of general sinfulness, of redemption, and the danger of eternal damnation, it would be a sign of weak intellect and lack of character *not* to become a priest, apostle or hermit, and to work only with fear and trembling for one's own salvation; it would be senseless thus to neglect eternal benefits for temporary comfort. Taking it for granted that there *is belief*, the commonplace Christian is a miserable figure, a man that really cannot add two and two together, and who, moreover, just because of his mental incapacity for responsibility, did not deserve to be so severely punished as Christianity has decreed.

117.

OF THE WISDOM OF CHRISTIANITY. — It is a clever stroke on the part of Christianity to teach the utter unworthiness, sinfulness, and despicableness of mankind so loudly that the disdain of their fellow-men is no longer possible. "He may sin as much as he likes, he is not essentially different from me, — it is I who am unworthy and despicable in every way," says the Christian to himself. But even this feeling has lost its sharpest sting, because the Christian no longer believes in his individual despicableness; he is bad as men are generally, and comforts himself a little with the axiom, "We are all of one kind."

118.

CHANGE OF FRONT. — As soon as a religion triumphs it has for its enemies all those who would have been its first disciples.

119.

THE FATE OF CHRISTIANITY. — Christianity arose for the purpose of lightening the heart; but now it must first make the heart heavy in order afterwards to lighten it. Consequently it will perish.

120.

THE PROOF OF PLEASURE. — The agreeable opinion is accepted as true, — this is the proof of the pleasure (or, as the Church says, the proof of the strength), of which all religions are so proud when they ought to be ashamed of it. If Faith did not make blessed it would not be believed in; of how little value must it be, then!

132.

OF THE CHRISTIAN NEED OF REDEMPTION. — With careful reflection it must be possible to obtain an explanation free from mythology of that process in the soul of a Christian which is called the need of redemption, consequently a purely psychological explanation. Up to the present, the psychological explanations of religious conditions and processes have certainly been held in some disrepute, inasmuch as a theology which called itself free carried on its unprofitable practice in this domain; for here from the beginning (as the mind of its founder, Schleiermacher, gives us reason to suppose) the preservation of the Christian religion and the continuance of Christian theology was kept in view; a theology which was to find a new anchorage in the psychological analyses of religious "facts," and above all a new occupation. Unconcerned about such predecessors we hazard the following interpretation of the phenomenon in question. Man is conscious of certain actions which stand far down in the customary rank of actions; he even discovers in himself a tendency towards similar actions, a tendency which appears to him almost as unchangeable as his whole nature. How willingly would he try himself in that other species of actions which in the general valuation are recognized as the loftiest and highest, how gladly would he feel himself to be full of the good consciousness which should follow an unselfish mode of thought! But unfortunately he stops short at this wish, and the discontent at not being able to satisfy it is added to all the other discontents which his lot in life or the consequences of those above-mentioned evil actions have aroused in him; so that a deep ill-humor is the result, with the search for a physician who could remove this and all its causes. This condition would not be felt so bitterly if man would only compare himself frankly with other men, — then he would have no reason for being dissatisfied with himself to a particular extent, he would only bear his share of the common burden of human dissatisfaction and imperfection. But he compares himself with a being who is said to be capable only of those actions which are called unegoistic, and to live in the perpetual consciousness of an unselfish mode of thought, i.e. with God; it is because he gazes into this clear mirror that his image appears to him so dark, so unusually warped. Then he is alarmed by the thought of that same creature, in so far as it floats before his imagination as a retributive justice; in all possible small and great events he thinks he recognizes its anger and menaces, that he even feels its scourge-strokes as judge and executioner. Who will help him in this danger, which, by the prospect of an immeasurable duration of punishment, exceeds in horror all the other terrors of the idea?

133.

Before we examine the further consequences of this mental state, let us acknowledge that it is not through his "guilt" and "sin" that man has got into this condition, but through a series of errors of reason; that it was the fault of the mirror if his image appeared so dark and hateful to him, and that that mirror was *his* work, the very imperfect work of human imagination and power of judgment. In the first place, a nature that is only capable of purely unegoistic actions is more fabulous than the phoenix; it cannot even be clearly imagined, just because, when closely examined, the whole idea "unegoistic action" vanishes into air. No man *ever* did a thing which was done only for others and without any personal motive; how should he be *able* to do anything which had no relation to himself, and therefore without inward obligation (which must always have its foundation in a personal need)? How could the *ego* act without *ego?* A God who, on the contrary, is *all* love, as such a one is often represented, would not be capable of a single unegoistic action, whereby one is reminded of a saying of Lichtenberg's which is certainly taken from a lower sphere: "We cannot possibly *feel* for others, as the saying is; we feel only for ourselves. This sounds hard, but it is not so really if it be rightly understood. We do not love father or mother or wife or child, but the pleasant sensations they cause us;" or, as Rochefoucauld says: "*Si on croit aimer sa maîtresse pour l'amour d'elle, on est bien trompé.*" To know the reason why actions of love are valued more than others, not on account of their nature, namely, but of their *usefulness*, we should compare the examinations already mentioned, *On the Origin of Moral Sentiments.* But should a man desire to be entirely like that God of Love, to do and wish everything for others and nothing for himself, the latter is impossible for the reason that he must do *very much* for himself to be able to do something for the love of others. Then it is taken for granted that the other is sufficiently egoistic to accept that sacrifice again and again, that living for him, — so that the people of love and sacrifice have an interest in the continuance of those who are loveless and incapable of sacrifice, and, in order to exist, the highest morality would be obliged positively to *compel* the existence of un-morality (whereby it would certainly annihilate itself). Further: the conception of a God disturbs and humbles so long as it is believed in; but as to how it arose there can no longer be any doubt in the present state of the science of comparative ethnology; and with a comprehension of this origin all belief falls to the ground. The Christian who compares his nature with God's is like Don Quixote, who under-valued his own bravery because his head was full of the marvellous deeds of the heroes of the chivalric romances, — the standard of measurement in both cases belongs to the domain of fable. But if the idea of God is removed, so is also the feeling of "sin" as a trespass against divine laws, as a stain in a creature vowed to God. Then, perhaps, there still remains that dejection which is intergrown and connected with the fear of the punishment of worldly justice or of the scorn of men; the dejection of the pricks of conscience, the sharpest thorn in the consciousness of sin, is always removed if we recognize that though by our own deed we have sinned against human descent, human laws and ordinances, still that we have not imperiled the "eternal salvation of the Soul" and its relation to the Godhead. And if man succeeds in gaining philosophic conviction of the absolute necessity of all actions and their entire irresponsibility, and absorbing this into his flesh and blood, even those remains of the pricks of conscience vanish.

134.

Now if the Christian, as we have said, has fallen into the way of self-contempt in consequence of certain errors through a false, unscientific interpretation of his actions and sensations, he must notice with great surprise how that state of contempt, the pricks of conscience and displeasure generally, does not endure, how sometimes there come hours when all this is wafted away from his soul and he feels himself once more free and courageous. In truth, the pleasure in himself, the comfort of his own strength, together with the necessary weakening through time of every deep emotion, has usually been victorious; man loves himself once again, he feels it, — but precisely this new love, this self-esteem, seems to him incredible, he can only see in it the wholly undeserved descent of a stream of mercy from on high. If he formerly believed that in every event he could recognize warning, menaces, punishments, and every kind of manifestation of divine anger, he now finds divine goodness in all his experiences, — this event appears to him to be full of love, that one a helpful hint, a third, and indeed, his whole happy mood, a proof that God is merciful. As formerly, in his state of pain, he interpreted his actions falsely, so now he misinterprets his experiences; his mood of comfort he believes to be the working of a power operating outside of himself, the love with which he really loves himself seems to him to be divine love; that which he calls mercy, and the prologue to redemption, is actually self-forgiveness, self-redemption.

135.

Therefore: A certain false psychology, a certain kind of imaginative interpretation of motives and experiences, is the necessary preliminary for one to become a Christian and to feel the need of redemption. When this error of reason and imagination is recognised, one ceases to be a Christian.

136.

OF CHRISTIAN ASCETICISM AND HOLINESS. — As greatly as isolated thinkers have endeavoured to depict as a miracle the rare manifestations of morality, which are generally called asceticism and holiness, miracles which it would be almost an outrage and sacrilege to explain by the light of common sense, as strong also is the inclination towards this outrage. A mighty impulse of nature has at all times led to a protest against those manifestations; science, in so far as it is an imitation of nature, at least allows itself to rise against the supposed inexplicableness and unapproachableness of these objections. So far it has certainly not succeeded: those appearances are still unexplained, to the great joy of the above-mentioned worshippers of the morally marvellous. For, speaking generally, the unexplained *must* be absolutely inexplicable, the inexplicable absolutely unnatural, supernatural, wonderful, — thus runs the demand in the souls of all religious and metaphysical people (also of artists, if they should happen to be thinkers at the same time); whilst the scientist sees in this demand the "evil principle" in itself. The general, first probability upon which one lights in the contemplation of holiness and asceticism is this, that their nature is a *complicated* one, for almost everywhere, within the physical world as well as in the moral, the apparently marvellous has been successfully traced back to the complicated, the many-conditioned. Let us venture, therefore, to isolate separate impulses from the soul of saints and ascetics, and finally to imagine them as intergrown.

137.

There is a *defiance of self*, to the sublimest manifestation of which belong many forms of asceticism. Certain individuals have such great need of exercising their power and love of ruling that, in default of other objects, or because they have never succeeded otherwise, they finally excogitate the idea of tyrannising over certain parts of their own nature, portions or degrees of themselves. Thus many a thinker confesses to views which evidently do not serve. either to increase or improve his reputation; many a one deliberately calls down the scorn of others when by keeping silence he could easily have remained respected; others contradict former opinions and do not hesitate to be called inconsistent — on the contrary, they strive after this, and behave like reckless riders who like a horse best when it has grown wild, unmanageable, and covered with sweat. Thus man climbs dangerous paths up the highest mountains in order that he may laugh to scorn his own fear and his trembling knees; thus the philosopher owns to views of asceticism, humility, holiness, in the brightness of which his own picture shows to the worst possible disadvantage. This crushing of one's self, this scorn of one's own nature, this *spernere se sperni*, of which religion has made so much, is really a very high degree of vanity. The whole moral of the Sermon on the Mount belongs here; man takes a genuine delight in doing violence to himself by these exaggerated claims, and afterwards idolising these tyrannical demands of his soul. In every ascetic morality man worships one part of himself as a God, and is obliged, therefore, to diabolise the other parts.

143.

That which gives the saint his historical value is not the thing he *is*, but the thing he *represents* in the eyes of the unsaintly. It was through the fact that errors were made about him, that the state of his soul was *falsely interpreted*, that men separated themselves from him as much as possible, as from something incomparable and strangely superhuman, that he acquired the extraordinary power which he exercised over the imagination of whole nations and whole ages. He did not know himself; he himself interpreted the writing of his moods, inclinations, and actions according to an art of interpretation which was as exaggerated and artificial as the spiritual interpretation of the Bible. The distorted and diseased in his nature, with its combination of intellectual poverty, evil knowledge, ruined health, and overexcited nerves, remained hidden from his own sight as well as from that of his spectators. He was not a particularly good man, and still less was he a particularly wise one; but he *represented* something that exceeded the human standard in goodness and wisdom. The belief in him supported the belief in the divine and miraculous, in a religious meaning of all existence, in an impending day of judgment. In the evening glory of the world's sunset, which glowed over the Christian nations, the shadowy form of the saint grew to vast dimensions, it grew to such a height that even in our own age, which no longer believes in God, there are still thinkers who believe in the saint.

144.

It need not be said that to this description of the saint which has been made from an average of the whole species, there may be opposed many a description which could give a more agreeable impression. Certain exceptions stand out from among this species, it may be through great mildness and philanthropy, it may be through the magic of unusual energy; others are attractive in the highest degree, because certain wild ravings have poured streams of light on their whole being, as is the case, for instance, with the famous founder of Christianity, who thought he was the Son of God and therefore felt himself sinless — so that through this idea — which we must not judge too hardly because the whole antique world swarms with sons of God — he reached that same goal, the feeling of complete sinlessness, complete irresponsibility, which every one can now acquire by means of science. Neither have I mentioned the Indian saints, who stand midway between the Christian saint and the Greek philosopher, and in so far represent no pure type. Knowledge, science — such as existed then — the uplifting above other men through logical discipline and training of thought, were as much fostered by the Buddhists as distinguishing signs of holiness as the same qualities in the Christian world are repressed and branded as signs of unholiness.

2. The Death of God

From *The Joyful Wisdom*

125.

THE MADMAN. — Have you ever heard of the madman who on a bright morning lighted a lantern and ran to the market-place calling out unceasingly: "I seek God! I seek God!" — As there were many people standing about who did not believe in God, he caused a great deal of amusement. Why! is he lost? said one. Has he strayed away like a child? said another. Or does he keep himself hidden? Is he afraid of us? Has he taken a sea voyage? Has he emigrated? — the people cried out laughingly, all in a hubbub. The insane man jumped into their midst and transfixed them with his glances. "Where is God gone?" he called out. "I mean to tell you! *We have killed him,* — you and I! We are all his murderers! But how have we done it? How were we able to drink up the sea? Who gave us the sponge to wipe away the whole horizon? What did we do when we loosened this earth from its sun? Whither does it now move? Whither do we move? Away from all suns? Do we not dash on unceasingly? Backwards, sideways, forewards, in all directions? Is there still an above and below? Do we not stray, as through infinite nothingness? Does not empty space breathe upon us? Has it not become colder? Does not night come on continually, darker and darker? Shall we not have to light lanterns in the morning? Do we not hear the noise of the grave-diggers who are burying God? Do we not smell the divine putrefaction? — for even Gods putrefy! God is dead! God remains dead! And we have killed him! How shall we console ourselves, the most murderous of all murderers? The holiest and the mightiest that the world has hitherto possessed, has bled to death under our knife, — who will wipe the blood from us? With what water could we cleanse ourselves? What lustrums, what sacred games shall we have to devise? Is not the magnitude of this deed too great for us? Shall we not ourselves have to become Gods, merely to seem worthy of it? There never was a greater event, — and on account of it, all who are born after us belong to a higher history than any history hitherto!" — Here the madman was silent and looked again at his hearers; they also were silent and looked at him in surprise. At last he threw his lantern on the ground, so that it broke in pieces and was extinguished. "I come too early," he then said, "I am not yet at the right time. This prodigious event is still on its way, and is travelling, — it has not yet reached men's ears. Lightning and thunder need time, the light of the stars needs time, deeds need time, even after they are done, to be seen and heard. This deed is as yet further from them than the furthest star, — *and yet they have done it!*" — It is further stated that the madman made his way into different churches on the same day, and there intoned his *Requiem aeternam deo.* When led out and called to account, he always gave the reply: "What are these churches now, if they are not the tombs and monuments of God?" —

130.

A DANGEROUS RESOLUTION. — The Christian resolution to find the world ugly and bad has made the world ugly and bad.

135.

ORIGIN OF SIN. — Sin, as it is at present felt wherever Christianity prevails or has prevailed, is a Jewish feeling and a Jewish invention; and in respect to this background of all Christian morality, Christianity has in fact aimed at "Judaising" the whole world. To what an extent this has succeeded in Europe is traced most accurately in the extent of our alienness to Greek antiquity — a world without the feeling of sin — in our sentiments even at present; in spite of all the good will to approximation and assimilation, which whole generations and many distinguished individuals have not failed to display. "Only when thou *repentest* is God gracious to thee" — that would arouse the laughter or the wrath of a Greek: he would say, "Slaves may have such sentiments." Here a mighty being, an almighty being, and yet a revengeful being, is presupposed; his power is so great that no injury whatever can be done to him except in the point of honor. Every sin is an infringement of respect, a *crimen laesae majestatis divinae* — and nothing more! Contrition, degradation, rolling-in-the-dust, — these are the first and last conditions on which his favour depends: the restoration, therefore, of his divine honour! If injury be caused otherwise by sin, if a profound, spreading evil be propagated by it, an evil which, like a disease, attacks and strangles one man after another — that does not trouble this honour-craving Oriental in heaven; sin is an offence against him, not against mankind! — to him on whom he has bestowed his favor he bestows also this indifference to the natural consequences of sin. God and mankind are here thought of as separated, as so antithetical that sin against the latter cannot be at all possible, — all deeds are to be looked upon *solely with respect to their supernatural consequences*, and not with respect to their natural results: it is thus that the Jewish feeling, to which all that is natural seems unworthy in itself, would have things. The *Greeks*, on the other hand, were more familiar with the thought that transgression also may have dignity, — even theft, as in the case of Prometheus, even the slaughtering of cattle as the expression of frantic jealousy, as in the case of Ajax; in their need to attribute dignity to transgression and embody it therein, they invented *tragedy*, — an art and a delight, which in its profoundest essence has remained alien to the Jew, in spite of all his poetic endowment and taste for the sublime.

343.

What our Cheerfulness Signifies. — The most important of more recent events — that "God is dead," that the belief in the Christian God has become unworthy of belief — already begins to cast its first shadows over Europe. To the few at least whose eye, whose *suspecting* glance, is strong enough and subtle enough for this drama, some sun seems to have set, some old, profound confidence seems to have changed into doubt: our old world must seem to them daily more darksome, distrustful, strange and "old." In the main, however, one may say that the event itself is far too great, too remote, too much beyond most people's power of apprehension, for one to suppose that so much as the report of it could have *reached* them; not to speak of many who already knew *what* had really taken place, and what must all collapse now that this belief had been undermined, —because so much was built upon it, so much rested on it, and had become one with it: for example, our entire European morality. This lengthy, vast and uninterrupted process of crumbling, destruction, ruin and overthrow which is now imminent: who has realised it sufficiently to-day to have to stand up as the teacher and herald of such a tremendous logic of terror, as the prophet of a period of gloom and eclipse, the like of which has probably never taken place on earth before? . . . Even we, the born riddle-readers, who wait as it were on the mountains posted 'twixt to-day and to-morrow, and engirt by their contradiction, we, the firstlings and premature children of the coming century, into whose sight especially the shadows which must forthwith envelop Europe *should* already have come—how is it that even we, without genuine sympathy for this period of gloom, contemplate its advent without any *personal* solicitude or fear? Are we still, perhaps, too much under the *immediate effects* of the event—and are these effects, especially as regards *ourselves,* perhaps the reverse of what was to be expected—not at all sad and depressing, but rather like a new and indescribable variety of light, happiness, relief, enlivenment, encouragement, and dawning day? . . . In fact, we philosophers and "free spirits" feel ourselves irradiated as by a new dawn by the report that the "old God is dead"; our hearts overflow with gratitude, astonishment, presentiment and expectation. At last the horizon seems open once more, granting even that it is not bright; our ships can at last put out to sea in face of every danger; every hazard is again permitted to the discerner; the sea, *our* sea, again lies open before us; perhaps never before did such an "open sea" exist. —

3. Mental Space and Religious Prisons

From Beyond Good and Evil

53.

Why Atheism nowadays? "The father" in God is thoroughly refuted; equally so "the judge," "the rewarder." Also his "free will": he does not hear—and even if he did, he would not know how to help. The worst is that he seems incapable of communicating himself clearly; is he uncertain? —This is what I have made out (by questioning, and listening at a variety of conversations) to be the cause of the decline of European theism; it appears to me that though the religious instinct is in vigorous growth,—it rejects the theistic satisfaction with profound distrust.

55.

There is a great ladder of religious cruelty, with many rounds: but three of these are the most important. Once on a time men sacrificed human beings to their God, and perhaps just those they loved the best—to this category belong the firstling sacrifices of all primitive religions, and also the sacrifice of the Emperor Tiberius in the Mithra-Grotto on the Island of Capri, that most terrible of all Roman anachronisms. Then, during the moral epoch of mankind, they sacrificed to their God the strongest instincts they possessed, their "nature"; *this* festal joy shines in the cruel glances of ascetics and "anti-natural" fanatics. Finally, what still remained to be sacrificed? Was it not necessary in the end for men to sacrifice everything comforting, holy, healing, all hope, all faith in hidden harmonies, in future blessedness and justice? Was it not necessary to sacrifice God himself, and out of cruelty to themselves to worship stone, stupidity, gravity, fate, nothingness? To sacrifice God for nothingness—this paradoxical mystery of the ultimate cruelty has been reserved for the rising generation; we all know something thereof already.

57.

The distance, and as it were the space around man, grows with the strength of his intellectual vision and insight: his world becomes profounder; new stars, new enigmas, and notions are ever coming into view. Perhaps everything on which the intellectual eye has exercised its acuteness and profundity has just been an occasion for its exercise, something of a game, something for children and childish minds. Perhaps the most solemn conceptions that have caused the most fighting and suffering, the conceptions "God" and "sin," will one day seem to us of no more importance than a child's plaything or a child's pain seems to an old man;—and perhaps another plaything and another pain will then be necessary once more for "the old man"—always childish enough, an eternal child!

60.

To love mankind *for God's sake*—this has so far been the noblest and remotest sentiment to which mankind has attained. That love to mankind, without any redeeming intention in the background, is only an *additional* folly and brutishness, that the inclination to this love has first to get its proportion, its delicacy, its grain of salt and sprinkling of ambergris from a higher inclination: — whoever first perceived and "experienced" this, however his tongue may have stammered as it attempted to express such a delicate matter, let him for all time be holy and respected, as the man who has so far flown highest and gone astray in the finest fashion!

62.

To be sure — to make also the bad counter-reckoning against such religions [as Buddhism and Christianity] and to bring to light their secret dangers — the cost is always excessive and terrible when religions do *not* operate as an educational and disciplinary medium in the hands of the philosopher, but rule voluntarily and *paramountly,* when they wish to be the final end, and not a means along with other means. Among men, as among all other animals, there is a surplus of defective, diseased, degenerating, infirm, and necessarily suffering individuals; the successful cases, among men also, are always the exception; and in view of the fact that man is *the animal not yet properly adapted to his environment,* the rare exception. But worse still. The higher the type a man represents, the greater is the improbability that he will *succeed;* the accidental, the law of irrationality in the general constitution of mankind, manifests itself most terribly in its destructive effect on the higher orders of men, the conditions of whose lives are delicate, diverse, and difficult to determine. What, then, is the attitude of the two greatest religions above-mentioned to the *surplus* of failures in life? They endeavour to preserve and keep alive whatever can be preserved; in fact, as the religions *for sufferers,* they take the part of these upon principle; they are always in favour of those who suffer from life as from a disease, and they would fain treat every other experience of life as false and impossible. However highly we may esteem this indulgent and preservative care (inasmuch as in applying to others, it has applied, and applies also to the highest and usually the most suffering type of man), the hitherto *paramount* religions — to give a general appreciation of them — are among the principal causes which have kept the type of "man" upon a lower level — they have preserved too much *that which should have perished.* One has to thank them for invaluable services; and who is sufficiently rich in gratitude not to feel poor at the contemplation of all that the "spiritual men" of Christianity have done for Europe hitherto! But when they had given comfort to the sufferers, courage to the oppressed and despairing, a staff and support to the helpless, and when they had allured from society into convents and spiritual penitentiaries the broken-hearted and distracted: what else had they to do in order to work systematically in that fashion, and with a good conscience, for the preservation of all the sick and suffering, which means, in deed and in truth, to work for *the deterioration of the European race?* To *reverse* all estimates of value — *that* is what they had to do! And to shatter the strong, to spoil great hopes, to cast suspicion on the delight in beauty, to break down everything autonomous, manly, conquering, and imperious — all instincts which are natural to the highest and most successful type of "man" — into uncertainty, distress of conscience, and self-destruction; forsooth, to invert all love of the earthly and of supremacy over the earth, into hatred of the earth and earthly things — *that* is the task the Church imposed on itself, and was obliged to impose, until, according to its standard of value, "unworldliness," "unsensuousness," and "higher man" fused into one sentiment. If one could observe the strangely painful, equally coarse and refined comedy of European Christianity with the derisive and impartial eye of an Epicurean god, I should think one would never cease marvelling and laughing; does it not actually seem that some single will has ruled over Europe for eighteen centuries in order to make a *sublime abortion* of man? He, however, who, with opposite requirements (no longer Epicurean) and with some divine hammer in his hand, could approach this almost voluntary degeneration and stunting of mankind, as exemplified in the European Christian (Pascal, for instance), would he not have to cry aloud with rage, pity, and horror: "Oh, you bungler, presumptuous pitiful bunglers, what have you done! Was that a work for your hands? How you have hacked and botched my finest stone! What have *you* presumed to do!" — I should say that Christianity has hitherto been the most portentous of presumptions. Men, not great enough, nor hard enough, to be entitled as artists to take part in fashioning *man;* men, not sufficiently strong and far-sighted to *allow,* with sublime self-constraint, the obvious law of the thousandfold failures and perishings to prevail; men, not sufficiently noble to see the radically different grades of rank and intervals of rank that separate man from man: — *such* men, with their "equality before God," have hitherto swayed the destiny of Europe; until at last a dwarfed, almost ludicrous species has been produced, a gregarious animal, something obliging, sickly, mediocre, the European of the present day.

4. The Antichrist

From *The Antichrist*

5

We must not deck out and adorn Christianity: it has waged a deadly war upon this *higher* type of man, it has set a ban upon all the fundamental instincts of this type, and has distilled evil and the devil himself out of these instincts: — the strong man as the typical pariah, the villain. Christianity has sided with everything weak, low, and botched; it has made an ideal out of *antagonism* against all the self-preservative instincts of strong life: it has corrupted even the reason of the strongest intellects, by teaching that the highest values of intellectuality are sinful, misleading and full of temptations. The most lamentable example of this was the corruption of Pascal, who believed in the perversion of his reason through original sin, whereas it had only been perverted by his Christianity.

7

Christianity is called the religion of *pity.* — Pity is opposed to the tonic passions which enhance the energy of the feeling of life: its action is depressing. A man loses power when he pities. By means of pity the drain on strength which suffering itself already introduces into the world is multiplied a thousandfold. Through pity, suffering itself becomes infectious; in certain circumstances it may lead to a total loss of life and vital energy, which is absurdly out of proportion to the magnitude of the cause (— the case of the death of the Nazarene). This is the first standpoint; but there is a still more important one. Supposing one measures pity according to the value of the reactions it usually stimulates, its danger to life appears in a much more telling light. On the whole, pity thwarts the law of development which is the law of selection. It preserves that which is ripe for death, it fights in favour of the disinherited and the condemned of life; thanks to the multitude of abortions of all kinds which it maintains in life, it lends life itself a sombre and questionable aspect. People have dared to call pity a virtue (— in every *noble* culture it is considered as a weakness —); people went still further, they exalted it to *the* virtue, the root and origin of all virtues, — but, of course, what must never be forgotten is the fact that this was done from the standpoint of a philosophy which was nihilistic, and on whose shield the device *The Denial of Life* was inscribed.

9

It is upon this theological instinct that I wage war. I find traces of it everywhere. Whoever has the blood of theologians in his veins, stands from the start in a false and dishonest position to all things. The pathos which grows out of this state, is called *Faith:* that is to say, to shut one's eyes once and for all, in order not to suffer at the sight of incurable falsity. People convert this faulty view of all things into a moral, a virtue, a thing of holiness. They endow their distorted vision with a good conscience, — they claim that no *other* point of view is any longer of value, once theirs has been made sacrosanct with the names "God," "Salvation," "Eternity." I unearthed the instinct of the theologian everywhere: it is the most universal, and actually the most subterranean form of falsity on earth. That which a theologian considers true, *must* of necessity be false: this furnishes almost the criterion of truth. It is his most profound self-preservative instinct which forbids reality ever to attain to honour in any way, or even to raise its voice. Whithersoever the influence of the theologian extends, *valuations* are topsyturvy, and the concepts "true" and "false" have necessarily changed places: that which is most deleterious to life, is here called "true," that which enhances it, elevates it, says Yea to it, justifies it and renders it triumphant, is called "false.". . . If it should happen that theologians, *via* the "conscience" either of princes or of the people, stretch out their hand for power, let us not be in any doubt as to what results therefrom each time, namely: — the will to the end, the *nihilistic* will to power. . . .

15

In Christianity, neither morality nor religion comes in touch at all with reality. Nothing but imaginary *causes* (God, the soul, the ego, spirit, free will — or even non-free will); nothing but imaginary *effects* (sin, salvation, grace, punishment, forgiveness of sins). Imaginary beings are supposed to have intercourse (God, spirits, souls); imaginary Natural History (anthropocentric: total lack of the notion, "natural causes"); an imaginary *psychology* (nothing but misunderstandings of self, interpretations of pleasant or unpleasant general feelings; for instance of the states of the *nervus sympathicus*, with the help of the sign language of a religio-moral idiosyncrasy, — repentance, pangs of conscience, the temptation of the devil, the presence of God); an imaginary teleology (the Kingdom of God, the Last Judgment, Everlasting Life). —This purely fictitious world distinguishes itself very unfavourably from the world of dreams: the latter *reflects* reality, whereas the former falsifies, depreciates and denies it. Once the concept "nature" was taken to mean the opposite of the concept God, the word "natural" had to acquire the meaning of abominable, — the whole of that fictitious world takes its root in the hatred of nature (— reality! —) it is the expression of profound discomfiture in the presence of reality. . . . *But this explains everything.* What is the only kind of man who has reasons for wriggling out of reality by lies? The man who suffers from reality. But in order to suffer from reality one must be a bungled portion of it. The preponderance of pain over pleasure is the *cause* of that fictitious morality and religion: but any such preponderance furnishes the formula for decadence.

45

— Let me give you a few examples of what these paltry people have stuffed into their heads, what they have laid *on the lips of their Master:* quite a host of confessions from "beautiful souls." —

"And whosoever shall not receive you, nor hear you, when ye depart thence, shake off the dust under your feet for a testimony against them. Verily I say unto you, It shall be more tolerable for Sodom and Gomorrah in the day of judgment, than for that city." (Mark vi. 11.) — *How evangelical!* . . .

"And whosoever shall offend one of these little ones that believe in me, it is better for him that a millstone were hanged about his neck, and he were cast into the sea." (Mark ix. 42.) — *How evangelical!* . . .

"And if thine eye offend thee, pluck it out: it is better for thee to enter into the kingdom of God with one eye, than having two eyes to be cast into hell fire: where their worm dieth not, and the fire is not quenched." (Mark ix. 47, 48.) — The eye is not precisely what is meant in this passage. . . .

"Verily I say unto you, That there be some of them that stand here, which shall not taste of death, till they have seen the kingdom of God come with power." (Mark ix. I.) — Well *lied,* lion! . . .)

"Whosoever will come after me, let him deny himself, and take up his cross, and follow me. *For* . . ." (A *psychologist's comment.* Christian morality is refuted by its "For's": its "reasons" refute, — this is Christian.) (Mark viii. 34.)

"Judge not, that ye be not judged. For with what judgment ye judge, ye shall be judged." (Matthew vii. I, 2.) — What a strange notion of justice on the part of a "just" judge! . . .

"For if ye love them which love you, what reward have ye? do not even the publicans the same? And if ye salute your brethren only, what do ye more *than others?* do not even the publicans so?" (Matthew v. 46, 47.) The principle of "Christian love": it insists upon being *well paid.* . . .

"But if ye forgive not men their trespasses neither will your Father forgive your trespasses." (Matthew vi. 15.) — Very compromising for the "Father" in question.

"But seek ye first the kingdom of God, and his righteousness; and all these things shall be added unto you." (Matthew vi. 33.) — "All these things" — that is to say, food, clothing, all the necessities of life. To use a moderate expression, this is an *error.* . . . Shortly before this God appears as a tailor, at least in certain cases. . . .

"Rejoice ye in that day, and leap for joy: for, behold, your reward *is* great in heaven: for in the like manner did their fathers unto the prophets." (Luke vi. 23.) — *Impudent* rabble! They dare to compare themselves with the prophets. . . .

"Know ye not that ye are the temple of God, and *that* the Spirit of God dwelleth in you? If any man defile the temple of God, *him shall God destroy;* for the temple of God is holy, which *temple ye are.*" (St Paul, I Corinthians iii. 16, 17.) — One cannot have too much contempt for this sort of thing. . . .

"Do ye not know that the saints shall judge the world? and if the world shall be judged by you, are ye unworthy to judge the smallest matters?" (St Paul, I Corinthians vi. 2.) — Unfortunately this is not merely the speech of a lunatic. . . . This *appealing impostor* proceeds thus: "Know ye not that we shall judge angels? How much more things that pertain to this life?"

"Hath not God made foolish the wisdom of this world? For after that in the wisdom of God, the world by wisdom knew not God, it pleased God by the foolishness of preaching to save them that believe . . . not many wise men after the flesh, not many mighty, not many noble *are called:* But God hath chosen the foolish things of the world to confound the wise; and God hath chosen the weak things of the world to confound the things which are mighty; And base things of the world, and things which are despised, hath God chosen; *yea,* and things which are not, to bring to nought things that are: That no flesh should glory in his presence." (St Paul, I Corinthians i. 20 *et seq.*) — In order to *understand* this passage, which is of the highest importance as an example of the psychology of every Chandala morality, the reader should refer to my *Genealogy of Morals:* in this book, the contrast between a *noble* and a Chandala morality born of *resentment* and impotent revengefulness, is brought to light for the first time. St Paul was the greatest of all the apostles of revenge. . . .

16

SIGMUND FREUD ON RELIGION AS WISH FULFILLMENT

Pathetic fallacy: "crediting inanimate things with human emotions"

—O.E.D.

Biographical Note

Sigmund Freud (1856–1939), the father of psychoanalysis and one of the dominant influences upon the cultural and literary ideas of the first half of the twentieth century, was brought up and spent most of his life in Vienna. In 1881 he obtained a degree in medicine from the university in Vienna, and after studying with the French neurologist Charcot and undergoing extensive clinical experience, Freud published numerous papers during the last decade of the nineteenth century in which he developed the basic theories of psychoanalysis. During the next forty years he published a huge body of work (the *Collected Works* amount to 24 volumes), which established a worldwide awareness of his psychoanalytic techniques. As a Jew, he fled Vienna in 1938 during the takeover by National Socialism. He died in London a year later.

Philosophical Note

Although brought up to observe Jewish religious customs, Freud seems never to have had any serious *belief* in God or in gods. But he has much to say about religion in a number of his published works (see bibliography). His frequently repeated contentions are that "the psychical origin of religious ideas . . . are illusions, fulfillments of the oldest, strongest, and most urgent wishes of mankind"; that "religion would thus be the universal obsessional neurosis of mankind"; and that "the primal father figure was the original image of God." Freud is thus very much in the tradition of reductionist accounts of religion ("religion is nothing but . . ."; "God is nothing but . . .") of the sort already seen in Hobbes, Marx, and particularly Feuerbach. But Freud's kind of reductionism is much more powerful than Feuerbach's. Freud does not merely argue for a possible semimetaphysical thesis to account for the phenomenon of religion. He argues in close detail, and with evidence, that human beings, being the sort of creatures they are, *need* to believe in gods. One of Freud's most effective developments of this contention is in *The Future of an Illusion* (1927). Section VI expresses the matter in the following typical and powerful way.

Religion as Wish Fulfillment
From *The Future of an Illusion*, Section 6

I think we have prepared the way sufficiently for an answer to both these questions. It will be found if we turn our attention to the psychical origin of religious ideas. These, which are given out as teachings, are not precipitates of experience or end-results of thinking: they are illusions, fulfillments of the oldest, strongest and most urgent wishes of mankind. The secret of their strength lies in the strength of those wishes. As we already know, the terrifying impression of helplessness in childhood aroused the need for protection — for protection through love — which was provided by the father; and the recognition that this helplessness lasts throughout life made it necessary to cling to the existence of a father, but this time a more powerful one. Thus the benevolent rule of a divine Providence allays our fear of the dangers of life; the establishment of a moral world-order ensures the fulfillment of the demands of justice, which have so often remained unfulfilled in human civilization; and the prolongation of earthly existence in a future life provides the local and temporal framework in which these wish-fulfillments shall take place. Answers to the riddles that tempt the curiosity of man, such as how the universe began or what the relation is between body and mind, are developed in conformity with the underlying assumptions of this system. It is an enormous relief to the individual psyche if the conflicts of its childhood arising from the father-complex — conflicts which it has never wholly overcome — are removed from it and brought to a solution which is universally accepted.

When I say that these things are all illusions, I must define the meaning of the word. An illusion is not the same thing as an error; nor is it necessarily an error. Aristotle's belief that vermin are developed out of dung (a belief to which ignorant people still cling) was an error; so was the belief of a former generation of doctors that *tabes dorsalis* is the result of sexual excess. It would be incorrect to call these errors illusions. On the other hand, it was an illusion of Columbus's that he had discovered a new sea-route to the Indies. The part played by his wish in this error is very clear. One may describe as an illusion the assertion made by certain nationalists that the Indo-Germanic race is the only one capable of civilization; or the belief, which was only destroyed by psycho-analysis, that children are creatures without sexuality. What is characteristic of illusions is that they are derived from human wishes. In this respect they come near to psychiatric delusions. But they differ from them, too, apart from the more complicated structure of delusions. In the case of delusions, we emphasize as essential their being in contradiction with reality. Illusions need not necessarily be false — that is to say, unrealizable or in contradiction to reality. For instance, a middle-class girl may have the illusion that a prince will come and marry her. This is possible; and a few such cases have occurred. That the Messiah will come and found a golden age is much less likely. Whether one classifies this belief as an illusion or as something analogous to a delusion will depend on one's personal attitude. Examples of illusions which have proved true are not easy to find, but the illusion of the alchemists that all metals can be turned into gold might be one of them. The wish to have a great deal of gold, as much gold as possible, has, it is true, been a good deal damped by our present-day knowledge of the determinants of wealth, but chemistry no longer regards the transmutation of metals into gold as impossible. Thus we call a belief an illusion when a wish-fulfillment is a prominent factor in its motivation, and in doing so we disregard its relations to reality, just as the illusion itself sets no store by verification.

Having thus taken our bearings, let us return once more to the question of religious doctrines. We can now repeat that all of them are illusions and insusceptible of proof. No one can be compelled to think them true, to believe in them. Some of them are so improbable, so incompatible with everything we have laboriously discovered about the reality of the world, that we may compare them — if we pay proper regard to the psychological differences — to delusions. Of the reality value of most of them we cannot judge; just as they cannot be proved, so they cannot be refuted. We still know too little to make a critical approach to them. The riddles of the universe reveal themselves only slowly to our investigation; there are many questions to which science to-day can give no answer. But scientific work is the only road which can lead us to a knowledge of reality outside ourselves. It is once again merely an illusion to expect anything from intuition and introspection; they can give us nothing but particulars about our own mental life, which are hard to interpret, never any information about the questions which religious doctrine finds it so easy to answer. It would be insolent to let one's own arbitrary will step into the breach and, according to one's personal estimate, declare this or that part of the religious system to be less or more acceptable. Such questions are too momentous for that; they might be called too sacred.

'At this point one must expect to meet with an objection. "Well then, if even obdurate sceptics admit that the assertions of religion cannot be refuted by reason, why should I not believe in them, since they have so much on their side—tradition, the agreement of mankind, and all the consolations they offer?" Why not, indeed? Just as no one can be forced to believe, so no one can be forced to disbelieve. But do not let us be satisfied with deceiving ourselves that arguments like these take us along the road of correct thinking. If ever there was a case of a lame excuse we have it here. Ignorance is ignorance; no right to believe anything can be derived from it. In other matters no sensible person will behave so irresponsibly or rest content with such feeble grounds for his opinions and for the line he takes. It is only in the highest and most sacred things that he allows himself to do so. In reality these are only attempts at pretending to oneself or to other people that one is still firmly attached to religion, when one has long since cut oneself loose from it. Where questions of religion are concerned, people are guilty of every possible sort of dishonesty and intellectual misdemeanor. Philosophers stretch the meaning of words until they retain scarcely anything of their original sense. They give the name of "God" to some vague abstraction which they have created for themselves; having done so they can pose before all the world as deists, as believers in God, and they can even boast that they have recognized a higher, purer concept of God, notwithstanding that their God is now nothing more than an insubstantial shadow and no longer the mighty personality of religious doctrines. Critics persist in describing as "deeply religious" anyone who admits to a sense of man's insignificance or impotence in the face of the universe, although what constitutes the essence of the religious attitude is not this feeling but only the next step after it, the reaction to it which seeks a remedy for it. The man who goes no further, but humbly acquiesces in the small part which human beings play in the great world—such a man is, on the contrary, irreligious in the truest sense of the word.

To assess the truth-value of religious doctrines does not lie within the scope of the present enquiry. It is enough for us that we have recognized them as being, in their psychological nature, illusions. But we do not have to conceal the fact that this discovery also strongly influences our attitude to the question which must appear to many to be the most important of all. We know approximately at what periods and by what kind of men religious doctrines were created. If in addition we discover the motives which led to this, our attitude to the problem of religion will undergo a marked displacement. We shall tell ourselves that it would be very nice if there were a God who created the world and was a benevolent Providence, and if there were a moral order in the universe and an after-life; but it is a very striking fact that all this is exactly as we are bound to wish it to be. And it would be more remarkable still if our wretched, ignorant and downtrodden ancestors had succeeded in solving all these difficult riddles of the universe.

Additional Note

One defect in Marx and Lenin's analysis of religion is that they can give no account of why religious belief persists in situations in which it is *not* of assistance to the ruling classes in upholding the *status quo.* The defect is, as we have seen, to some extent remedied by Freud. But another great Austrian psychiatrist, Wilhelm Reich, takes the analysis in a different and more radical direction. In the *Mass Psychology of Fascism* (1933) Reich suggests that the *energy* that underlies religious emotions can be seen as displaced or redirected sexual energy.

17

BERTRAND RUSSELL ON A WISE MAN'S BELIEFS AND VALUES

A wise man, therefore, proportions his belief to
the evidence. In such conclusions as are founded
on an infallible experience, he expects the event
with the last degree of assurance, and regards his
past experience as a full proof of the future
existence of that event. In other cases he proceeds
with more caution: He weighs the opposite
experiments: He considers which side is supported
by the greater number of experiments: to that
side he inclines, with doubt and hesitation; and
when at last he fixes his judgment, the evidence
exceeds not what we properly call probability.

David Hume, in "Of Miracles"

Biographical Note

Bertrand Russell was born in 1872. His parents died before he could remember them, and he was brought up by his aristocratic grandparents, one of whom was Lord John Russell, twice prime minister of Great Britain. Russell read mathematics and philosophy at Trinity College, Cambridge. Among his early books was a specialist work on *The Philosophy of Leibniz* (1900). But his best-known early work was on logic and mathematics, particularly that done in collaboration with A. N. Whitehead and published as *Principia Mathematica* (three volumes, 1910–13). In later life Russell produced a number of important and original contributions to epistemology and general philosophy, e.g., *Our Knowledge of the External World* (1914), *The Analysis of Mind* (1921), and *The Analysis of Matter* (1927), as well as a large collection of more popular works on general philosophy, the history of philosophy, religion, and on scientific, political, moral, and social issues. He was a pacifist during World War I, but not during World War II. Between the wars he conducted an experimental school while continuing his vast literary activities. In 1940 he enjoyed the distinction of being prevented from teaching at the College of the City of New York—the charge against him being not dissimilar to that upheld against Socrates in Athens 2,339 years earlier. In 1950 Russell was awarded the Nobel Prize for Literature. In the last years before his death he was much involved with the Campaign for Nuclear Disarmament. His autobiography was published in three volumes in 1967–1969, but there is also a charming "epitome" written by him at the beginning of *Portraits from Memory* (1956).

Philosophical Note

Russell has probably exerted more influence in the twentieth century than any other contemporary academic philosopher. His influence has been both in terms of his radical ideas and his practical example. Thus his unbelief did not merely issue in endorsements of the arguments of Epicurus, Hume, D'Holbach *et al.*, but in a very real advocacy of a practical liberal ethic that could stand in the ideological void perceived by Nietzsche. In fact Russell's critique of religion in general and of Christianity in particular adds almost nothing to the positions represented in this book from Hobbes onward. But his style, clarity, and persistence, and, above all, his cool pursuit of the reasonable and the justifiable make Russell, in Hume's sense, the wise man of the century —the positive advocate of reason and of a free individual's values. In this and in other points of comparison, he is the Voltaire of the twentieth century.

Russell wrote a good deal on religion. His earliest significant essay is "A Free Man's Worship" (*The Independent Review*, December 1903, reprinted in *Mysticism and Logic*, 1918). A somewhat dated discussion, *Science and Religion*, came out in 1935 and Russell has a lot to say on the subject of religion in *Human Society in Ethics and Politics* (1954), as well as in numerous lesser pamphlets and essays some of which were grouped together under the title *Why I Am Not a Christian* (1957), edited by Paul Edwards. Two of his works are presented here. The first consists of the opening section of his booklet "What I Believe," which was first published in 1925 and has been reprinted several times with updated political references. This work shows Russell as the wise man proportioning his beliefs (and hopes) to the evidence. The second selection is taken from Chapter VII of *Human Society in Ethics and Politics.* It shows Russell as the wise man arguing *against* the claims of moral and social excellence often voiced on behalf of religion, and *for* the humanistic "we are alone" values of the unbeliever: values that he cherished to the end. As he put it in the last few sentences of "Reflections on My Eightieth Birthday" — "I have lived in the pursuit of a vision, both personal and social. Personal: to care for what is noble, for what is beautiful, for what is gentle; to allow moments of insight to give wisdom at more mundane times. Social: to see in imagination the society that is to be created, where individuals grow freely, and where hate and greed and envy die because there is nothing to nourish them.

These things I believe, and the world, for all its horrors, has left me unshaken."

1. A Wise Man's Beliefs

From "What I Believe"

Man is a part of Nature, not something contrasted with Nature. His thoughts and his bodily movements follow the same laws that describe the motions of stars and atoms. The physical world is large compared with Man — larger than it was thought to be in Dante's time, but not so large as it seemed a hundred years ago. Both upward and downward, both in the large and in the small, science seems to be reaching limits. It is thought that the universe is of finite extent in space, and that light could travel round it in a few hundred millions of years. It is thought matter consists of electrons and protons, which are of finite size and of which there are only a finite number in the world. Probably their changes are not continuous, as used to be thought, but proceed by jerks, which are never smaller than a certain minimum jerk. The laws of these changes can apparently be summed up in a small number of very general principles, which determine the past and the future of the world when any small section of its history is known.

Physical science is thus approaching the stage when it will be complete, and therefore uninteresting. Given the laws governing the motions of electrons and protons, the rest is merely geography — a collection of particular facts telling their distribution throughout some portion of the world's history. The total number of facts of geography required to determine the world's history is probably finite; theoretically they could all be written down in a big book to be kept at Somerset House with a calculating machine attached which, by turning a handle, would enable the inquirer to find out the facts at other times than those recorded. It is difficult to imagine anything less interesting or more different from the passionate delights of incomplete discovery. It is like climbing a high mountain and finding nothing at the top except a restaurant where they sell ginger beer, surrounded by fog but equipped with wireless. Perhaps in the times of Ahmes the multiplication table was exciting.

Of this physical world, uninteresting in itself, Man is a part. His body, like other matter, is composed of electrons and protons, which, so far as we know, obey the same laws as those not forming part of animals or plants. There are some who maintain that physiology can never be reduced to physics, but their arguments are not very convincing and it seems prudent to suppose that they are mistaken. What we call our "thoughts" seem to depend upon the organization of tracks in the brain in the same sort of way in which journeys depend upon roads and railways. The energy used in thinking seems to have a chemical origin;

for instance, a deficiency of iodine will turn a clever man into an idiot. Mental phenomena seem to be bound up with material structure. If this be so, we cannot suppose that a solitary electron or proton can 'think'; we might as well expect a solitary individual to play a football match. We also cannot suppose that an individual's thinking survives bodily death, since that destroys the organization of the brain, and dissipates the energy which utilized the brain tracks.

God and immortality, the central dogmas of the Christian religion, find no support in science. It cannot be said that either doctrine is essential to religion, since neither is found in Buddhism. (With regard to immortality, this statement in an unqualified form might be misleading, but it is correct in the last analysis.) But we in the West have come to think of them as the irreducible minimum of theology. No doubt people will continue to entertain these beliefs, because they are pleasant, just as it is pleasant to think ourselves virtuous and our enemies wicked. But for my part I cannot see any ground for either. I do not pretend to be able to prove that there is no God. I equally cannot prove that Satan is a fiction. The Christian God may exist; so may the Gods of Olympus, or of ancient Egypt, or of Babylon. But no one of these hypotheses is more probable than any other: they lie outside the region of even probable knowledge, and therefore there is no reason to consider any of them. I shall not enlarge upon this question, as I have dealt with it elsewhere.*

The question of personal immortality stands on a somewhat different footing. Here evidence either way is possible. Persons are part of the everyday world with which science is concerned, and the conditions which determine their existence are discoverable. A drop of water is not immortal; it can be resolved into oxygen and hydrogen. If, therefore, a drop of water were to maintain that it had a quality of aqueousness which would survive its dissolution we should be inclined to be sceptical. In like manner we know that the brain is not immortal, and that the organized energy of a living body becomes, as it were, demobilized at death, and therefore not available for collective action. All the evidence goes to show that what we regard as our mental life is bound up with brain structure and organized bodily energy. Therefore it is rational to suppose that mental life ceases when bodily life ceases. The argument is only one of probability, but it is as strong as those upon which most scientific conclusions are based.

There are various grounds upon which this conclusion might be attacked. Psychical research professes to have actual scientific evidence of survival, and undoubtedly its procedure is, in principle, scientifically correct. Evidence of this sort might be so overwhelming that no one with a scientific temper could reject it. The weight to be attached

* See my *Philosophy of Leibniz,* Chapter XV.

to the evidence, however, must depend upon the antecedent probability of the hypothesis of survival. There are always different ways of accounting for any set of phenomena and of these we should prefer the one which is antecedentally least improbable. Those who already think it likely that we survive death will be ready to view this theory as the best explanation of psychical phenomena. Those who, on other grounds, regard this theory as implausible will seek for other explanations. For my part, I consider the evidence so far adduced by psychical research in favor of survival much weaker than the physiological evidence on the other side. But I fully admit that it might at any moment become stronger, and in that case it would be unscientific to disbelieve in survival.

Survival of bodily death is, however, a different matter from immortality: it may only mean a postponement of psychical death. It is immortality that men desire to believe in. Believers in immortality will object to physiological arguments, such as I have been using, on the ground that soul and body are totally disparate, and that the soul is something quite other than its empirical manifestations through our bodily organs. I believe this to be a metaphysical superstition. Mind and matter alike are for certain purposes convenient terms, but are not ultimate realities. Electrons and protons, like the soul, are logical fictions; each is really a history, a series of events, not a single persistent entity. In the case of the soul, this is obvious from the facts of growth. Whoever considers conception, gestation, and infancy cannot seriously believe that the soul is an indivisible something, perfect and complete throughout this process. It is evident that it grows like the body, and that it derives both from the spermatozoon and from the ovum, so that it cannot be indivisible. This is not materialism: it is merely the recognition that everything interesting is a matter of organization, not of primal substance.

Metaphysicians have advanced innumerable arguments to prove that the soul must be immortal. There is one simple test by which all these arguments can be demolished. They all prove equally that the soul must pervade all space. But as we are not so anxious to be fat as to live long, none of the metaphysicians in question have ever noticed this application of their reasonings. This is an instance of the amazing power of desire in blinding even very able men to fallacies which would otherwise be obvious at once. If we were not afraid of death, I do not believe that the idea of immortality would ever have arisen.

Fear is the basis of religious dogma, as of so much else in human life. Fear of human beings, individually or collectively, dominates much of our social life, but it is fear of nature that gives rise to religion. The antithesis of mind and matter is, as we have seen, more or less illusory; but there is another antithesis which is more important—that, namely, between things that can be affected by our desires and things that cannot be so affected. The line between the two is neither sharp nor immutable — as science advances, more and more things are brought under human control. Nevertheless there remain things definitely on the other side. Among these are all the *large* facts of our world, the sort of facts that are dealt with by astronomy. It is only facts on or near the surface of the earth that we can, to some extent, mould to suit our desires. And even on the surface of the earth our powers are very limited. Above all, we cannot prevent death, although we can often delay it.

Religion is an attempt to overcome this antithesis. If the world is controlled by God, and God can be moved by prayer, we acquired a share in omnipotence. In former days, miracles happened in answer to prayer; they still do in the Catholic Church, but Protestants have lost this power. However, it is possible to dispense with miracles, since Providence has decreed that the operation of natural laws shall produce the best possible results. Thus belief in God still serves to humanize the world of nature, and to make men feel that physical forces are really their allies. In like manner immortality removes the terror from death. People who believe that when they die they will inherit eternal bliss may be expected to view death without horror, though, fortunately for medical men, this does not invariably happen. It does, however, soothe men's fears somewhat even when it cannot allay them wholly.

Religion, since it has its source in terror, has dignified certain kinds of fear, and made people think them not disgraceful. In this it has done mankind a great disservice: *all* fear is bad. I believe that when I die I shall rot, and nothing of my ego will survive. I am not young, and I love life. But I should scorn to shiver with terror at the thought of annihilation. Happiness is none the less true happiness because it must come to an end, nor do thought and love lose their value because they are not everlasting. Many a man has borne himself proudly on the scaffold; surely the same pride should teach us to think truly about man's place in the world. Even if the open windows of science at first make us shiver after the cosy indoor warmth of traditional humanizing myths, in the end the fresh air brings vigour, and the great spaces have a splendour of their own.

The philosophy of nature is one thing, the philosophy of value is quite another. Nothing but harm can come of confusing them. What we think good, what we should like, has no bearing whatever upon what is, which is the question for the philosophy of nature. On the other hand, we cannot be forbidden to value this or that on the ground that the non-human world does not value it, nor can we be compelled to admire anything because it is a "law of nature." Undoubtedly we are part of nature, which has produced our desires, our hopes and fears, in accordance with laws which the physicist is beginning to discover. In this sense we are part of nature, we are subordinated to nature, the outcome of natural laws, and their victims in the long run.

The philosophy of nature must not be unduly terrestrial; for it, the earth is merely one of the smaller planets of one of the smaller stars of the Milky Way. It would be ridiculous to warp the philosophy of nature in order to bring out results that are pleasing to the tiny parasites of this insignificant planet. Vitalism as a philosophy, and evolutionism, show, in this respect, a lack of sense of proportion and logical relevance. They regard the facts of life, which are personally interesting to us, as having a cosmic significance, not a significance confined to the earth's surface. Optimism and pessimism, as cosmic philosophies, show the same naïve humanism; the great world, so far as we know it from the philosophy of nature, is neither good nor bad, and is not concerned to make us happy or unhappy. All such philosophies spring from self-importance, and are best corrected by a little astronomy.

But in the philosophy of value the situation is reversed. Nature is only a part of what we can imagine; everything, real or imagined, can be appraised by us, and there is no outside standard to show that our valuation is wrong. We are ourselves the ultimate and irrefutable arbiters of value, and in the world of value Nature is only a part. Thus in this world we are greater than Nature. In the world of values, Nature in itself is neutral, neither good nor bad, deserving of neither admiration nor censure. It is we who create value and our desires which confer value. In this realm we are kings, and we debase our kingship if we bow down to Nature. It is for us to determine the good life, not for Nature —not even for Nature personified as God.

2. A Wise Man's Political Values

From *Human Society in Ethics and Politics*, Chapter 7

But let us leave the details of politics and consider our question more generally. Christians hold that their faith does good, but other faiths do harm. At any rate, they hold this about the Communist faith. What I wish to maintain is that *all* faiths do harm. We may define "faith" as a firm belief in something for which there is no evidence. Where there is evidence, no one speaks of "faith." We do not speak of faith that two and two are four or that the earth is round. We only speak of faith when we wish to substitute emotion for evidence. The substitution of emotion for evidence is apt to lead to strife, since different groups substitute different emotions. Christians have faith in the Resurrection, Communists have faith in Marx's Theory of Value. Neither faith can be defended rationally, and each therefore is defended by propaganda and, if necessary, by war. The two are equal in this respect. If you think it immensely important that people should believe something which cannot be rationally defended, it makes no difference what the something is. Where you control the government, you teach the something to the immature minds of children and you burn or prohibit books which teach the contrary. Where you do not control the government, you will, if you are strong enough, build up armed forces with a view to conquest. All this is an inevitable consequence of any strongly-held faith unless, like the Quakers, you are content to remain forever a tiny minority.

It is completely mysterious to me that there are apparently sane people who think that a belief in Christianity might prevent war. Such people seem totally unable to learn anything from history. The Roman State became Christian at the time of Constantine, and was almost continually at war until it ceased to exist. The Christian States which succeeded to it continued to fight each other, though, it must be confessed, they also from time to time fought states which were not Christian. From the time of Constantine to the present day there has been no shred of evidence to show that Christian States are less warlike than others. Indeed, some of the most ferocious wars have been due to disputes between different kinds of Christianity. Nobody can deny that Luther and Loyola were Christians; nobody can deny that their differences were associated with a long period of ferocious wars.

There are those who argue that Christianity, though it may not be true, is very useful as promoting social cohesion, and, though it may not be perfect, is better than any other faith that has the same social effectiveness. I will admit that I would rather see the whole world Christian than Marxist. I find the Marxist faith more repellent than any other that has been adopted by civilized nations (except perhaps the Aztecs). But I am quite unwilling to accept the view that social cohesion is impossible except by the help of useful lies. I know that this view has the sanction of Plato and of a long line of practical politicians, but I think that even from a practical point of view it is mistaken. It is not necessary for purposes of self-defence where rational arguments suffice. It is necessary for a crusade, but I cannot think of any case in which a crusade has done any good whatever. When people regard Christianity as part of re-armament they are taking out of it whatever spiritual merit it may have. And, in order that it may be effective as re-armament, it is generally thought that it must be pugnacious, dogmatic and narrow-minded. When people think of Christianity as a help in fighting the Russians, it is not the Quaker type of Christianity that they have in view, but something more in the style of Senator McCarthy. What makes a creed effective in war is its negative aspect, that is to say, its hatred of those who do not adopt it. Without this hatred it serves no bellicose purpose. But as soon as it is used as a weapon of war, it is the hatred of un-believers that becomes prominent. Consequently, when two faiths fight each other each develops its worst aspects, and even copies whatever it imagines to be effective in the faith that it is combating.

The belief that fanaticism promotes success in war is one that is not borne out by history, although it is constantly assumed by those who

cloak their ignorance under the name of "realism." When the Romans
conquered the Mediterranean world, fanaticism played no part in their
success. The motives of Roman Generals were either to acquire the
gold reserves of temples with a view to keeping half for themselves and
giving half to their soldiers, or, as in the case of Caesar, to gain the
prestige which would enable them to win elections in Rome and defy
their creditors. In the early contests of Christians and Mohammedans it
was the Christians who were fanatical and the Mohammedans who
were successful. Christian propaganda has invented stories of Moham-
medan intolerance, but these are wholly false as applied to the early
centuries of Islam. Every Christian has been taught the story of the
Caliph destroying the Library of Alexandria. As a matter of fact, this
Library was frequently destroyed and frequently re-created. Its first
destroyer was Julius Caesar, and its last antedated the Prophet. The
early Mohammedans, unlike the Christians, tolerated those whom they
called "people of the Book", provided they paid tribute. In contrast to
the Christians, who persecuted not only pagans but each other, the
Mohammedans were welcomed for their broadmindedness, and it was
largely this that facilitated their conquests. To come to later times,
Spain was ruined by fanatical hatred of Jews and Moors; France was
disastrously impoverished by the persecution of Huguenots; and one
main cause of Hitler's defeat was his failure to employ Jews in atomic
research. Ever since the time of Archimedes war has been a science,
and proficiency in science has been a main cause of victory. But proficiency in science is very difficult to combine with fanaticism. We all
know how, under the orders of Stalin, Russian biologists were compelled to subscribe to Lysenko's errors. It is obvious to every person
capable of free scientific inquiry that the doctrines of Lysenko are less
likely to increase the wheat supply of Russian than those of orthodox
geneticists are to increase the wheat supply of the West. I think it is
also very doubtful whether nuclear research can long continue to
flourish in such an atmosphere as Stalin produced in Russia. Perhaps
Russia is now going to become liberal, and perhaps it will be in the
United States that bigotry will hamper atomic research. As to this, I
express no opinion. But, however this may be, it is clear that, without
intellectual freedom, scientific warfare is not likely to remain long
successful.

But let us look at this matter of fanaticism somewhat more broadly.
The contention of those who advocate fanaticism without being fanatics
is, to my mind, not only false, but ignoble. It seems to be thought that
unless everybody in a nation is compelled, either by persecution or by
an education which destroys the power of thought, to believe things
which no rational man can believe, that nation will be so torn by
dissensions or so paralyzed by hesitant doubts that it will inevitably
come to grief. Not only, as I have already argued, is there no historical

evidence for this view, but it is also quite contrary to what ought to be expected. When a British military expedition marched to Lhasa in 1905, the Tibetan soldiers at first opposed it bravely, because the Priests had pronounced charms which afforded protection against lead. When the soldiers nevertheless were killed, the Priests excused themselves on the ground that the bullets contained nickel, against which their charms had been powerless. After this, the British troops encountered little opposition. Philip II of Spain was so persuaded that Heaven must bless his warfare against the heretics that he neglected entirely to consider the difference between fighting the English and fighting the Turks, and so he was defeated. There is a very widespread belief that people can be induced to believe what is contrary to fact in one domain while remaining scientific in another. This is not the case. It is by no means easy to keep one's mind open to fresh evidence, and it is almost impossible to achieve this in one direction, if, in another, one has a carefully fostered blindness.

There is something feeble, and a little contemptible, about a man who cannot face the perils of life without the help of comfortable myths. Almost inevitably some part of him is aware that they are myths and that he believes them only because they are comforting. But he dare not face this thought, and he therefore cannot carry his own reflections to any logical conclusion. Moreover, since he is aware, however dimly, that his opinions are not rational, he becomes furious when they are disputed. He therefore adopts persecutions, censorship, and a narrowly cramping education as essentials of statecraft. In so far as he is successful, he produces a population which is timid and unadventurous and incapable of progress. Authoritarian rules have always aimed at producing such a population. They have usually succeeded, and by their success have brought their countries to ruin.

Many of the objections to what is called "faith" do not depend in any way upon what the faith in question may be. You may believe in the verbal inspiration of the Bible or of the Koran or of Marx's *Capital*. Whichever of these beliefs you entertain, you have to close your mind against evidence; and if you close your mind against evidence in one respect, you will also do so in another, if the temptation is strong. The Duke of Wellington never allowed himself to doubt the value of the playing fields of Eton, and was therefore never able to accept the superiority of the rifle to the old-fashioned musket. You may say that belief in God is not as harmful as belief in the playing fields of Eton. I will not argue on this point, except to say that it becomes harmful in proportion as you secretly doubt whether it is in accordance with the facts. The important thing is not what you believe, but how you believe it. There was a time when it was rational to believe that the earth is flat. At that time this belief did not have the bad consequences belonging to what is called "faith." But the people who, in our day, persist in believing that the earth is flat, have to close their minds against reason and to open them to every kind of absurdity in addition to the one from which they start. If you think that your belief is based upon reason, you will support it by argument, rather than by persecution, and will abandon it if the argument goes against you. But if your belief is based on faith, you will realize that argument is useless, and will therefore resort to force either in the form of persecution or by stunting and distorting the minds of the young in what is called "education." This last is peculiarly dastardly, since it takes advantage of the defencelessness of immature minds. Unfortunately it is practised in a greater or less degree in the schools of every civilized country.

In addition to the general argument against faith, there is something peculiarly odious in the contention that the principles of the Sermon on the Mount are to be adopted with a view to making atom bombs more effective. If I were a Christian, I should consider this the absolute extreme of blasphemy.

I do not believe that a decay of dogmatic belief can do anything but good. I admit at once that new systems of dogma, such as those of the Nazis and the Communists, are even worse than the old systems, but they could never have acquired a hold over men's minds if orthodox dogmatic habits had not been instilled in youth. Stalin's language is full of reminiscences of the theological seminary in which he received his training. What the world needs is not dogma, but an attitude of scientific inquiry, combined with a belief that the torture of millions is not desirable, whether inflicted by Stalin or by a Deity imagined in the likeness of the believer.

18

SIR ALFRED AYER ON THE LACK OF SIGNIFICANCE IN RELIGIOUS LANGUAGE

In a life of Bishop John Robinson, author of *Honest to God*, to be published next month, there is an account of a visit to Robinson in a Cambridge hospital by Sir Herman Bondi, now Master of Churchill College Cambridge, then chairman of the National Environment Research Council.

"God," said Bondi to Robinson, "was recently applying for a grant from a scientific institution to study the origins of Creation. It was declined on three grounds: first that there was no visible evidence that He had done any work on the subject for a long time; second because no one had been able to replicate the experiment; and third because the only records of it had not been published in any recognized scientific journal. . . . "

Times Higher Education Supplement,
September 18, 1987

Biographical Note

A. J. Ayer was born in 1910 and educated at Eton and Christ Church, Oxford. Greatly influenced by the logical positivist philosophy that was then concentrated in the University of Vienna, he published in 1936, while teaching at Christ Church, *Language, Truth and Logic*, a book of exceptional clarity and vigor that firmly established a logical positivist influence in English language philosophy. In 1940 Ayer joined the Welsh Guards but was employed for most of the war in military intelligence. From 1946 to 1959 he held the Grote Professorship of the Philosophy of Mind and Logic at London University, and from 1959 until his retirement in 1978 he was Wykeham Professor of Logic at the University of Oxford. His numerous and important publications include *The Problem of Knowledge* (1956), *The Concept of a Person* (1963), and *Probability and Evidence* (1972). Sir Alfred was knighted in 1970.

Philosophical Note

Ayer has not written extensively on religion. Apart from a number of incidentally related discussions in larger works, his place in this book depends upon three short but seminal discussions: the last chapter of *The Central Questions of Philosophy* (1973), where, in addition to discussing the arguments for the existence of God, he argues with characteristic elegance and precision that morality does not depend upon religion; the essay "Chance," *Scientific American* 1965 (reprinted in *Metaphysics and Common Sense*, 1967, which deals with aspects of the design argument; and, above all, the section on religious language from *Language, Truth and Logic*. (This is reprinted here with the author's generous permission.) The philosophy of logical positivism, with its demand that verifiability should be the criterion of the significance of propositions, has been in full retreat for more than twenty years. But its critique of religious language, particularly in Ayer's presentation, exerted very considerable pressure toward academic and philosophical unbelief in the period following World War II. In particular, a variant of its thesis was employed to great effect in Antony Flew's much-anthologised thousand-word essay "Theology and Falsification," which was first published in 1950. The challenge with which Flew ends almost sets the seal on contemporary unbelief: "I therefore put to the succeeding symposiasts the simple central questions, 'What would have to occur or to have occurred to constitute for you a disproof of the love of, or of the existence of, God?'"

The Lack of Significance in Religious Language

From *Language Truth and Logic*, Chapter 6

It is now generally admitted, at any rate by philosophers, that the existence of a being having the attributes which define the god of any non-animistic religion cannot be demonstratively proved. To see that this is so, we have only to ask ourselves what are the premises from which the existence of such a god could be deduced. If the conclusion that a god exists is to be demonstratively certain, then these premises must be certain; for, as the conclusion of a deductive argument is already contained in the premises, any uncertainty there may be about the truth of the premises is necessarily shared by it. But we know that no empirical proposition can ever be anything more than probable. It is only *a priori* propositions that are logically certain. But we cannot deduce the existence of a god from an *a priori* proposition. For we know that the reason why *a priori* propositions are certain is that they are tautologies. And from a set of tautologies nothing but a further tautology can be validly deduced. It follows that there is no possibility of demonstrating the existence of a god.

What is not so generally recognised is that there can be no way of proving that the existence of a god, such as the God of Christianity, is even probable. Yet this also is easily shown. For if the existence of such a god were probable, then the proposition that he existed would be an empirical hypothesis. And in that case it would be possible to deduce from it, and other empirical hypotheses, certain experiential propositions which were not deducible from those other hypotheses alone. But in fact this is not possible. It is sometimes claimed, indeed, that the existence of a certain sort of regularity in nature constitutes sufficient evidence for the existence of a god. But if the sentence "God exists" entails no more than that certain types of phenomena occur in certain sequences, then to assert the existence of a god will be simply equivalent to asserting that there is the requisite regularity in nature; and no religious man would admit that this was all he intended to assert in asserting the existence of a god. He would say that in talking about God, he was talking about a transcendent being who might be known through certain empirical manifestations, but certainly could not be defined in terms of those manifestations. But in that case the term "god" is a metaphysical term. And if "god" is a metaphysical term, then it cannot be even probable that a god exists. For to say that "God exists" is to make a metaphysical utterance which cannot be either true or false. And by the same criterion, no sentence which purports to describe the nature of a transcendent god can possess any literal significance.

It is important not to confuse this view of religious assertions with the view that is adopted by atheists, or agnostics.[1] For it is characteristic of an agnostic to hold that the existence of a god is a possibility in which there is no good reason either to believe or disbelieve; and it is characteristic of an atheist to hold that it is at least probable that no god exists. And our view that all utterances about the nature of God are nonsensical, so far from being identical with, or even lending any support to, either of these familiar contentions, is actually incompatible with them. For if the assertion that there is a god is nonsensical, then the atheist's assertion that there is no god is equally nonsensical, since it is only a significant proposition that can be significantly contradicted. As for the agnostic, although he refrains from saying either that there is or that there is not a god, he does not deny that the question whether a transcendent god exists is a genuine question. He does not deny that the two sentences "There is a transcendent god" and "There is no transcendent god" express propositions one of which is actually true and the other false. All he says is that we have no means of telling which of them is true, and therefore ought not to commit ourselves to either. But we have seen that the sentences in question do not express propositions at all. And this means that agnosticism also is ruled out.

---

[1] This point was suggested to me by Professor H. H. Price.

Thus we offer the theist the same comfort as we gave to the moralist. His assertions cannot possibly be valid, but they cannot be invalid either. As he says nothing at all about the world, he cannot justly be accused of saying anything false, or anything for which he has insufficient grounds. It is only when the theist claims that in asserting the existence of a transcendent god he is expressing a genuine proposition that we are entitled to disagree with him.

It is to be remarked that in cases where deities are identified with natural objects, assertions concerning them may be allowed to be significant. If, for example, a man tells me that the occurrence of thunder is alone both necessary and sufficient to establish the truth of the proposition that Jehovah is angry, I may conclude that, in his usage of words, the sentence "Jehovah is angry" is equivalent to "It is thundering." But in sophisticated religions, though they may be to some extent based on men's awe of natural process which they cannot sufficiently understand, the "person" who is supposed to control the empirical world is not himself located in it; he is held to be superior to the empirical world, and so outside it; and he is endowed with super-empirical attributes. But the notion of a person whose essential attributes are non-empirical is not an intelligible notion at all. We may have a word which is used as if it named this "person," but, unless the sentences in which it occurs express propositions which are empirically verifiable, it cannot be said to symbolize anything. And this is the case with regard to the word "god," in the usage in which it is intended to refer to a transcendent object. The mere existence of the noun is enough to foster the illusion that there is a real, or at any rate a possible entity corresponding to it. It is only when we enquire what God's attributes are that we discover that "God," in this usage, is not a genuine name.

It is common to find belief in a transcendent god conjoined with belief in an after-life. But, in the form which it usually takes, the content of this belief is not a genuine hypothesis. To say that men do not ever die, or that the state of death is merely a state of prolonged insensibility, is indeed to express a significant proposition, though all the available evidence goes to show that it is false. But to say that there is something imperceptible inside a man, which is his soul or his real self, and that it goes on living after he is dead, is to make a metaphysical assertion which has no more factual content than the assertion that there is a transcendent god.

It is worth mentioning that, according to the account which we have given of religious assertions, there is no logical ground for antagonism between religion and natural science. As far as the question of truth or falsehood is concerned, there is no opposition between the natural scientist and the theist who believes in a transcendent god. For since the religious utterances of the theist are not genuine propositions at all, they cannot stand in any logical relation to the propositions of science. Such antagonism as there is between religion and science appears to consist in the fact that science takes away one of the motives which make men religious. For it is acknowledged that one of the ultimate sources of religious feeling lies in the inability of men to determine their own destiny; and science tends to destroy the feeling of awe with which men regard an alien world, by making them believe that they can understand and anticipate the course of natural phenomena, and even to some extent control it. The fact that it has recently become fashionable for physicists themselves to be sympathetic towards religion is a point in favour of this hypothesis. For this sympathy towards religion marks the physicists' own lack of confidence in the validity of their hypotheses, which is a reaction on their part from the anti-religious dogmatism of nineteenth-century scientists, and a natural outcome of the crisis through which physics has just passed.

It is not within the scope of this enquiry to enter more deeply into the causes of religious feeling, or to discuss the probability of the continuance of religious belief. We are concerned only to answer those questions which arise out of our discussion of the possibility of religious knowledge. The point which we wish to establish is that there cannot be any transcendent truths of religion. For the sentences which the theist uses to express such "truths" are not literally significant.

An interesting feature of this conclusion is that it accords with what many theists are accustomed to say themselves. For we are often told that the nature of God is a mystery which transcends the human understanding. But to say that something transcends the human understanding is to say that it is unintelligible. And what is unintelligible cannot significantly be described. Again, we are told that God is not an object of reason but an object of faith. This may be nothing more than an admission that the existence of God must be taken on trust, since it cannot be proved. But it may also be an assertion that God is the object of a purely mystical intuition, and cannot therefore be defined in terms which are intelligible to the reason. And I think there are many theists who would assert this. But if one allows that it is impossible to define God in intelligible terms, then one is allowing that it is impossible for a sentence both to be significant and to be about God. If a mystic admits that the object of his vision is something which cannot be described, then he must also admit that he is bound to talk nonsense when he describes it.

For his part, the mystic may protest that his intuition does reveal truths to him, even though he cannot explain to others what these truths are; and that we who do not possess this faculty of intuition can have no ground for denying that it is a cognitive faculty. For we can hardly maintain *a priori* that there are no ways of discovering true propositions except those which we ourselves employ. The answer is that we set no limit to the number of ways in which one may come to formulate a true proposition. We do not in any way deny that a synthetic truth may be discovered by purely intuitive methods as well as by the rational method of induction. But we do say that every synthetic proposition, however it may have been arrived at, must be subject to the test of actual experience. We do not deny *a priori* that the mystic is able to discover truths by his own special methods. We wait to hear what are the propositions which embody his discoveries, in order to see whether they are verified or confuted by our empirical observations. But the mystic, so far from producing propositions which are empirically verified, is unable to produce any intelligible propositions at all. And therefore we say that his intuition has not revealed to him any facts. It is no use his saying that he has apprehended facts but is unable to express them. For we know that if he really had acquired any information, he would be able to express it. He would be able to indicate in some way or other how the genuineness of his discovery might be empirically determined. The fact that he cannot reveal what he "knows," or even himself devise an empirical test to validate his "knowledge," shows that his state of mystical intuition is not a genuinely cognitive state. So that in describing his vision the mystic does not give us any information about the external world; he merely gives us indirect information about the condition of his own mind.

These considerations dispose of the argument from religious experience, which many philosophers still regard as a valid argument in favour of the existence of a god. They say that it is logically possible for men to be immediately acquainted with God, as they are immediately acquainted with a sense-content, and that there is no reason why one should be prepared to believe a man when he says that he is seeing a yellow patch, and refuse to believe him when he says that he is seeing God. The answer to this is that if the man who asserts that he is seeing God is merely asserting that he is experiencing a peculiar kind of sense-content, then we do not for a moment deny that his assertion may be true. But, ordinarily, the man who says that he is seeing God is saying not merely that he is experiencing a religious emotion, but also that there exists a transcendent being who is the object of this emotion; just as the man who says that he sees a yellow patch is ordinarily saying not merely that his visual sense-field contains a yellow sense-content, but also that there exists a yellow object to which the sense-content belongs. And it is not irrational to be prepared to believe a man when he asserts the existence of a yellow object, and to refuse to believe him when he asserts the existence of a transcendent god. For whereas the sentence "There exists here a yellow-coloured material thing" expresses a genuine synthetic proposition which could be empirically verified, the sentence "There exists a transcendent god" has, as we have seen, no literal significance.

We conclude, therefore, that the argument from religious experience is altogether fallacious. The fact that people have religious experiences is interesting from the psychological point of view, but it does not in any way imply that there is such a thing as religious knowledge, any more than our having moral experiences implies that there is such a thing as moral knowledge. The theist, like the moralist, may believe that his experiences are cognitive experiences, but, unless he can formulate his "knowledge" in propositions that are empirically verifiable, we may be sure that he is deceiving himself. It follows that those philosophers who fill their books with assertions that they intuitively "know" this or that moral or religious "truth" are merely providing material for the psycho-analyst. For no act of intuition can be said to reveal a truth about any matter of fact unless it issues in verifiable propositions. And all such propositions are to be incorporated in the system of empirical propositions which constitutes science.

19

SARTRE ON THE INCONSEQUENCE OF MODERN RELIGION

> People may say what they like about the decay of
> Christianity; the religious system that produced
> green Chartreuse can never really die.
>
> *Saki: H. H. Munro*

Biographical Note

Jean-Paul Sartre (1905–1980) is best known as the French literary advocate of the philosophy of existentialism. His novels and plays deal with political and social issues. His large (and largely unreadable) book *Being and Nothingness* (1943) had considerable influence among the intelligentsia of post-war France. His political sympathies were Marxist, but after 1968 he adopted far-left solutions to issues on an *ad hoc* basis.

Philosophical Note

It is fitting that our survey of some of the great contributions to unbelief should end, not with an impassioned rejection of religious beliefs or with the elevation of some secular system to the position of an ideological substitute for religion, but with the commitment to religion reduced to a triviality. In the following passage from the *War Diaries*, Sartre does not rebel or reject or affirm. Religion has simply become irrelevant. It survives as a social occasion or an aesthetic experience. Its content has become so thin that it can readily be shrugged off by a twelve-year-old boy. It remains a mildly benevolent but ineffectual background to the real affairs of life: benevolent because it has no longer the power to compel or to frighten; ineffectual because it has become a museum of culture rather than a gateway to everlasting life.

212

The Inconsequence of Modern Religion

From *The War Diaries*

I lost my faith at the age of twelve. But I don't imagine I ever believed very strongly. My grandfather was Protestant, my grandmother Catholic. But so far as I could see, their religious feelings if decent were frigid. With my grandfather, there was a rejection on principle of the whole religious business, as a great cultural phenomenon, combined with a "dissenter's" contempt for clerics. I think he cracked anti-clerical jokes at table and my grandmother rapped him on the fingers, saying: "Be quiet, Dad!" My mother made me take my first communion, but I think it was more out of respect for my future freedom than from true conviction. Rather as certain people have their children circumcised for reasons of hygiene. She has no religion, but rather a vague religiosity, which consoles her a bit when necessary and leaves her strictly in peace the rest of the time.

I hardly have any religious memories: however, I can still see myself at the age of seven or eight, in Rue Le Goff, burning the lace curtains on the window with a match; and this memory is connected with the Good Lord, I don't know why. Perhaps because this incendiary act had no witness, and yet I was thinking: "The Good Lord can see me." I remember too that I wrote an essay on Jesus at Abbé Dibildos's catechism class (this was on the premises of the École Bossuet), and that I won a silver-paper medal. I am still filled with admiration and delight when I think of that essay and that medal, but there's nothing religious about this. The fact is my mother had copied out my composition in her beautiful hand, and I imagine the impression that seeing my prose transcribed in this way made on me was more or less comparable to the sense of wonder I felt at seeing myself in print for the first time. Moreover, the silver medal, which was a beautiful, glistening, pale-grey colour, had to be stuck on to the first page of the exercise so that the whole formed a superb and precious object. In addition to this, the abbé who'd corrected my work was very young, a pretty boy with red hair, a pale face and beautiful hands. I seek in vain, I can find nothing else within me.

Oh yes! They used still to take me quite often to church, but (and this, which comes back to me, is a pretty good indication of the type of bourgeoisie I belong to) it was primarily in order to hear fine music — the organ of St-Sulpice or Notre-Dame. It is clear to me what feelings of high spirituality were provoked, in my mother and grandmother, by this union between the purest forms of art and the most elevated forms of faith; and it is also clear to me that, with these teachers' wives and daughters, religion touched them only if it decked itself out with the charms of music. They no longer had any very clear idea, I imagine, whether the music thrilled them because it was religious or the religion because it was harmonious. And their respect for religion merged with their academic cult of spiritual values. For my own part I understood nothing of that music, those great moaning winds that used suddenly to fill the church. Yet, in spite of everything, those masses were linked in my mind with the idea of virtue. Since I used to grow very bored, my mother had discovered how to handle me by explaining that a *really* good little boy had to sit like a statue at mass. So, at little cost, I achieved that perfect goodness for the hour that the service lasted, in order to be able afterwards to ask my mother, sure of her reply: "Have I been good, Mummy?" I even used to overdo things, intent on avoiding even the smallest creak of my chair or scuffling of my feet. But I used to hate kneeling down, since for some reason I have two rather sensitive bumps on my knees.

So there you are. It's pretty thin. God existed, but I didn't concern myself with him at all. And then one day at La Rochelle, while waiting for the Machado girls who used to keep me company every morning on my way to lycée, I grew impatient at their lateness and, to while away the time, decided to think about God. "Well," I said, "he doesn't exist." It was something authentically self-evident, although I have no idea any more what it was based on. And then it was over and done with. I never thought about it again; I was no more concerned with that dead God than I had been bothered about the living God. I imagine it would be hard to find a less religious nature than mine. I settled the question once and for all at the age of twelve. Much later I studied religious proofs and atheist arguments. I appraised the fortunes of their disputes. I was fond of saying that Kant's objections did not affect Descartes's ontological proof. But all that struck me as hardly any more alive than the Quarrel of Ancients and Moderns. I think I ought to say all this because, as I have said, I am affected by moralism, and because moralism often has its source in religion. But with me it was nothing of the kind. Besides, the truth is I was brought up and educated by relatives and teachers most of whom were champions of secular morality and everywhere sought to replace religious morality by it.

20

EPILOGUE: MORTALITY

Ask not ('tis forbidden knowledge), what our
  destined term of years,
Mine and yours; nor scan the tables of your
  Babylonish seers.
Better far to bear the future, my Leuconoe,
  like the past,
Whether Jove has many winters yet to give,
  or this our last:
This, that makes the Tyrrhene billows spend
  their strength against the shore.
Strain your wine and prove your wisdom!
  Life is short; should hope be more?
In the moment of our talking, envious time
  has ebb'd away.
Seize the present; trust tomorrow e'en as little
  as you may.

Horace, Odes, I xi., c. 30 B.C.

Philosophical Note

By far the majority of the authors represented in this collection have
tried to show either that a true account of the nature of things is
incompatible with belief in gods, that the reasons given for belief in
gods are defective, that the phenomenon of religion can be fully accounted for without recourse to questions about the truth of what
religions proclaim, or that religion is socially pernicious and morally
distorting. But (as was pointed out in the Introduction) unbelief has
three typical aspects. These are (a) — the one with which we have
mostly been concerned — lack of belief in supernatural agents; (b) lack
of belief in miracles — a necessary consequence of the first if miracles
are taken to be interventions in natural processes by gods or by lesser
supernatural agents; and (c) lack of belief in the continuance of any
individual person after death. But this last aspect of unbelief has far
more importance for the position of the unbeliever than does a lack of
belief in miracles, because although few of us expect to encounter
putative miracles, *all* of us expect to encounter death.

The first and obvious thing to note — although it is not always noted
— is that belief in individual survival after death is logically independent of (and on historical occasions has been entertained as a distinct

215

belief from) belief in gods. The writer of the Old Testament book *Ecclesiastes* does believe in the God of the Jews, but does *not* believe in his own survival; where the tree falls, there shall it lie (see p. 53). Conversely it is entirely possible for persons who do not believe in gods to be convinced, rightly or wrongly, for example from the data of parapsychology, that individuals survive death, at least for a period and in a locality. So people can be, and have been, unbelievers in life after death and believers in gods, and vice versa.

Nevertheless everyone will recognize that belief in personal survival after death is commonly — and almost always in the cases of Christianity and Islam — associated with belief in the God. It is the power of the God that sustains the conditions which are supposed to make possible our survival, and the God's promise or revelation which assures us that we do in fact survive. Similarly, a lack of belief in gods is commonly accompanied with a lack of belief in personal survival after death, and it is this association which is the reason for concluding the selection of unbelief with two seminal accounts of human mortality, that of Lucretius and Hume's. The final item — A. E. Housman's poem — is the most perfect short statement known to me of the outcome of Epicurean unbelief: the acute awareness of the fantasy of unguided matter which made *me*, and of the friendship to *you* which I can offer *now* but never again.

1. The Epicurean Argument

From Lucretius, *De Rerum Natura*, III

Two of the principal purposes of Lucretius' philosophical poem *De Rerum Natura* (*On the Nature of Things*) are the delivery of humanity from fear of gods and the delivery of humanity from fear of death. Book III is a sustained assault upon the latter fear. It both argues and urges that people are mortal and concludes with the great hymn to mortality which has attracted poets and translators from Dryden onward. The 1,094 lines of Latin verse in Book III fall into four sections. There is a brief address (the first 30 lines) to Epicurus giving thanks to him for opening the secrets of nature and thus delivering humanity from fear. Lines 31 to 416 deal with the relations between mind, body, and the principle of life. This opens the way for the dense collection of arguments (28 can be distinguished) in lines 417 to 829 designed to show that mind and body disintegrate together at death. Lines 830 to the end are the unique hymn to mortality.

These are poetic and philosophic glories of the first order. They express most of the grounds — both in argument and sentiment — for subsequent and particularly modern belief in mortality (compare, for example, Russell's "What I Believe," p. 197). But for the reader of today, Lucretius, whether rendered in prose or poetry, sounds strange.

The problem is the medium he uses—blank verse—and the problem is made worse by translation. In prose versions one seems to be reading philosophy gratuitously embellished with adjectives and pictorial images. In verse, one seems to be reading poetry curiously cramped with tight little philosophical arguments. In rendering the hymn to mortality, a prose translation is given based on that of H. A. J. Munro, which was first published in 1864. But the translation gives way to verse where the original lines were rendered into quatrains in the meter of Omar Khayyam by W. H. Mallock in 1900. The translation is preceded by a summary of the argument to line 830. The mixture of verse and prose is meant to remind the reader of the double character —poetry and philosophy—in the original.

MIND AND BODY (summary, lines 31–416)   After the initial thanksgiving address to Epicurus, lines 31 to 93 express Lucretius' preliminary statement of the view that undue love of life that arises from a fear of death is personally and morally stultifying. Line 94 begins the discussion of the relation between mind and body. Mind (*animus*—whatever thinks or wills) is usually taken to be the same as the intelligence (*mens*) and is a localized part of a person in the same sense that his or her eye or foot is a part of the person. Likewise the vital principle of the body (*anima*—the soul or breath of the body; that which makes it live) is a part of the body but dispersed throughout its members. Mind and the vital principle have one nature in common and can be spoken of as one thing. They function as causes of bodily states (e.g., acute fear can cause fainting). Moreover, since bodily movements are only communicated by the impact—in some sense—of matter on matter, and mind can move body, mind must be a form of matter. But the material of the mind must be very tenuous since at death no physical change of weight is detectable, just as the departure of the bouquet of a wine leaves the apparent bulk of the liquid undiminished. (Lucretius is speaking in the old mode that assumes that at a person's last breath, the *anima* literally departs from the person leaving behind the decomposing body. Lucretius' radical assertion is that part of that decomposing body is the mind. It is like saying that at death *life* leaves an individual, but, of course, this *life* is not identical with the person of the individual: *that* is all ended in the dead body.)

THE ARGUMENTS FOR MORTALITY (summary, lines 417–829)   There are three main lines of argument in Lucretius' welter of proofs of mortality. These are (a) proofs from the previously described structure of mind and body; (b) proofs from death, disease, and the influence of drugs, showing the close concomitant variation between mind and body; and (c) arguments from the incoherence of supposing that the mind exists apart from the body. A few of the arguments under each head are:

   (a) The mind is a physical part of the body, and like any other part of the body (an eye or an ear, for example) it can only putrify apart from the living whole. (Lucretius is here—lines 548–557—using "mind" as equivalent to "(active) brain"). The mind is located in an identifiable part of the body just as sight is, and can be damaged like any other bodily organ.

(b) Mind and body grow and grow old together. Bodily health influences the function of the mind and vice versa. Wine affects the mind *via* the body. Medicine affects both mind and body, *etc.*

(c) If the mind survives the body, "We must, I think, assume that it is equipped with the five senses," but this is unintelligible apart from something which is or has a body (lines 624–633). If the mind is immortal, then it *always* existed. Why then do we remember nothing of its previous existence? (Lines 670–678), *etc.*

The Hymn to Mortality (translation, lines 830–1094)

Death is for us, then, nothing—a mere name
   For the mere noiseless ending of a flame.
It hurts us not, for there is nothing left
To hurt: and as of old, when Carthage came

To battle, we and ours felt nought at all,
   Nor quailed to see city and farm and stall
      Flare into dust, and all our homeless fields
Trampled beneath the hordes of Hannibal,

But slumbered on and on, nor cared a jot,
   Deaf to the stress and tumult, though the lot
      Of things was doubtful, to which lords should fall
The rule of all—but we, we heeded not—

So when that wedlock of the flesh and mind
   Which makes us what we are, shall cease to bind,
      And mind and flesh, being mind and flesh no more,
Powdered to dust go whistling down the wind,

Even as our past was shall our future be.
   Others may start and tremble, but not we,
      Though heaven with the disbanded dust of earth
Be dark, or earth be drowned beneath the sea.

And even supposing the nature of the mind and power of the vital spirit do feel after they have been severed from our body, yet that is nothing to us who by the binding tie of marriage between body and mind are formed each into one single being. And if time should gather up our matter after our death and put it once more into the position in which it now is, and the light of life be given to us again, this result would concern us not at all, when the chain of our recollection has once been snapped asunder. So now we give ourselves no concern about any self which we have been before, nor do we feel any distress on the score of that self. For when you look back on the whole past course of immeasurable time and think how various are the shapes which the motions of matter take, you may easily credit this too, that these very same seeds of which we now are formed, have often before been placed in the same order in which they now are; and yet we cannot recover this in memory. A break in our existence has been interposed, and all the motions have wandered to and fro far astray from the sensations they produced. For he whom evil is to befall, must in his own person exist at the very time it comes, if the misery and suffering are haply to have any place at all. But since death takes away this possibility, and forbids him to exist upon whom the ills can be brought, you may be sure that we have nothing to fear after death, and that he who exists not, cannot become miserable, and that it matters not a whit whether he has been born into life at any other time, when immortal death has taken away his mortal life.

Therefore when you see a man bemoaning his hard case, that after death he shall either rot with his body laid in the grave or be devoured by flames or the jaws of wild beasts, you may be sure that he rings false, and that there lurks in his heart a secret dread though he himself declare that he does not believe that any sense will remain to him after death. He does not, I think, really grant the conclusion which he professes to grant, nor the principle on which he so professes, nor does he take and force himself root and branch out of life, but all unconsciously imagines something of himself to survive. For when any one in life suggests to him that birds and beasts will rend his body after death, he makes moan for himself: he does not separate himself from that self, nor withdraw himself fully from the body so thrown out. He fancies himself that other self, and stands by and gives it a share of his own feeling. Hence he makes much moan that he has been born mortal, and does not see that after real death there will be no other self to remain in life and lament that he has met death, or to stand and grieve that his own self, there lying, is mangled or burnt. For if it is an evil after death to be pulled about by the devouring jaws of wild beasts, I cannot see why it should not be a cruel pain to be laid on fires and burn in hot flames, or to be placed in honey and stifled, or to stiffen with cold, stretched on the smooth surface of an icy slab of stone, or to be pressed down and crushed by a load of earth above.

> And yet — ah thou who art about to cease
> From toil, and lapse into perpetual peace,
>   Why will the mourners stand about thy bed,
> And sting thy parting hour with words like these? –
>
> "Never shalt thou behold thy dear home more,
> Never thy wife await thee at thy door,
>   Never again thy little climbing boy
> A father's kindness in thine eyes explore.

"All you have toiled for, all you have loved," they say,
"Is gone, is taken in a single day;"
    But never add, "All memory, all desire,
All love—these likewise shall have passed away."

Ah ignorant mourners! Did they only see
The fate which Death indeed lays up for thee,
    How would they sing a different song from this—
"Beloved, not thou the sufferer—not thou; but we.

"Thou hast lost us all; but thou, redeemed from pain,
Shalt sleep the sleep that kings desire in vain.
    Thou hast left us all; and lo, for us, for us,
A void that never shall be filled again.

"Not thine, but ours, to see the sharp flames thrust
Their daggers through the hands we clasped in trust;
    To see the dear lips crumble, and at last
To brood above a bitter pile of dust.

"Not thine, but ours is this. All pain is fled
From thee, and we are wailing in they stead,
    Not for the dead that leave the loved behind,
But for the living that must lose their dead."

This question therefore should be asked of this speaker: what there is in it so passing bitter, if it come in the end to sleep and rest, that any one should pine in never-ending sorrow?

This too men often, when they recline at table, cup in hand and shading their brows with garlands, love to say from the heart: "Short is this enjoyment for poor weak men; presently it will have been, and never after may it be called back." As if after their death it is to be one of their chiefest afflictions that thirst and parching drought is to burn them up, or a craving for any thing else is to beset them. What folly! No one feels the want of himself and life at the time when mind and body are together sunk in sleep; for all we know this sleep might be everlasting, no craving whatever for ourselves then moves us. And yet by no means do those first-beginnings throughout our frame wander at that time far away from their sense-producing motions, at the moment when a man starts up from sleep and collects himself. Death therefore must be thought to concern us much less, if less there can be than what we see to be nothing; for a greater dispersion of the mass of matter follows after death, and no one wakes up, upon whom the chill cessation of life has once come.

Oh ye of little faith, who fear to scan
    The inevitable hour that ends your span,
If me you doubt, let Nature find a voice;
And Will not nature reason thus with man?

"Fools," she will say, "whose petulant hearts and speech
Dare to arraign, and long to overreach,
    Mine ordinance—I see two schools of fools.
Silent be both, and I will speak with each.

"And first for thee, whose whimpering lips complain
That all life's wine for thee is poured in vain,
    That each hour spills it like a broken cup—
Life is for thee the loss, and Death the gain.

"Death shall not mock thee. Death at last shall slake
Your life's thirst from a cup that will not break.
    Cease then your mutterings. Drain that wine-cup dry,
Nor fear the wine. Why should you wish to wake?

"And next for thee, who hast eaten and drunk with zest
At my most delicate table of the best,
    Yet when the long feast ends art loth to go,
Why not, oh fool, rise like a sated guest—

"Rise like some guest who has drunk well and deep,
And now no longer can his eyelids keep
    From closing; rise and hie thee home to rest,
And enter calmly on the unending sleep?

"What, will you strive with me, and say me 'No,'
Like some distempered child; and whisper low,
    'Give me but one life more, one hour, to drink
One draught of some new sweetness ere I go'?

"Oh three times fool! For could I only do
The impossible thing you ask, and give to you
    Not one life more, but many, 'twere in vain.
You would find nothing sweet, and nothing new.

"Pleasure and power, the friend's, the lover's kiss,
Would bring you weariness in place of bliss.
    You would turn aside, and say, 'I have known them all,
And am long tired of this, and this, and this.'

"Nature can nothing do she has not done—
Nature, to whom a thousand lives are one:
    And though a thousand lives were yours to endure,
You would find no new thing beneath the Sun.

"Children of ended joy, and ended care,
I tell you both, take back, take back your prayer;
    For one life's joys and loves, or one life's load,
Are all, are all, that one man's bones can bear."

Such, if the mute Omnipotence were free
To speak, which it is not, its words would be.
    Could you gainsay them? Lend your ears once more,
Not to the mute Omnipotence, but me.

If one of greater age, and more advanced in years, should complain
and lament (poor wretch!) his death more than is right, would nature
not with greater cause raise her voice and rally him in sharp accents,
"Away with your tears, rascal; a truce to your complainings. You are
withering after full enjoyment of all the prizes of life. But because you
ever yearn for what is not present, and despise what is, life has slipped
from your grasp unfinished and unsatisfying, and death has taken his
stand at your pillow, before you can take your departure sated and
filled with good things. So now resign all things unsuited to your age,
and with a good grace up and depart: for go you must!"

With good reason I think nature would bring her charge, with reason
rally and reproach; for old things ever give way to new, and one thing
must ever be replenished out of other things; and no one is delivered
over to the pit and black Tartarus: matter is needed for after generations to grow. And yet all of them will follow you when they have
finished their term of life; and thus it is that all these, no less than you,
have before this come to an end, and hereafter will come to an end.
Thus one thing will never cease to rise out of another, and life is
granted freehold to none, to all as tenants. Think too how the bygone
antiquity of everlasting time before our birth was nothing to us. Nature
therefore holds this up to us as a mirror of the time yet to come after
our death. Is there aught in this that looks appalling, aught that wears
an aspect of gloom? Is it not more untroubled than any sleep?

But I, if still you are haunted by the fear
    Of Hell, have one more secret for your ear.
    Hell is indeed no fable; but, my friends,
Hell and its torments are not there, but here.

No Tantalus down below with craven head
Cowers from the hovering rock: but here instead
    A Tantalus lives in each fond wretch who fears
An angry God, and views the heavens with dread.

No Tityos there lies prone, and lives to feel
The beak of the impossible vulture steal
    Day after day out of his bleeding breast
The carrion of the insatiable meal.

But you and I are Tityos, when the dire
Poison of passion turns our blood to fire;
    For despised love is crueller than the pit,
And bitterer than the vulture's beak desire.

Hell holds no Sisyphus who, with toil and pain,
Still rolls the huge stone up the hill in vain.
  But he is Sisyphus who, athirst for power,
Fawns on the crowd, and toils and fails to gain

The crowd's vile suffrage. What a doom is his—
Abased and unrewarded! Is not this
  Ever to roll the huge stone up the hill,
And see it still rebounding to the abyss?

Then to be ever feeding the thankless nature of the mind, and never
to fill it full and sate it with good things, as the seasons of the year do for
us, when they come round and bring their fruits and varied delights,
though after all we are never filled with the enjoyments of life: this I
think is what is meant by the maidens in the flower of their age who
keep pouring water into a perforated vessel which in spite of all can
never be filled full. Moreover Cerberus and the furies and yon priva-
tion of light [are idle tales, as well as all the rest, Ixion's wheel and
black] Tartarus belching forth hideous fires from his throat: things
which nowhere are nor could exist. But there is in life a dread of
punishment for evil deads, signal as the deeds are signal, and for atonement of guilt, the prison and the frightful hurling down from the rock,
scourgings, executioners, the dungeon of the doomed, the pitch, the
metal plate, torches. And even though these are lacking, yet the guilty
mind, through boding fears, applies to itself goads and frightens itself
with whips, and sees not meanwhile what end there can be of ills or
what limit at last is to be set to punishments, and fears lest these very
evils be enhanced after death. The conclusion of it all is that the fool's
life becomes a hell on earth.
  This too you may sometimes say to yourself, even worthy Ancus has
quitted the light with his eyes, who was far far better than you, uncon-
scionable man. And since then many other kings and potentates have
been laid low, who lorded it over mighty nations. He too, even he—
Xerxes—who paved a way over the great sea and made a path for his
legions to march over the deep, and taught them to pass on foot over
the salt pools and set at naught the roarings of the sea, trampling on
them with his horses, even he had the light taken from him and shed
forth his spirit from his dying body. The son of the Scipios, thunderbolt
of war, terror of Carthage, yielded his bones to earth just as if he were
the lowest menial. Think too of the inventors of all sciences and grace-
ful arts, think of the companions of the Heliconian maids; among whom
Homer bore the sceptre without a peer: he now sleeps the same sleep
as others. Then there is Democritus who, when a ripe old age had
warned him that the memory-waking motions of his mind were waning,
by his own spontaneous act offered up his head to death. Even Epicurus
passed away, when his light of life had run its course, he who surpassed

in intellect the race of man and quenched the light of all, as the ethereal sun arisen quenches the stars. Will you then hesitate and think it a hardship to die? You for whom life is well nigh dead while yet you live and see the light, you who spend the greater part of your time in sleep, and snore wide awake, and cease not to see visions and have a mind troubled with groundless terror and cannot discover often what it is that ails you, when, besotted man, you are sore pressed on all sides with full many cares and go astray tumbling about in the wayward wanderings of thy mind!

Plainly enough men feel a heavy burden on their minds whose weight wears them out. If only they saw equally clearly the causes of this wearyness, the origin of this pile of evil, they would not spend their lives as for the most part they do—no one knowing what he really wants and everyone continually trying to be somewhere else. The man who is sick of home often issues forth from his large mansion, and as suddenly comes back to it, finding as he does that he has been no better off abroad.

> "Bring me my chariot," to his slaves he cries.
> The chariot comes. With thundering hoofs he flies—
>   Flies to his villa, where the calm arcades
> Prophesy peace, and fountains cool the skies.
>
> Vain are the calm arcades, the fountain's foam,
> Vain the void solitude he calls a home.
>   "Bring me my chariot," like a hunted thing
> He cries once more, and thunders back to Rome.
>
> So each man strives to flee that secret foe
> Which is himself. but move he swift or slow,
>   That Self, for ever punctual at his heels,
> Never for one short hour will let him go.
>
> How, could he only teach his eyes to see
> The things that can, the things that cannot be,
>   He would hail the road by which he shall at last
> Escape the questing monster, and be free!

Moreover we are ever engaged, ever involved in the same pursuits, and no new pleasure is struck out by living on; but whilst what we crave is wanting, it seems to transcend all the rest; then, when it has been gotten, we crave something else, and ever does the same thirst of life possess us, as we gape for it open-mouthed. Quite doubtful it is what fortune the future will carry with it or what chance will bring us or what end is at hand. Nor by prolonging life do we take one tittle from the time spent in death, nor can we fret anything away, whereby we may haply be a less long time in the condition of the dead. Therefore you may complete as many generations as you please during your life;

but everlasting death will still await you; and for no less long a time will he be no more in being, who beginning with today has ended his life, than the man who has died many months and years ago.

2. The Enlightenment Epitome

Hume, "Of the Immortality of the Soul"

Hume's essay "Of the Immortality of the Soul" is the other of the two suppressed essays of 1757. As with the essay "Of Suicide" (see pp. 74–80) the essay has never before been printed with Hume's final corrections. His debt to Epicurean arguments is at times obvious but the theme is now redirected at the sort of after life traditionally associated with Christianity, and the Epicurean axiom that matter alone exists is abandoned. Hume's own personal disbelief, if it were ever in doubt, was confirmed by his death bed conversation with Boswell and other evidence (see *Private Papers of James Boswell*, eds. Scott and Pottle, vol. XII, Harvard, 1931). The initial and concluding references to the gospels and revelation should be regarded as prudent pieties not sincere directions.

OF THE IMMORTALITY OF THE SOUL   By the mere light of reason it seems difficult to prove the Immortality of the Soul. The arguments for it are commonly derived either from *metaphysical* topics, or *moral* or *physical*. But in reality, it is the gospel, and the gospel alone, that has brought life and immortality to light.

1. Metaphysical topics are founded on the supposition that the soul is immaterial, and that it is impossible for thought to belong to a material substance.

But just metaphysics teach us, that the notion of substance is wholly confused and imperfect, and that we have no other idea of any substance than as an aggregate of particular qualities, inhering in an unknown something. Matter, therefore, and spirit are at bottom equally unknown; and we cannot determine what qualities may inhere in the one or in the other.

They likewise teach us, that nothing can be decided *a priori* concerning any cause or effect; and that experience being the only source of our judgments of this nature, we cannot know from any other principle, whether matter, by its structure or arrangement, may not be the cause of thought. Abstract reasonings cannot decide any question of fact or existence.

But admitting a spiritual substance to be dispersed throughout the universe, like the ethereal fire of the *Stoics,* and to be the only inherent subject of thought; we have reason to conclude from *analogy,* that nature uses it after the same manner she does the other substance, matter. She employs it as a kind of paste or clay; modifies it into a variety of forms and existences; dissolves after a time each modification; and from its substance erects a new form. As the same material substance may successively compose the body of all animals, the same spiritual substances may compose their minds: Their consciousness, or that system of thought, which they formed during life, may be continually dissolved by death; and nothing interest them in the new modification. The most positive asserters of the mortality of the soul, never denied the immortality of its substance. And that an immaterial substance, as well as a material, may lose its memory or consciousness appears, in part, from experience, if the soul be immaterial.

Reasoning from the common course of nature, and without supposing any *new* interposition of the supreme cause, which ought always to be excluded from philosophy; what is incorruptible must also be ingenerable. The soul, therefore, if immortal, existed before our birth: And if the former state of existence no wise concerned us, neither will the latter.

Animals undoubtedly feel, think, love, hate, will, and even reason, tho' in a more imperfect manner than man. Are their souls also immaterial and immortal?

II. Let us now consider the *moral* arguments, chiefly those arguments derived from the justice of God, which is supposed to be farther interested in the farther punishments of the vicious, and reward of the virtuous.

But these arguments are grounded on the supposition, that God has attributes beyond what he has exerted in this universe, with which alone we are acquainted. Whence do we infer the existence of these attributes?

It is very safe for us to affirm, that, whatever we know the diety to have actually done, is best; but it is very dangerous to affirm, that he must always do what to us seems best. In how many instances would this reasoning fail us with regard to the present world?

But if any purpose of nature be clear, we may affirm, that the whole scope and intention of man's creation, so far as we can judge by natural reason, is limited to the present life. With how weak a concern, from the original, inherent structure of the mind and passions, does he ever look farther? What comparison, either for steadiness or efficacy, between so floating an idea, and the most doubtful persuasion of any matter of fact, that occurs in common life.

There arise, indeed, in some minds, some unaccountable terrors with regard to futurity: But these would quickly vanish, were they not artificially fostered by precept and education. And those, who foster them; what is their motive? Only to gain a livelihood, and to acquire power and riches in the world. Their very zeal and industry, therefore, are an argument against them.

What cruelty, what iniquity, what injustice in nature, to confine thus all our concern, as well as all our knowledge, to the present life, if there be another scene still awaiting us, of infinitely greater consequence? Ought this barbarous deceit to be ascribed to a beneficent and wise being?

Observe with what exact proportion the task to be performed and the performing powers are adjusted throughout all nature. If the reason of man gives him a great superiority above other animals, his necessities are proportionably multiplied upon him. His whole time, his whole capacity, activity, courage, passion, find sufficient employment, in fencing against the miseries of his present condition. And frequently, nay almost always, are too slender for the business assigned them.

A pair of shoes, perhaps, was never yet wrought to the highest degree of perfection, which that commodity is capable of attaining. Yet it is necessary, at least very useful, that there should be some politicians and moralists, even some geometers, historians, poets, and philosophers among mankind.

The powers of men are no more superior to their wants, considered merely in this life, than those of foxes and hares are, compared to *their* wants and *their* period of existence. The inference from parity of reason is therefore obvious.

On the theory of the soul's mortality, the inferiority of women's capacity is easily accounted for: Their domestic life requires no higher faculties of mind or body. This circumstance vanishes and becomes absolutely insignificant, on the religious theory: The one sex has an equal task to perform with the other: Their powers of reason and resolution ought also to have been equal, and both of them infinitely greater than at present.

As every effect implies a cause, and that another, till we reach the first cause of all, which is the *Diety*; every thing, that happens, is ordained by him; and nothing can be the object of his punishment or vengeance.

By what rule are punishments and rewards distributed? What is the divine standard of merit and demerit? Shall we suppose, that human sentiments have place in the diety? However bold that hypothesis, we have no conception of any other sentiments.

According to human sentiments, sense, courage, good manners, industry, prudence, genius, etc. are essential parts of personal merit. Shall we therefore erect an elysium for poets and heroes, like that of the ancient mythology? Why confine all rewards to one species of virtue?

Punishment, without any proper end or purpose, is inconsistent with *our* ideas of goodness and justice; and no end can be served by it after the whole scene is closed.

Punishment, according to *our* conceptions, should bear some proportion to the offense. Why then eternal punishment for the temporary offenses of so frail a creature as man? Can any one approve of *Alexander's* rage, who intended to exterminate a whole nation, because they had seized his favorite horse, Bucephalus?[a]

Heaven and hell suppose two distinct species of men, the good and the bad. But the greatest part of mankind float between vice and virtue.

Were one to go round the world with an intention of giving a good supper to the righteous and a sound drubbing to the wicked, he would frequently be embarrassed in his choice, and would find, that the merits and demerits of most men and women scarcely amount to the value of either.

To suppose measures of approbation and blame, different from the human, confounds every thing. Whence do we learn, that there is such a thing a moral distinctions but from our own sentiments?

What man, who has not met with personal provocation (or what good natur'd man who has) could inflict on crimes, from the sense of blame alone, even the common, legal, frivolous punishments? And does any thing steel the breast of judges and juries against the sentiments of humanity but reflections on necessity and public interest?

By the Roman law, those who had been guilty of parricide and confessed their crime, were put into a sack, along with an ape, a dog, and a serpent; and thrown into the river: Death alone was the punishment of those, who denied their guilt, however fully proved. A criminal was tryed before *Augustus*, and condemned after full conviction: But the humane emperor, when he put the last interrogatory, gave it such a turn as to lead the wretch into a denial of his guilt. *You surely*, said the prince, *did not kill your father*.[b] This lenity suits our natural ideas of RIGHT, even towards the greatest of all criminals, and even tho' it prevents so inconsiderable a sufferance. Nay, even the most bigotted priest would naturally, without reflection, approve of it; provided the crime was not heresy or infidelity. For as these crimes hurt himself in his *temporal* interests and advantages; perhaps he may not be altogether so indulgent to them.

The chief source of moral ideas is the reflection on the interests of human society. Ought these interests, so short, so frivolous, to be guarded by punishments, eternal and infinite? The damnation of one man is an infinitely greater evil in the universe, then the subversion of a thousand million of kingdoms.

Nature has rendered human infancy peculiarly frail and mortal; as it were on purpose to refute the notion of a probationary state. The half of mankind dye before they are rational creatures.

III. The *physical* arguments from the analogy of nature are strong for the mortality of the soul; and these are really the only philosophical

---

[a]Quint. Curtius, lib., vi, chap. 5.
[b]Sueton. August. chap. 3.

arguments, which ought to be admitted with regard to this question, or indeed any question of fact.

Where any two objects are so closely connected, that all alterations, which we have ever seen in the one, are attended with proportionable alterations in the other; we ought to conclude, by all rules of analogy, that, when there are still greater alterations produced in the former, and it is totally dissolved, there follows a total dissolution of the latter.

Sleep, a very small effect on the body, is attended with a temporary extinction; at least a great confusion in the soul.

The weakness of the body and that of the mind in infancy are exactly proportioned; their vigor in manhood; their sympathetic disorder in sickness; their common gradual decay in old age. The step farther seems unavoidable; their common dissolution in death.

The last symptoms, which the mind discovers, are disorder, weakness, insensibility, stupidity, the forerunners of annihilation. The farther progress of the same causes, increasing the same effects, totally extinguish it.

Judging by the usual analogy of nature, no form can continue, when transferred to a condition of life very different from the original one, in which it was placed. Trees perish in the water; fishes in the air; animals in the earth. Even so small a difference as that of climate is often fatal. What reason then to imagine, that an immense alteration, such as is made on the soul by the dissolution of its body and all its organs of thought and sensation, can be effected without the dissolution of the whole?

Every thing is common between soul and body. The organs of the one are all of them the organs of the other. The existence therefore of the one must be dependent on that of the other.

The souls of animals are allowed to be mortal; and these bear so near a resemblance to the souls of men, that the analogy from one to the other forms a very strong argument. Their bodies are not more resembling; yet no one rejects the arguments drawn from comparative anatomy. The *Metempsychosis* is therefore the only system of this kind, that philosophy can so much as hearken to.

Nothing in this world is perpetual. Every being, however seeming firm, is in continual flux and change: The world itself gives symptom of frailty and dissolution: How contrary to analogy, therefore, to imagine, that one single form, seemingly the frailest of any, and, from the slightest causes, subject to the greatest disorders, is immortal and indissoluble? What a daring theory is that! How lightly, not to say, how rashly entertained!

How to dispose of the infinite number of posthumous existences ought also to embarrass the religious theory. Every planet, in every solar system, we are at liberty to imagine peopled with intelligent, mortal beings: At least, we can fix on no other supposition. For these, then, a new universe must, every generation, be created, beyond the bounds of the present universe; or one must have been created at first so progidiously wide as to admit of this continual influx of beings. Ought such bold suppositions to be received by any philosophy; and that merely on pretence of bare possibility?

When it is asked, whether *Agamemnon, Thersites, Hannibal, Nero*, and every stupid clown, that ever existed in *Italy, Scythia, Bactria*, or *Guinea*, are now alive; can any man think, that a scrutiny of nature will furnish arguments strong enough to answer so strange a question in the affirmative? The want of arguments, without revelation, sufficiently establishes the negative.

Quanto facilius, says *Pliny*,[a] *certiusque sibi quemque credere, ac specimen securitatis antigenitali sumere experimento.* Our insensibility, before the composition of the body, seems to natural reason of proof of a like state after is dissolution.

Were our horror of annihilation an original passion, not the effect of our general love of happiness, it would rather prove the mortality of the soul. For as nature does nothing in vain, she would never give us a horror against an impossible event. She may give us a horror against an unavoidable event, provided our endeavors, as in the present cause, may often remove it to some distance. Death is in the end unavoidable; yet the human species could not be preserved, had not nature inspired us with an aversion towards it.

All doctrines are to be suspected, which are favored by our passions. And the hopes and fears which give rise to this doctrine, are very obvious.

It is an infinite advantage in every controversy, to defend the negative. If the question be out of the common experienced course of nature, this circumstance is almost, if not altogether, decisive. By what arguments or analogies can we prove any state of existence, which no one ever saw, and which no wise resembles any that ever was seen? Who will repose such trust in any pretended philosophy, as to admit upon its testimony the reality of so marvellous a scene? Some new species of logic is requisite for that purpose; and some new faculties of the mind, which may enable us to comprehand that logic.

Nothing could set in a fuller light the infinite obligations, which mankind have to devine revelation; since we find, that no other medium could ascertain this great and important truth.

---

[a]Lib., vii, chap. 55.

3. The Final Word

From far, from eve and morning
    And yon twelve-winded sky,
The stuff of life to knit me
    Blew hither: here am I.

Now — for a breath I tarry
    Nor yet disperse apart —
Take my hand quick and tell me,
    What you have in your heart.

Speak now, and I will answer;
    How shall I help you, say;
Ere to the wind's twelve quarters
    I take my endless way.

                A. E. Houseman, *A Shropshire Lad,* **XXXII**

ANNOTATED BIBLIOGRAPHY

General Works

[a] *Histories of unbelief* include J. M. Robertson, *A History of Free-thought in the Nineteenth Century*, 2 vols (London, 1929) and *A History of Freethought, Ancient and Modern, to the Period of the French Revolution*, 2 vols. (London, 1936). Both are invaluable mines of information. The most recent scholarly examination of a portion of this topic is D. Berman, *A History of Atheism in Britain: from Hobbes to Russell* (London, Sydney and New York, 1988). This is particularly helpful in understanding the scale of suppressed atheism in the eighteenth century. A measured, learned (and vast) account of many of the historical ideas associated with unbelief can be found in W. E. H. Lecky, *History of the Rise and Influence of the Spirit of Rationalism in Europe* (London, 1865 with numerous reprints). J. B. Bury, *A History of Freedom of Thought* (originally published 1913, second ed. Oxford, 1952) provides a short, exciting, well-informed account of the dialectic between religious intolerance and freedom of thought.

[b] Recent *Philosophical Surveys* of the topics that adopt or lead to unbelief include Antony Flew, *God: A Critical Enquiry* (La Salle, 1984); John Mackie, *The Miracle of Theism* (Oxford, 1982) and J. C. A. Gaskin, *The Quest for Eternity* (Hammondsworth and New York, 1984). The first two are sharply critical of theistic beliefs; the third is somewhat less so.

[c] *Moral Critiques* of religion include J. Kahl, *The Misery of Christianity* (Hammondsworth, 1971)—a vigorous but highly personal denunciation—and R. Robinson, *An Atheist's Values* (Oxford, 1964) which is one of the best recent philosophical discussions of the issues.

[d] *General or Survey* works on unbelief include *The Encyclopedia of Unbelief* ed. G. Stein, 2 vols (Buffalo, 1985) whose individual articles are useful in many ways, and P. Kurtz, *The Transcendental Temptation* (Buffalo, 1986). This is particularly valuable for its critical discussion of that beguiling source of modernistic belief: the paranormal. The current progress of unbelief is chronicled and facilitated by such periodicals as: in the United States *Free Inquiry* and *Skeptical Inquirer*, and in the United Kingdom *The New Humanist* (originally established in 1885).

232

1. Classical Materialism: Epicurus and Lucretius

Apart from short quotations of sometimes dubious authenticity in Cicero, Seneca, Plutarch, and others, the only complete works (and they are short) which survive from Epicurus' voluminous writings are preserved in the compilation of philosophies put together by Diogenes Laertius in the second century A.D.. For this work see the Loeb edition (Harvard and Heinemann, 1925). A complete, readable, and usefully annotated translation (from which the sections printed here are taken) is in the Bobb-Mervill Library of Liberal Arts (Macmillan Inc., 1964) translated by R. M. Geer. Lucretius' *De Rerum Natura* (*On the Nature of Things* or *The Nature of the Universe*) is readily available in modern translations, for example, in the Library of Liberal Arts (Macmillan Inc., 1964) or from Penguin Books (Harmondsworth, 1951) or in the Loeb edition (1982).

Secondary works on the Epicureans do not generally follow out their thought as the precursors of modern atheistical materialism in the way suggested here. Karl Marx's doctoral thesis "The difference between the natural philosophy of Democritus and the natural philosophy of Epicurus" (Berlin, 1841) is interesting. A standard work on the whole area is *The Greek Atomists and Epicurus* by C. Bailey (Oxford, 1928). Works on the influence of Lucretius include G. D. Hadzsits, *Lucretius and His Influence* (New York, 1935), W. B. Fleischmann, *Lucretius and His Influence 1680–1740* (Paris, 1964) and A. D. Winspear, *Lucretius and Scientific Thought* (Montreal, 1963). The best short philosophical account of Epicureanism is in A. A. Long. *Hellenistic Philosophy* (London and New York, 1974), Chapter 2. A fuller general account is J. M. Rist, *Epicurus, An Introduction* (Cambridge, 1972).

General works on religion and unbelief in the anncient world include C. Bailey, *Phases in the Religion of Ancient Rome* (Berkeley, 1932), J. Thrower, *The Alternative Tradition: Religion and the Rejection of Religion in the Ancient World* (The Hague, 1981). A short and beautifully written account of Greek religion in relation to philosophy can be found in the great classical and humanist scholar Gilbert Murray's *Five Stages of Greek Religion* (London, 1935).

The concept of matter is examined philosophically and historically in S. Toulmin and J. Goodfield, *The Architecture of Matter* (London, 1962). F. A. Lange's magisterial *The History of Materialism* (originally three volumes, London 1877 translated from the German, but the best edition is in one volume, London 1925, with an Introduction by Bertrand Russell) has chapters of historical and philosophical interest on almost every development of materialism.

2. Classical Skepticism: Cicero and Sextus Empiricus

The main sources for classical skepticism are Cicero and Sextus Empiricus. Cicero's *De Academica* and *De Natura Deorum* are available in the Loeb edition (Harvard and Heinemann, 1933) translated by H. Rackham. The translation is very readable and is the one used previously. Sextus Empiricus, *Outlines of Pyrrhonism etc.*, four volumes, is also available in the Loeb edition (1933). Once again A. A. Long, *Hellenistic Philosophy* (London and New York, 1974) provides an admirable short account. A more detailed account is in Charlotte Stough, *Greek Skepticism* (Berkeley, 1969). But the most sophisticated and scholarly recent examination of the skeptical arguments is J. Barnes and J. Annas, *The Modes of Skepticism* (Cambridge, 1985).

The best modern work on the more recent history of skepticism is Richard H. Popkin, *The History of Skepticism from Erasmus to Spinoza* (Berkeley and Los Angeles, 1979). An illuminating account of the peculiar process, whereby a skeptical argument came to be misused as a religious apology for fideism, can be found in T. Penelhum, *God and Skepticism* (Dordrecht, 1983). After Hume (q.v.) the skeptical tradition is fused into the general critical apparatus of modern philosophy, particularly in twentieth-century writings.

3. Edward Gibbon

Gibbon is an end in himself and all that is needed is that one should read more of him, preferably in one of the editions annotated by later scholars such as J. B. Bury. The classic work on the rise and progress of Christianity is *The Expansion of Christianity in the First Three Centuries*, 2 vols. (London and New York, 1904–5), by A. Harnack. The scale and character of early martyrdom are reexamined in W. H. C. French, *Martyrdom and Persecution in the Early Church* (Oxford, 1965). A very readable and well-informed account of the early church by the same author is *The Early Church* (Philadelphia, 1982).

4. Thomas Hobbes

Hobbes has been worse served with complete editions of his works than any other British philosopher of comparable distinction. The Molesworth edition (*English Works*, 11 vols., *Latin Works*, 5 vols.) came out in 1839–45. Since then numerous individual items have been published including many editions of *Leviathan*. The Clarendon Press, Oxford, is apparently undertaking a new complete edition, but thus far only volumes 2 and 3 (*De Cive*) have appeared.

Most secondary works on Hobbes concentrate on his political theory, but a delightful short biography can be found in (John) *Aubrey's Brief Lives* (many editions) and in the first chapter of *Hobbes* by Sir Leslie Stephen (London, 1904). Comments on Hobbes' attitude to religion are found in the following: S. J. Mintz, *The Hunting of Leviathan* (Cambridge, 1962), which relates the contemporary reactions to what everyone then took to be Hobbes' unbelief, a unanimous misunderstanding (?), which F. C. Hood in *The Divine Politics of Thomas Hobbes* (Oxford, 1964) attempts to correct by interpreting Hobbes as a religious reformer. A useful article by W. B. Glover on Hobbes' god can be found in *Hobbes Studies* (Oxford, 1965) ed. by K. Brown. A scholarly discussion of Hobbes' atheism is in D. P. Gauthier, *The Logic of Leviathan* (Oxford, 1969) Chap. 5.

5. Anthony Collins

The legal and social restraints that were laid upon the free criticism of religious beliefs in England in the early eighteenth century have led to the underestimation of Collins as a philosopher. At his best he is the equal of Locke; but Collins cannot aim straight at his targets, and his oblique attacks now need sympathetic decoding. In recent years only two writers, J. O'Higgins and D. Berman, have taken Collins seriously, and the former not very sympathetically. Their works are: J. O'Higgins, *Anthony Collins: The Man and His Works* (The Hague, 1970) and *Determination and Freewill: Anthony Collins's A*

Philosophical Inquiry Concerning Human Liberty (The Hague, 1976); D. Berman "Anthony Collins and the Question of Atheism in the Early Part of the Eighteenth Century," in *Proceedings of the Royal Irish Academy*, 1975, and the entry "Anthony Collins" in *The Encyclopedia of Unbelief*, ed. G. Stein (Buffalo, 1985). Several of Collins's own works have been reprinted recently by Garland Publishing, Inc. (New York and London), including *A Discourse of the Grounds and Reasons of the Christian Religion* (1724, reprint 1976) and *A Discourse of Free-Thinking* (1713, reprint 1978). A masterful survey of the whole scene of thought of which Collins was a part is provided (despite Stephen's unjustifiable belittling of the critical deists) by Sir Leslie Stephen's *History of English Thought in the Eighteenth Century*, originally published in 1876.

6. François-Marie Voltaire

The writings of Voltaire himself together with those about or concerning him would fill a reasonably sized library, and since very many of these writings touch upon religion to a greater or lesser extent a selection among them is a little difficult. The most extended discussions occur in the *Treatise on Metaphysics*, the *Philosophical Dictionary*, and the *Ignorant Philosopher*. The *Philosophical Dictionary*, probably the most famous of Voltaire's books next to *Candide*, is currently available in two translations, by Peter Gay (New York, 1962) and T. Besterman (London, 1970). Gay's translation is somewhat free, but it brilliantly succeeds in preserving the spirit of the original. A six-volume edition—the text used in the selection in Chapter 6—also bearing the title "Philosophical Dictionary" was published in London in 1824. This edition contains the whole text of the original *Philosophical Dictionary* as well as selections from Voltaire's later *Questions Concerning the Encyclopedia* and miscellaneous other writings. In the *Questions Concerning the Encyclopedia*, Voltaire reprinted numerous of the original articles from the *Philosophical Dictionary* with additional sections, some of them much more radical and provocative than those in the original version. The entire *Treatise on Metaphysics*, selections from the *Philosophical Dictionary*, *The Ignorant Philosopher*, and *Questions Concerning the Encyclopedia* are available in P. Edwards (ed.), *Voltaire*, a volume in "The Great Philosophers" (New York, 1989). Among recent books on Voltaire, those by A. J. Ayer (London, 1986) and two books by Haydn Mason (both entitled *Voltaire*, London 1975 and 1981, respectively) may be especially recommended. Earlier substantial biographies are those by Gustave Lanson (1906), Georg Brandes (1930), and Alfred Noyes (1936).

7. David Hume

The best source for Hume is himself, in any of the many editions of the *Dialogues Concerning Natural Religion*, the *Natural History of Religion*, and the *Enquiry Concerning Human Understanding* (notably Sections X and XI). The only comprehensive discussion of Hume on religion in J. C. A. Gaskin's *Hume's Philosophy of Religion* (second ed., London and New York, 1988), but there are scores of articles on the subject for which consult Rowland Hall's *Fifty Years of Hume Scholarship* (Edinburgh, 1978) together with its continuations in various issues of *Hume Studies*. Other books with much of importance to say about

Hume's arguments concerning religion include N. Kemp Smith's famous edition of the *Dialogues* (edition of 1947 in Library of Liberal Arts, Macmillan Inc.), Antony Flew, *Hume's Philosophy of Belief* (London, 1961), and Richard H. Popkin, *The High Road to Pyrrhonism* (San Diego, 1980). The most thorough biography is E. C. Mossner, *The Life of David Hume* (second ed. Oxford, 1980).

8. Baron D'Holbach

There is remarkably little recent material on D'Holbach that is worth recommending. His own *System of Nature* appeared again in an English translation in New York in 1970 (itself a reprint of an 1868 edition). A recent account of his position in eighteenth-century France can be found in A. C. Kors, *D'Holbach's Coterie: An Early Enlightenment in Paris* (Princeton, 1976). The standard, very readable, biography is W. H. Wickwar, *Baron D'Holbach: A Prelude to the French Revolution* (London, 1935). This also contains a valuable "provisional" attempt at a chronological list of his publications together with editions of English translations. F. A. Lange, *The History of Materialism* (London, 1925 and New York, 1950), Bk. I, Sect. 4, Chap. III, is clear, vigorous, and remarkably helpful; so is the short article on D'Holbach in *The Encyclopedia of Philosophy* (London and New York, 1967).

9, 10 and 11. Thomas Paine, Elihu Palmer, and Percy Bysshe Shelley

There are three interesting biographies of Paine: M. C. Conway, *The Life of Thomas Paine*, 2 vols. (New York, 1982); A. O. Aldridge, *Man of Reason: The Life of Thomas Paine* (New York, 1959), and A. Williamson, *Thomas Paine, His Life, Work and Times* (London, 1973). For the observations of one agitator about another, see the article in Bertrand Russell, *Why I Am Not a Christian* (London and New York, 1957) ed. by P. Edwards.

Works on Palmer are almost exclusively historical. R. S. French's "Elihu Palmer, Radical Deist, Radical Republican: A Reconsideration of American Freethought" is worth reading. It is in *Studies in Eighteenth-Century Culture*, Vol. VIII (Wisconsin, 1979). For more critiques of Christian morality, see General Works (c).

Shelley is the object of a huge amount of literary and biographical research, but his atheistical arguments as such have never been taken seriously by philosophers of religion. Indeed his prose essays are hard to come by and the only good modern edition is that edited by D. L. Clarke, *Shelley's Prose or the Trumpet of Prophecy* (New Mexico, 1966). Paul Foot, *Red Shelley* (London, 1980) is very readable, but for Shelley's unbelief see K. N. Cameron, *Shelley, The Golden Years* (Cambridge, Mass., 1974) and D. Berman, *A History of Atheism in Britain from Hobbes to Russell* (London, 1988), Chap. 6.

12. Arthur Schopenhauer

Among a multitude of books dealing with Schopenhauer the philosopher, two are outstanding. They are P. Gardiner, *Schopenhauer* (Harmondsworth, 1963) and B. Magee, *The Philosophy of Schopenhauer* (Oxford, 1983). The former is short and penetrating; the latter is wide-ranging, scholarly, and remarkably lively. There is a dearth of material exclusively on Schopenhauer on religion, perhaps understandably, given that Schopenhauer's writings on the subject form only a small proportion of his total output.

13 and 14. Feuerbach, Marx, and Lenin

A heavy but thorough review of these thinkers' views on religion can be found in D. DeGrood, *Dialectics and Revolution* (Amsterdam, 1982). W. B. Chamberlain, *Heaven Wasn't His Destination: The Philosophy of Ludwig Feuerbach* (London, 1941) is a valuable general account. A scholarly examination of Feuerbach's account of religion is contained in M. W. Wartofsky, *Feuerbach* (Cambridge, 1977), Chapters VIII to X. A very idiosyncratic but exciting account of this area of atheism is in V. Gardavsky, *God Is Not Yet Dead*, Part III (Harmondsworth, 1973).

For the genesis of Marxism, see Sidney Hook, *From Hegel to Marx: Studies in the Intellectual Development of Karl Marx* (Princeton, 1962). The short critical article, "The Marxist-Leninist Theory of Religion" by H. B. Acton (*Ratio*, 1957/8) is very helpful, as is one of the most recent commentaries: D. McLellan, *Marxism and Religion* (London, 1987). A judicious philosophical critique of Marxism can be found in H. B. Action, *The Illusion of the Epoch* (London, 1955) Allen Wood (ed.), *Marx*, a volume in "The Great Philosophers" (New York, 1988) contains Marx's major writings on philosophical and religious topics together with commentary by the editor.

15. Friedrich Nietzsche

A well-established account of Nietzsche and his ideas is Walter Kaufmann, *Nietzsche* (4th ed., Princeton, 1974). Highly recommended books include A. C. Danto, *Nietzsche as Philosopher* (New York, 1965) a heavy but penetrating account; J. P. Stern, *Nietzsche* (Glasgow, 1978), a sound introduction; R. Hayman, *Nietzsche: A Critical Life* (London, 1980), which approaches its subject from the literary side of ideas. One of the oldest but still most readable accounts of Niétzsche and his works is H. L. Mencken, *The Philosophy of Friedrich Nietzsche* (London, 1908); more recently G. J. Stack, *Lange and Nietzsche* (Berlin and New York, 1983) has much to say on Nietzsche's views on Christianity.

16. Sigmund Freud

For those who wish to follow the thoughts of Freud about religion, the index volume to the *Standard Edition of the Complete Psychological Works of Sigmund Freud* provides an invaluable key. The most important separate items are the early essay "Obsessive Actions and Religious Practices" (1907); some parts of *Leonardo da Vinci and a Memory of His Childhood* (1910); *Totem and Taboo* (1913); *The Future of an Illusion* (1927); and *Moses and Monotheism*, three essays (1939). An excellent article on Freud on religion "Psychoanalysis and Theism" by Adolf Grünbaum appeared in *The Monist* for April 1987 (pp. 152–192). Some of Freud's responses to criticism of *The Future of an Illusion* can be found in *Psychoanalysis and Faith: The Letters of Sigmund Freud and Oskar Pfister* (London, 1963), edited by H. Meng and E. L. Freud.

One aspect of Freud's views on religion is developed by Wilhelm Reich, mainly in *The Mass Psychology of Fascism*. By far the best and most easily accessible route to a further understanding of Reich, and incidentally to an expertly assembled bibliography, is the article on Reich in *The Encyclopedia of Philosophy* (New York and London, 1967).

A useful recent book on this area, as indicated by its title, is J. S. Preus, *Explaining Religion* (Yale, 1987). Works on the psychology and sociology of religion are as numerous as those concerning any other prevalent aspect of human activity, but William Sargent's account of conversion techniques in *Battle for the Mind* (London, et al., 1957) and Michael Argyle and B. Beit-Hallahmi's account of the correlations between belief systems and social classes in *The Social Psychology of Religion* (London, 1975) are both particularly thought provoking.

17. Bertrand Russell

Russell's own publications on religion are very readable. The main collection is *Why I Am Not a Christian* (London and New York, 1957), ed. P. Edwards; for other items see above pp. 195. There is much concerning Russell's lack of belief in his witty and lucidly written *The Autobiography of Bertrand Russell*, particularly in the first volume, 1872–1914 (London, 1967). Among secondary sources, A. J. Ayer's *Russell* (London, 1972) is a good, short general guide, but Russell's comments on religion, being more influential than original, have attracted little critical discussion outside the main body of his philosophical work. A detailed identification of his essays and pieces on religion is found in the section of the bibliography headed "Ethics and Religion" at the end of the article on Russell in *The Encyclopedia of Philosophy* (New York and London, 1967).

18. Sir Alfred Ayer

Apart from Ayer's own works listed in the text (pp. 206), which directly concern religion, the principal influence of *Language Truth and Logic* was as an exceptionally effective statement of views of the logical positivist school of philosophy. A selection of leading essays in the school can be found in *Logical Positivism*, ed. A. J. Ayer (Illinois, 1959). With some adaptation, its most influential use against religion is to be found in Antony Flew's brief essay "Theology and Falsification," which would certainly have had a place in this book had it not already been so much anthologized. It is available with Flew's later comments in *The Presumption of Atheism* (London, 1976). It is from the logical positivist concern with meaning—with input from Wittgenstein and others—that the concern with religious language (so evident in the 1960s and 1970s) derives. An excellent account of what went on can be found in K. Nielsen, *Contemporary Critiques of Religion* (London, 1971), which is also furnished with a well-chosen bibliography of books and articles.

19. Jean-Paul Sartre

Sartre's prolix and undisciplined style; his preference for literary, political, or social attitudes rather than arguments; and the facility with which metaphor and object are conflated by him have found little favor with critical philosophers. The most careful account of Sartre given from within the analytic tradition is Mary Warnock, *The Philosophy of Sartre* (London, 1965); the most critical is probably in two articles by A. J. Ayer, "Novelist-Philosophers: J.-P. Sartre," *Horizon*, 1945. A sympathetic, highly praised, but unprofound account of his life and works will be found in A. Cohen-Solal, *Sartre 1905–1980* (Paris, 1987).

20. Epilogue: Mortality

Mortality, or some sort of personal survival into a postmortem state, is a question that has both conceptual and matter-of-fact problems attached to it, and both philosophers, and scientists concerned with the paranormal, have given it close attention. A very careful presentation of some of the philosophical issues is found in T. Penelhum, *Survival and Disembodied Existence* (London, 1970). A vigorous, highly entertaining and well-informed case against three possible accounts of personal survival is in Antony Flew, *The Logic of Morality* (Oxford and New York, 1987). An opposite view, powerfully argued, is in Richard Swinburne, *The Evolution of the Soul* (Oxford, 1986). A survey of the medical evidence and accounts of relevant investigations is found in P. and L. Badham, *Immortality or Extinction?* (London, 1982) and M. B. Sabom, *Recollections of Death* (New York, 1982). On a somewhat different tack, "The Case against Reincarnation" has been effectively argued by P. Edwards in *Free Inquiry* (fall 1986 to summer 1987).

GLOSSARY

Uses and misuses of all but one among the following terms are discussed in full in the Introduction (pp. 1 – 5) but for convenience a brief restatement of the meanings of the terms as understood in the editorial matter to the present text is given.

Atheism: Historically a vague and contentious term meaning lack of belief in god(s) or impiety toward the god(s). Abandoned in favor of "unbelief" (q.v.) in all editorial matter in this book.

Attenuated Deism: Acknowledgment of the possibility of some inconceivably remote and unknowable creator-god who is neither concerned with nor of concern to the human race, nor thinkably like a human person.

Deism: Belief in a god who ordered the universe and masterminds its general laws but has no concern with such particular effects as individual men and women and has made no special revelation of its (his or her) nature or purposes to the human race.

Epicureanism: A complete (and the original) humanistic-materialistic philosophy whose particular stance with regard to gods is to acknowledge that inactive, uncreating gods exist *as a part of* the material universe. However, these inactive gods have no care for us nor we any duty to or dependence on them.

Fideism: The position that the teachings of Christianity or of Islam or whatever are justified because all knowledge rests on premises accepted by faith.

Theism: Belief in a single God who created and sustains the ordered universe and who also knows about and cares about each individual human being (Jews, Christians, and Muslims are all, in this sense, theists).

Unbelief: At least (a) lack of belief in any supernatural agents and, by implication, (b) lack of belief in miracles, and often, but connected with (a) and (b) only contingently, (c) lack of belief in personal survival after death (see pp. 215ff).